This Book must be returned to
the Library on, or before, the
last date shown below.

SERVICES

11 JAN. 1966

10 JUL 1968

ACROSS
THE BUSY YEARS

Ceux qui vivent, ce sont ceux qui luttent; ce sont
Ceux dont un dessein ferme emplit l'âme et le front,
Ceux qui d'un haut destin gravissent l'âpre cime,
Ceux qui marchent pensifs, épris d'un but sublime,
Ayant devant les yeux sans cesse, nuit et jour,
Ou quelque saint labeur ou quelque grand amour.

VICTOR HUGO

Les Châtiments, Livre IV, 9

Nicholas Murray Butler, painted by Sir William Orpen for the
Trustees of Columbia University, 1925

ACROSS
THE BUSY YEARS

Recollections and Reflections

I

By

NICHOLAS MURRAY BUTLER

President of Columbia University
President of the American Academy of Arts and Letters
President of the Carnegie Endowment for International Peace
Membre de l'Institut de France

CHARLES SCRIBNER'S SONS · NEW YORK
CHARLES SCRIBNER'S SONS · LTD · LONDON
MCMXXXIX

Such portions of this book as have heretofore appeared in whole or in part in *Scribner's Magazine*, in *The Columbia University Quarterly*, in *The Teachers College Record* or in *The Saturday Evening Post* are published here with their consent and approval.

CONTENTS

LIST OF ILLUSTRATIONS

ACROSS
THE BUSY YEARS

I
APOLOGIA

ONE who has had and is having the inestimable pleasure and satisfaction of a busy, an interesting and a happy life, and who has enjoyed and is enjoying worldwide contacts and associations of the greatest possible charm and importance, may easily overestimate the value to others of even an imperfect record of those things which he has seen and heard. On the other hand, there is no more interesting branch of literature than biography, with its record, often ingenuous and vain, of the interplay of heredity and environment, of natural capacity and opportunity, with their resulting activities and achievements in the field of reflective thought or in letters or in science or in public service, whether official or unofficial. In the case of a really great personality one does not rest satisfied until every minutest detail of his personal history and activity has been explored, recorded and explained. Two illustrations will suffice. How greedy are men to know something more authentic and definite of William Shakespeare! For Americans in particular, Abraham Lincoln is a magnet of irresistible attraction, and no spoken or written word of his, no act or happening, is allowed to escape attention and chronicle.

There are always some details which are omitted from these biographies and character studies, probably because they are taken for granted, and yet they are both interesting and important. When Admiral Peary returned from his successful expedition to the North Pole it was my good fortune to be present in a small company where he gave, quite informally, the first account of his experiences during that expedition. After his fascinating and absorbingly interesting story had been told, I said to him that there were some things that I was yet more anxious to hear about than any of which he had spoken. If the temperature near the Pole is forty-five degrees below zero, how can one carry on the ordinary activities of daily personal life? how can one sleep at such a temperature without the face becoming frozen? how can food be prepared and eaten? what sort of underclothing is worn? These and a score of similar inquiries were pressed upon him. Admiral Peary's answers to these questions were most illuminating, but he had not included them in his own account of the journey because they seemed to him so matter of fact and so ordinary that they might be taken for granted. Yet they were the very first questions which one unfamiliar with Arctic exploration wished-to ask.

Something like this is true of biography. Rarely is enough told of the subject's ancestry, of the domestic and social environment in which he was brought up, of the details of his formal education and of other supposedly minor events in his life before he became a character of public significance and importance.

There is still another characteristic of the best and most helpful writing in the field of biography. Almost any man of active mind and busy life finds himself for a longer or a shorter period or more or less frequently involved in the consideration and discussion of disputed questions or associated with important undertakings which for one reason or another, good or bad, it is desired to keep secret and confidential. No biographical record could possibly be complete without including whatever material of this kind may be available. Yet if unpleasant and often bitter criticism and controversy are to be avoided, the treatment of matters of this sort must be carefully documented. One of the most attractive biographies of modern times is John Morley's *Life of Gladstone,* and not a little of its charm and satisfaction is due to the fact that the story of Mr. Gladstone's career is interwoven with citations from his own spoken and written words in a way that makes those three volumes a most delightful blending of biography and autobiography. There is a marked distinction to be drawn between autobiography and biography on the one hand and a critical study and examination of an individual's character and achievements on the other. The one will resemble so far as possible a well-focused photograph, while the other will resemble in its originality and detachment a fortunate portrait or a noble statue.

Even in the case of less important personalities, there is one other way in which their biographies become of larger importance. If by chance they have been associated more or less intimately with leaders of thought and action in their own or other lands, then some account of those contacts and friendships will often assist in giving a more complete picture of those personalities themselves than might otherwise be possible. All men, including the greatest, are at their best in the intimate and informal relationships of life when their minds and characters are freely at play with perfect naturalness.

When I begin to recall those truly great minds and spirits which it has been my good fortune to meet and to know, often very intimately, I am astounded at the length and high significance of the list. It is literally true, I think, that beginning with Mr. Gladstone, Prince Bismarck,

Cardinal Newman and Pope Leo XIII, it has been my happy fortune to meet, to talk with and often to know in warm friendship almost every man of light and leading who has lived in the world during the past half-century. This has been made possible, first, by my early introductions and contacts when going to Europe as a mere youth, and second, by the range and character of my interests and occupations. To Mr. Gladstone I was presented in 1884 by Lord Chief Justice Coleridge, who was my father's cousin and who received me with great kindness and hospitality on the occasion of my first visit to England. Prince Bismarck I met in the autumn of the same year, and several times afterwards, first through the kindly courtesy of the American Minister at Berlin, Mr. John A. Kasson of Iowa. It was my privilege to be received by Cardinal Newman through the thoughtful kindness of Dean Church and some Oxford friends. In June, 1893, I was received in audience by Pope Leo XIII by reason of the generous offices of the head of the American College in Rome. The impression made upon me by that truly saintly and spiritual personality can never be effaced.

These were all old men, particularly so in my youthful eyes, and their names, their personalities and their achievements have been through life the base-line from which I have been in the habit of measuring the minds, the characters and the achievements of other men. It goes without saying that with such a standard of measurement one easily becomes critical, perhaps too much so. It is now fashionable to scoff at the Victorian Era—but what an era it was! Surely one would have to search long and hard to find men who, whether in number or in quality, equalled the group which gave that era its character.

In England my acquaintances and friends have included every Prime Minister since Mr. Gladstone except only Lord Salisbury and Andrew Bonar Law. Outstanding is Arthur Balfour, of whom it is still difficult to learn to think as the Earl of Balfour and whom for nearly fifty years I knew and admired for his mind and character. I look upon him as the most accomplished gentleman of his generation. The last time that I ever saw Balfour was just before leaving London for New York in July, 1928, when, with my wife and daughter, I lunched with him and his sister at his familiar house, 4 Carlton Gardens. We had a most interesting talk and as usual he pressed me with questions as to whom I had seen, what they had said and what impressions I was gaining as to movements and problems which were affecting public policy in Europe. Since he was about to go to the House of Lords, he accompanied us to our automobile as we were leaving his house. Standing there and bidding us good-by, he said: "Farewell, old friend, until next year. Remember that you have been coming to my house for forty-three years!" Believe me, those years are crowded with happy and interesting memories of a great personality.

Lord Rosebery, too, had a charm of manner and of mind which was quite unique. What he lacked, apparently, was that which Mr. Gladstone described as "his unwillingness to fight with his back against the wall." Sir Henry Campbell-Bannerman, if not of the very first rank in statesmanship, was a well-balanced, courageous and indefatigable Liberal. He once told me that his greatest failing was that he was "that somewhat unusual thing—a Scotsman with a sense of humor." Mr. Asquith, who, like Bryce, Morley and Balfour, became a peer late in life, had a quiet, sober, powerful mind and character which were never fully understood or appreciated until after he had passed from earth. He was a truly great Englishman.

Mr. Lloyd George I have known well. I was his guest at Chequers on a famous occasion, in 1921, when during the Imperial Conference the chief representatives of the Dominions met there—I being the only foreigner—to consider in confidence the possible future use of the phrase British Commonwealth of Nations instead of the familiar British Empire. The intimate conversations and happenings during that visit can never be forgotten. His Welsh alertness and eagerness, his amazing command of language and his quick and efficient method of dealing with practical problems are the explanation of the great power which he has had over men and policies. Then there was Ramsay MacDonald, who was quite as much a poet and a dreamer as he was a statesman, and Stanley Baldwin, now a peer, whose ability and mental poise are worthy of England at its best. Neville Chamberlain, whose father I knew slightly, is less well known to me than was his half-brother, Sir Austen Chamberlain.

I early met John Morley, most fascinating of men, who had a gift of conversation and of historical interpretation quite unsurpassed. At the close of his second and last visit to America in 1904, he did me the honor to say that that visit had brought him many new acquaintances and one new friend. We were familiar and intimate correspondents for a full quarter-century. Much the same may be said of Lord Haldane, to whom I became attached early in life by reason of his philosophical insight and power, and whose friendship I enjoyed and whose house I visited for many, many years. Of the first Lord Coleridge I have already spoken. His personal charm was quite equal to his legal authority and learning. James Bryce, of course, had a host of American friends and correspondents, among whom I was glad to be numbered. It was at his house, when he lived in Portland Place long before his marriage, that I met Mr. Gladstone several times and Sir Henry Campbell-Bannerman more than once. Another Englishman whom I greatly admired was Sir Edward Grey, afterwards Viscount Grey of Fallodon. No statesman of our time excelled him in serene reasonableness, in unselfish detachment or in lofty patriotism and fine human feeling. He well earned the acclaim in which future generations will hold him.

Of those active and commanding in later British public life I knew best Sir Austen Chamberlain, once Foreign Secretary. The last time that I ever saw Austen Chamberlain was just as I was leaving London in July, 1936, when we met at Claridge's Hotel. He said, with the utmost seriousness: "You and I have been working for the same high international ends for forty years, and now for the first time I find myself hopelessly discouraged." Among the notable churchmen I greatly value my warm friendships with the present Archbishop of Canterbury and with his predecessor, Archbishop Davidson, as well as with the present Archbishop of York, from all of whom I have frequent and most interesting letters. Differing in background and in mental process, these churchmen are one in their deep spirituality and in their sense of heavy responsibility both for the Church of England and for their country.

The list of men of science and of letters and of university leaders and representatives is almost too long to mention. It would include Tennyson, Browning, Matthew Arnold, Robert Louis Stevenson and Rudyard Kipling. It would include five masters of Balliol—Benjamin Jowett, Edward Caird, Strachan Davidson, A. L. Smith and A. D. Lindsay, as well as Principal John Rhys of Jesus, Sir William Anson, Warden of All Souls, President Warren of Magdalen, Provost Magrath of Queen's, William

Waller Merry, Rector of Lincoln, and Henry T. Gerrans, Fellow of Worcester. In later years I have known and greatly admired Herbert A. L. Fisher, Warden of New College, whose great *History of Europe* has already become an outstanding classic. At Cambridge I had the honor of knowing the accomplished Master of Trinity College, Henry Montague Butler, and a number of his contemporaries. Others whom I met and with whom I talked were Professor John Caird of Glasgow, whose *Philosophy of Religion* seems to me the very best book ever written on that subject, and Professor Blackie of Edinburgh, whose quaint sayings and doings were only the natural reflection of a personality of singular charm and sweetness. Then there was Professor John P. Mahaffy of Trinity College, Dublin, whose scholarship and wit were combined in delightful harmony. Of my own contemporaries my warmest friend has been Sir Michael Sadler, who, unfortunately to my thinking, interrupted his university career for years of great public service to the governmental Department of Education, first in England and then in India. Among men of science and their interpreters my acquaintanceship included Professor Huxley and Professor Tyndall, both master teachers, Herbert Spencer, whom I used to see at the Athenæum and who seemed to me singularly unlovely, and Lord Kelvin, who was as fascinating as he was great.

Of our American men of consequence nearly every one has played some part either in shaping my life and thought or in guiding and inspiring my activities. I recall well Longfellow, whom I first met while still an undergraduate; Whittier, with whom I talked at his house in New Hampshire; James Russell Lowell, whose host and escort I was when he came as the representative of Harvard to the Columbia celebration of 1887; Mark Twain, of whom I saw much through a full quarter-century; and Richard Watson Gilder, who was friend and companion for a like period. President Barnard of Columbia is responsible in large measure for the direction that my lifework has taken. I look back upon him as a truly great man, gravely handicapped in his relations with other men by his extreme deafness. Doctor Andrew D. White had a mind of the first order of excellence, and had his voice and physical strength been adequate, he would have made a much deeper impression upon the general public than he actually did. President Eliot of Harvard, a warm and glowing heart under a cold and severe exterior, was an odd combination of Puritan and enthusiast. He was frankness personified, courageous in high degree and a true intellectual leader and guide of his generation. President Gilman, who organized and shaped Johns Hopkins University, while not himself a profound scholar, had high ideals of scholarship, fine human feeling and instincts and was tireless in the task of organization. It was of him that Professor Gildersleeve, when asked how he liked his transfer from the quiet shades of the University of Virginia to the city of Baltimore, replied that President Gilman's idea of a university was the same as the Presbyterian's idea of heaven, namely, "a place where meetings ne'er break up and congregations have no end." President Harper of the University of Chicago was a very intimate friend. He was an odd mixture of serious scholar, vigorous administrator and *bon vivant*. He loved good things to eat and drink, and told me, toward the close of his all too short life, that he never would be happy until he had taken me to a certain café in Moscow where he assured me would be found better food and drink than anywhere in Paris.

My lifelong active participation in the work of political

organization and political education has brought me and kept me in contact with political leaders, particularly those of the Republican Party. Thirty-one persons have been President of the United States and, therefore, there have been thirty-one Presidents—not thirty-two, as the *World Almanac* and various public records persist in misstating. A President who serves a second term does not thereby become two different Presidents or two different persons, whether the terms be consecutive or not. Of the thirty-one, I have known thirteen—all who have held that high office beginning with President Hayes. Of the thirteen, I have known seven more or less intimately and have been in constant correspondence and discussion with them over public questions of the moment. My personal correspondence with these several Presidents, dealing with almost every phase of our nation's life, is now collected in twelve stout volumes, which some day will be available for reference in the library of Columbia University.

President Hayes I never knew until after he had left the White House, but he then took an interest in my work in connection with the Industrial Education Association's College for the Training of Teachers and came to see me several times at 9 University Place, New York. President Garfield I knew slightly and James G. Blaine very well indeed. He stopped several times at my father's house in Paterson, New Jersey, when engaged in political-speaking tours, and it was in that way that I came under the spell of his personal magnetism. For President Harrison I had very great admiration, believing him to be the strongest intellect that has been in the White House since John Quincy Adams. His personality lacked the charm which would have greatly increased his power.

President Cleveland I met through my friend, Francis Lynde Stetson of the New York bar. Of him I saw less than of any other of the Presidents whom I have known. President McKinley was not my first choice at the Convention of 1896. I enjoyed the intimate friendship of Speaker Thomas B. Reed and believed him to be so outstanding an intellect and public servant as to make his election to the Presidency a matter of high public importance. President McKinley never cherished any ill will because of this fact and quickly took me into his confidence, both during his campaign and more especially after his election. President Theodore Roosevelt, whose close personal friend I was, as well as most intimate political adviser from 1898 to 1908, urged high public office upon me again and again. Of President Harding I have written somewhat fully in another chapter.[1] President Taft I knew quite intimately and likewise President Coolidge.

During the administrations of Presidents Theodore Roosevelt, Harding and Coolidge it was my invariable custom to stop at the White House on the occasion of all my visits to Washington. These three Presidents were kind enough to ask me to make my coming known in advance and then simply to come as if I were a member of the family. During these administrations, however, my visits to Washington steadily grew fewer as the pressure upon me in New York City increased. In earlier years, particularly during the administrations of Presidents Harrison, Cleveland and McKinley, it was my custom to go to Washington two or three times each month. On these occasions I was usually a guest at the house of Doctor William T. Harris, Commissioner of Education.

President Wilson I had known since we were young lecturers together at the Johns Hopkins University in the winter of 1886, and I was associated with him on many

[1]See p. 392, *On Keeping Out of Public Office.*

educational boards and committees, including particularly
the Carnegie Foundation for the Advancement of Teaching. We were, however, never sympathetic, either intellectually or temperamentally. I could understand and
appreciate his intellect and his power of speech, but I
never was able to feel confidence in his mental processes
or in his standards of judgment.

Later in life the list of those whose friendship meant
much to me grew steadily longer and more outstanding.
Among philosophers it includes Henri Bergson of France
and Benedetto Croce of Italy, both original and most
stimulating leaders of thought. In the world of political
policy and action it includes the German Emperor, who
was much more than the mere occupant of an imperial
throne; President Diaz of Mexico and his exceptionally
able Secretary of the Treasury, M. Limantour; President
Hindenburg, whose dignity of mind and manner was most
impressive; Doctor Stresemann, who, had his life been
spared for ten years more, might well have changed the
course of European history; M. Aristide Briand, whose
subtlety of mind, persuasiveness and clearness of vision
meant so much both to France and to Europe; M. Veni-
zelos, outstanding statesman with a clear grasp on the
problems which faced not only Greece but the whole
world; the able and accomplished Hungarians, Count
Apponyi, Count Teleki, Count Bethlen and Admiral
Horthy, who were left a hard job to do by the Treaties
of Trianon and Saint-Germain; President Masaryk and
Doctor Benes, brave and untiring builders of a new government for their people whose history has, unfortunately,
not been happy; General Jan Smuts, a statesman with
genuine vision and noble courage; Mussolini, with whom
I had long and frank political discussions in 1927, 1930
and 1934, and who has done really great things for the

Italian people, but whose intellectual power is overestimated by both himself and his friends; His Holiness Pope
Pius XI, whose place among the leaders and interpreters
of thought—whether religious or secular—is wholly secure;
and Cardinal Paccelli, now Pope Pius XII, whose prompt
and unanimous election to the Papacy is one of the outstanding events of recent years.

One who has been so closely associated with political
life and work finds some difficulty in keeping himself from
cynicism and from playing the role of *laudator temporis
acti*. The average man in public life is so set upon immediate success that he is willing and able to find ways
and means to bend his principles, his convictions and his
ideals to the passing whim of the moment, if only he can
thereby win an election and gain a post of power and
patronage. The number of men who are willing to stand
for a principle and to fall for it rather than to surrender,
is not very large. A clever man will always find ways and
means of explaining how it is that, while changing, he
has not really changed. Grover Cleveland once said that
there was no use in standing as a candidate unless you
stood for something. That has always been my view, but
it is not a popular view or one widely held.

Running the eye back over this impressive list of
friends and acquaintances, it is plain that the intellectual
life, when combined with interest in public affairs, may
bring personal rewards and satisfactions in the form of
friendships and associations which nothing else could possibly do. The intellectual life, university service, deep
interest in international relationships and international
understanding and active participation in public affairs,
are the foundation upon which these fortunate friendships and associations have been built. It is not possible
to be too grateful for them or to express too emphatically

my sense of dependence upon them for help and for stimulus in carrying on the work of a lifetime. The fact that they have existed is ample excuse for the recollections and reflections that are to follow.

In looking back across the busy years it is plain that both their interest and whatever importance those years may be thought to possess are due to the fact that they have been so largely occupied with ideas and policies of public moment. There are many busy lives, to be sure, but if these deal simply with things or with interests narrowly personal, they cannot give either the stimulus or the satisfaction that comes from contact with ideas as well as from constant association with men and women to whom ideas are precious. Every activity has been secondary and even incidental to the self-chosen task of planning and building, upon the foundations of historic Columbia College, a university in the fullest sense of that word, which should respond not only to the highest ideals of the intellectual and spiritual life but to the insistent and many-sided needs of modern democratic society. That task, chosen with deliberation and adhered to persistently and stubbornly despite every possible temptation and allurement, both financial and political, has dominated these busy years from first to last.

Apart from constant and often very intense activity in the work of Republican Party organization and in successive political struggles, there comes to mind a long series of undertakings, each one of which at the moment seemed to have exceptional interest and importance. The first of these was the beginning of my lifelong struggle against the evils of the saloon and against the power of the organized liquor traffic in politics. This began while a freshman in college, when in the spring of 1879 my father was nominated for mayor of Paterson by the Republicans on this precise issue. In that short and sharp campaign I worked hard but in vain, for the power of the organized liquor traffic was then too great. In 1886 when a delegate from Passaic County to the Republican State Convention at Trenton which nominated Captain Benjamin F. Hovey of Warren County for governor, I was a member of the Committee on Resolutions, consisting of twenty-one members, and cast the eleventh and deciding vote in favor of the declaration against the saloon and the organized liquor traffic, which the platform adopted by that convention contained. Later, on removing to New York City, I became quickly associated with those who were working for the restriction of the saloon by high license and other methods of control. The prohibition movement always offended my intelligence, my moral sense and my political principles and from first to last I opposed it as vigorously and as emphatically as I knew how. That movement, while it lasted, brought our American public morality to its lowest level.

Another very early interest was in the library system and the public-school system of the State of New Jersey. I took part in drafting the act which was passed by the legislature of 1886[1] relative to the organization and support of public libraries and which is the basis of the excellent public-library system which the State of New Jersey now enjoys. One year later I drew the act[2] for the introduction of manual training into the public schools of the state and also became by appointment of the governor a member of the State Board of Education. As such I undertook a vigorous campaign to reorganize the State Normal School at Trenton, to remove the county superintendents of schools from politics and generally to

[1] *Laws of New Jersey,* 1886, Chapter 50.
[2] *Laws of New Jersey,* 1887, Chapter 173.

strengthen and vivify the administration of the educational system of New Jersey. As chairman of the Committee on Education of the State Board of Education, I was for several years in a very favorable position to exert quick and constructive influence in respect to all of these matters.

It was also my good fortune to draw the act[1] which provided for non-partisan boards of education in cities of the second class, of which my home city of Paterson was one. The mayor of that city straightway insisted upon my accepting appointment to the first non-partisan Board of Education of Paterson, which elected me its president. Already, however, my academic duties in New York were so overwhelming that I could no longer retain my residence in New Jersey, and therefore after about a year's service I resigned this office and changed my legal residence to the city of New York.

My interest in the public-school system followed me there and I quickly organized the Public Education Society, forerunner of the present Public Education Association, for the purpose of reforming the administration of the school system of the city of New York, getting rid of the local district boards of trustees which were a grave obstacle to progress, putting real power in the hands of the City Superintendent and his associates and generally removing the system so far as possible from the danger of purely partisan control. This was a long and a hard fight and was not accomplished without arousing much bitterness and ill feeling.

My last effective participation in matters of this kind was when, in 1903, I supported to the full extent of my ability the bill to unify the administration of the educational system of the State of New York,[2] which had been

[1]*Laws of New Jersey*, 1892, Chapter 49.
[2]*Laws of New York State*, 1904, Chapter 40, pp. 94–97.

ineffective and abundant in conflicting tendencies and policies for twenty-five years, primarily because of faulty organization. This statute, too, was hotly contested and violently opposed by many excellent persons, but by reason of the effective support of Governor Odell, of Senators Stranahan of Oswego and White of Onondaga and of Assemblyman Lewis of Monroe, it became a law. Governor Odell authorized me to tender to Andrew S. Draper, formerly New York State Superintendent of Education but at that time President of the University of Illinois, appointment as first Commissioner of Education under the new act. This I did by telephone one cold winter night, speaking from the Century Club in New York. Mr. Draper accepted the appointment and entered upon the very brilliant and constructive administration with which his name and public service will always be associated.

Through the influence of Doctor William T. Harris, I was drawn early into the activities of the National Education Association, and after the Toronto meeting of 1891 attended these annual gatherings with great regularity for fifteen years. In 1892 at Saratoga I brought forward the plan to interest the association in research and proposed the appointment of the Committee of Ten on Secondary School Studies which paved the way for much of the improvement in secondary-school conditions that has since resulted. As chairman of the committee to select the members of this Committee of Ten, I nominated President Eliot as its chairman and persuaded him to accept. The committee held its first meeting for conference at my apartment, then 225 East Seventeenth Street, New York, and afterwards met for most of its sessions in the Trustees' Room of old Columbia College at Madison Avenue and Forty-ninth Street.

At Asbury Park in 1894 I was, to my great surprise,

unanimously elected President of the National Education Association and presided at the annual meeting of the following year which was held at Denver, Colo. That same year I was chosen President of the Association of Colleges and Preparatory Schools of the Middle States and Maryland which I had been instrumental in organizing a few years earlier, and presided at its annual meeting held at Lafayette College, Easton, Pa., in the month of November, 1895. It was then that I developed the essentials of my plan for a College Entrance Examination Board which should bring order out of chaos in the matter of college admission, more closely relate the work of the colleges to that of the secondary schools and raise the standards of secondary-school instruction throughout the country.

It will be worth while to go somewhat fully into the ideas and ideals which led to my organizing in 1886 the New York College for the Training of Teachers, now Teachers College,[1] as well as my plans for the *Educational Review,* for the Great Educators Series, published by Charles Scribner's Sons, and for the Teachers Professional Library, published by the Macmillan Company, all of which were parts of one large and well-matured plan for educational stimulus and reform and all of which became effective at about the same time. These various undertakings appealed so strongly to Doctor William T. Harris, then United States Commissioner of Education, that he made them the subject of a very kindly article which was printed in the *New York School Journal* for December 15, 1894.

My trip to Europe in 1905 and the numerous trips thereafter were of very different character from those which had preceded them. They brought opportunity for

[1]See Chapter VIII.

contacts, associations and insights which it will be appropriate to record in some detail. Finally, my work as Director of the Division of Intercourse and Education of the Carnegie Endowment for International Peace, and in these later years as President of the Endowment, has been of absorbing interest and has had to do with many things that have an importance and significance far beyond the life of any one individual or of any one land.

It is across such busy years as these that I am glad indeed to be able to look.

II
BACKGROUND OF INHERITANCE

AMONG a people like ours, built up from so many different national origins and recording every sort of commingling of race and blood and language, not much attention is paid to genealogy. To go far back beyond one's own parentage with any hope of getting information that is both detailed and accurate is rarely possible. At most, information as to the genealogy of the present-day American usually ends with the grandparents. Few persons keep any family records whatsoever. It so happens that my inheritance is a matter of record and can be easily traced a long distance back in the case of three of the four grandparental strains. Speaking some years ago in England, I said jokingly that if any one was entitled to fly the Union Jack, I should be at liberty to do so, since there was in my inheritance a strain of Scottish, a strain of English, a strain of Welsh and a strain of Irish. This particular combination is doubtless unusual even in Great Britain itself, but the facts are easily established.

My father, Henry Leny Butler, was an only son, born in the district of Lambeth, London, England, on March 11, 1833. His father was John Thomas Butler Buchanan, fifth child and third son of the Reverend Doctor Gilbert Buchanan, Rector of Woodmansterne, Surrey, a beautifully quiet country parish now at the very edge of the city

of London. This grandfather was born at the Woodmansterne Rectory in 1804, and in 1831 married Elizabeth
Lower of Lyme Regis, whose family is the only one of the
grandparental groups which I have not been able to
trace. My grandfather and grandmother sailed from Liverpool to New York, dropping the name Buchanan, by
the ship *John Taylor* in December, 1834, and arrived at
the Port of New York on February 13, 1835. On January
22, 1913, through the courtesy of Collector Loeb and
Deputy Collector Swords, I had opportunity to inspect,
in the Division of Records of the New York Custom House,
the manifest of the ship *John Taylor,* Captain Thayer,
which arrived at the Port of New York from Liverpool on
the date already given, February 13, 1835. It appears that
the *John Taylor* was a ship of 535¼ tons and carried on
that trip sixteen passengers. The first three names of
passengers as entered on the manifest are as follows:

> John Butler, age 31, mariner
> Betsey Butler, age 26
> Henry Butler, age 2

These data are correct except as to the age of Betsey
Butler who was born Elizabeth Lower at Lyme Regis,
Dorset, England, on April 23, 1812, and was, therefore,
at this time not quite twenty-three years of age. The
occupation of John Butler is correctly given as mariner,
since he had been an officer in the service of the East
India Company from his youth.

This grandfather and grandmother lived for a time in
a house on Pearl Street in the city of New York, not far
from Franklin Square. At that time Pearl Street, then
called Queen Street, appears to have been an excellent
residential street with a number of boarding houses, at
one of which they may have made their first American

home. My information is that my grandfather Butler again went to sea as an officer in the coastwise trade and lost his life through a collision taking place in a heavy fog somewhere between Long Island and Nantucket. It was never possible for me to learn whether his body was recovered and, if so, whether he was buried either at New London or on the island of Nantucket, between which points the vessel on which he was an officer apparently cruised. Search of the public records, made at my request, has failed to yield any information either at New London or at Nantucket.

Immediately afterwards my grandmother removed to Paterson, N. J., then just beginning its vigorous career as a manufacturing town and attracting a large number of English and Scottish immigrants. In fact these constituted, if not the dominant element of the population numerically, yet easily the dominant element industrially and socially. Grandmother Butler, as she then was, moved from New York to Paterson about 1840 and for her support and protection took lodgers in the brown stone-faced house on the north side of Market Street almost opposite Clark Street. Here she lived from about 1840 until Mr. Meldrum, her second husband, erected the house at 27 Clark Street, which was their home for nearly thirty years. The old house was torn down and in its stead the apartment house now standing on the site was erected about 1907 or 1908. My grandmother, who married John Balfour Meldrum of St. Andrews, Fife, on April 26, 1849, lived until March 12, 1893. She is buried in the family plot at Cedar Lawn Cemetery, Paterson. Mr. Meldrum, her second husband, came of the best Scottish stock and had a very remarkable mind and character. He was graduated from St. Andrew's University and immediately entered upon manufacturing in the city of Dundee. He is said to have been the first person to spin jute successfully and thereby to have become, in a sense, the founder of the great jute industry of Dundee. On coming to America he settled in Paterson as general manager of the mills of the Dolphin Manufacturing Company and so remained for twenty years, when he accepted a similar post with the Barbour Brothers Flax Spinning Company. In 1875 his health became insecure and he wished to have relief from active business, so that he withdrew from the service of Barbour Brothers and remained inactive for some little time. A year or two later, however, he accepted an invitation to become general manager of the mills of Buchanan and Lyall in South Brooklyn and removed to 389 Sackett Street, Brooklyn, where he and my grandmother lived for a number of years until the condition of his health compelled him to retire permanently from active business. He died in Paterson in 1883 and is buried in Cedar Lawn Cemetery there.

During much of my early youth and school days I spent a great deal of time in the house of my stepgrandfather and grandmother in Clark Street. They had a charming garden with flowers and fruit which my stepgrandfather cultivated with great care and about which he had gained a great deal of technical knowledge. He was a constant reader of the severest sort of literature. He read not only the classical writers in English and in other languages, but he read a great deal of theology and philosophy and accumulated a number of books of this type in his library. He had no patience with the more frivolous literature that was already becoming popular and followed with keenest interest and attention the rapidly developing controversy between the representatives of science and those of religion. I well remember his tremendous interest in Renan's *Vie de Jésus,* in the notable volume *Ecce Homo,* published anonymously but afterwards known to be the work of Professor J. R. Sceley, and in the writings of Professor Huxley, Professor Tyndall and Herbert Spencer. His example and influence were wholly good, since his intellectual standards were very high and he had no patience with the tawdry or the vulgar. The Meldrum house was the center of the most interesting social life that there was in Paterson from about 1850 to about 1875. It became the custom for twenty or thirty of their intimate friends, all men and women of good education and the best breeding, to come to them regularly on Wednesday evenings. Sometimes there was music and sometimes the hours were passed in conversation. I can just recollect being privileged to look in for a few moments at one or two of these gatherings, but I have no clear impression of anything more than that.

The Buchanan genealogy is quite easy to trace. My great-grandfather, the Reverend Doctor Gilbert Buchanan of Woodsmansterne, was born November 22, 1750, and was graduated from Queen's College, Cambridge, which university subsequently gave him the honorary degree of Doctor of Divinity in 1806. In 1784 he was presented to the Rectory of Woodmansterne, Surrey, by William Pitt and in 1796 also to the Vicarage of Northfleet, Kent, by the Lord Chancellor. He married Miss Frances Reed, daughter of Henry R. Reed of Bromley, Kent, who was born in 1763 and died in 1856 at Chiselhurst. She is buried beside her husband in the churchyard at Woodmansterne. Of her there is a very charming sketch in the volume entitled *This for Remembrance,* written by the second Lord Coleridge and published by T. Fisher Unwin, London, 1925:

I was taken at times to visit my great-grandmother, Mrs. Buchanan, who lived in Devonshire Street, leading out of Portland Place on the western side. She was the mother of my grandmother—Lady Coleridge, and the widow of the Reverend Doctor Gilbert Buchanan, Rector of Woodmansterne, Surrey. She died on July 23, 1856, at the age of ninety-three, and lies buried with her husband under an altar-tomb in Woodmansterne Churchyard. Her maiden name was Reed, and she was the daughter of Doctor Reed, a physician at Hayes, who attended to the great Earl of Chatham and used to swathe up his gouty limbs. I know not what was the regimen prescribed by Doctor Reed for the gout, let us hope it was not that of Doctor Addington, the father of the Prime Minister, who writes thus to Lady Chatham:

"My Lord, I hope, goes on with animal food for dinner and abates not of his wine. I cannot recommend exercise in the air at present. I am very glad my Lord has begun to drink old Hock. I own I wish him to double his quantity of Hock for dinner, *i.e.,* to drink two glasses of plain Hock and two glasses of red Port every day, over and above the Madeira which he drinks, unmixed with water, and over and above the Port which is taken in sago."

Doctor Addington's desire was to induce "friendly visits" of the gout, and he congratulates Lord Chatham "on its first faint appearance, the prelude of the long-wished-for fit."

Mrs. Buchanan was an interesting link with the past. She well remembered Chatham at Hayes, and possessed a fine diamond ring given by him to her father as a mark of gratitude. This is the "Chatham Ring" which we value in the family. She also could recall Doctor Johnson, whom, through her father, she knew well, and had sat on his knee when a child. I can still recollect her, white-haired, mob-capped, shrunken, with her thin, old voice and kindly smile, and, above all, her side cupboards which held sweet biscuits.

Doctor Buchanan himself, who was obviously a person of much consequence, was a son of John Buchanan of Glasgow. The latter was, therefore, my grandfather's grandfather. He was born in 1709 and died in 1779. He was a merchant of Glasgow who came to America and remained in this country for some time. He arrived probably between 1735 and 1740. It has not been possible to get any information fixing the date of his arrival or the length of his stay on this side of the Atlantic. He appears to have been the first of my direct ancestors to cross the ocean, but plainly he did not remain very long.

I have among my papers a copy of the Buchanan genealogy from this point back for several centuries. It begins with the first Laird of Buchanan in the eleventh century. The branch of the large and widely distributed Buchanan family from which I spring is that known as the Buchanans of Leny, also spelled Lenny. Leny House, which I have visited, stands in the Pass of Leny, a short distance north of Callander at the very entrance to the Highlands. This house or its predecessors on the same spot has been occupied by the family since the middle of the fourteenth century. Sir Walter Scott's description of the spot is finely given in *The Lady of the Lake:*

At length they came where, stern and steep,
The hill sinks down upon the deep.
Here Vennachar in silver flows,
There, ridge on ridge, Benledi rose;
Ever the hollow path twined on,
Beneath steep bank and threatening stone;
A hundred men might hold the post
With hardihood against a host.
The rugged mountain's scanty cloak
Was dwarfish shrubs of birch and oak,
With shingles bare, and cliffs between,
And patches bright of bracken green,
And heather black, that waved so high,
It held the copse in rivalry.
But where the lake slept deep and still,
Dank osiers fringed the swamp and hill;
And oft both path and hill were torn,
Where wintry torrent down had borne,
And heaped upon the cumbered land
Its wreck of gravel, rocks, and sand.

A full account of the Buchanan clan and genealogy will be found in the volume written by William Buchanan and published in 1820.[1] In this volume the Buchanans of Leny are described on pages 243–258. Two other references of importance are: The Buchanans of Leny, in Burke's *Landed Gentry of Great Britain* (1914—pp. 261–262), and William Buchanan, *History of the Ancient Surname Buchanan* (Glasgow, 1793).

Of the Lower family in Dorsetshire from which my grandmother came, I have been able to get no equally definite trace. The parish records of Lyme Regis yield nothing, but it may well be that the family lived in some rural parish near by. It is a curious coincidence that on the occasion of one of my visits to Woodmansterne, which by the way is not easy to find despite its nearness to London, my attention was attracted by a street in this little village called Lyme Regis Avenue. The fact at once flashed into my mind that some day I might find in the name of this street a clue as to how it happened that a youth of the parish of Woodmansterne met and married a young woman so far away as Dorset, for in the early part of the nineteenth century the distance between these two places must have seemed very great indeed.

On my mother's side the ancestry is likewise very easy to follow. She was Mary Jones Murray, born at Elizabeth, N. J., June 7, 1838, the fourth child of the Reverend Doctor Nicholas Murray, Pastor of the First Presbyterian Church at Elizabeth, and his wife, Eliza Jones Rhees. My grandfather Murray is so well known in the history of New Jersey and of the Presbyterian church throughout the nation that

[1]*An Inquiry into the Genealogy and Present State of Ancient Scottish Surnames; with the Origin and Descent of the Highland Clans, and Family of Buchanan*—by William Buchanan of Auchmar, Glasgow: John Wylie & Company, 1820, 310 pages.

not much need be said of him here. So marked was his leadership and so great was his authority that he was often humorously referred to as the Presbyterian Pope. He was Moderator of the General Assembly of the Presbyterian Church in 1849. The story of his life and an appreciation of his personality and service will be found in the volume written by the Reverend Doctor Samuel Irenæus Prime.[1] He was born on Christmas Day, 1802, in Ballynaskea, County Westmeath, Ireland, the son of Nicholas and Judith Manger Murray, who were persons of some consequence in their community, his father being a farmer of some property and a leading influence in the social and public life of that part of Ireland. The story of my grandfather's coming to America on the ship *Martha* from Dublin sailing in July, 1818, is told in Doctor Prime's volume. Unfortunately, the records of the Custom House in the city of New York do not go back so far as that year and I have been quite unable to learn anything of the vessel itself or of his fellow voyagers. My grandfather's very distinguished career and the large part which he played in the social, religious and public life of his community, his state and his nation remain a highly prized possession of his grandchildren. He has always been thought of by us as an elderly man, but as a matter of fact he died in his fifty-ninth year of angina pectoris, so that judged by present-day standards he never became an old man at all.

My maternal grandmother, Eliza Jones Rhees, was the daughter of a very celebrated Welshman, Morgan John Rhys. He was born in Glamorganshire, Wales, on December 8, 1760, of parents who are described as "respectable and pious" in the volume on Doctor Rhys's

[1]Samuel Irenæus Prime, *Memoirs of the Rev. Nicholas Murray, D.D. (Kirwan)*, New York: Harper & Brothers, 1862.

life and work by the Reverend John T. Griffith, pastor
of the First Baptist Church of Lansford, Pa.[1] My great-
grandfather is called in this volume "the Welsh Baptist hero of civil and religious liberty of the 18th century." He was plainly a very remarkable person and
a liberal to the core. He was persecuted for his views and
on that account came to America in February, 1794, and
settled in Pennsylvania. He travelled extensively through
the southern and western states preaching the Gospel,
and was married on February 22, 1796, to Ann Loxley,
daughter of Colonel Benjamin Loxley of Philadelphia and
Catherine Cox of Freehold, N. J. She was born in Philadelphia, June 18, 1775, and died on April 14, 1849, in
the seventy-fourth year of her age. Her father was captain of the First Artillery Company of Philadelphia in the
War of Independence, and of all my ancestors he is the
only one who took any part in the Revolution. He was
the son of Benjamin Loxley of Wakefield, Yorkshire, who
was born December 20, 1720, and came to America about
1740, settling in Philadelphia. He is, therefore, the first of
my direct ancestors to come to the United States and
to remain.[2]

My great-grandmother, Mrs. Rhys, was profoundly
revered by her children and those of her grandchildren
who were old enough to remember her, and left a deep
impression on their minds and hearts. Morgan John Rhys
himself lived a most active and eager life, although a very
short one. Deeply affected by the French Revolution and

[1]John T. Griffith, *The Rev. Morgan John Rhys.* Lansford, Pa.,
1899, Leader Job Print.
[2]A detailed history of the Loxley family has long since been
printed. See Loxley Family Records in the Pennsylvania *Magazine of
History and Biography,* Philadelphia, published by the Historical Society of Pennsylvania, 1899, Vol. XXIII, pp. 265-6, 272; also Journal of Benjamin Loxley in *Collections of the Historical Society of
Pennsylvania,* Vol. I, No. 4, November, 1852, pp. 223 and following.

its philosophy, he became in this country the friend of Doctor Priestley and of Thomas Jefferson, whose political philosophy he accepted although differing sharply with their religious opinions. Following some years of residence in Philadelphia he, in connection with the celebrated Doctor Benjamin Rush, purchased a large tract of land in Pennsylvania which in honor of his native country he called Cambria. He also located and planned the capital of the county to which he gave the name of Beulah. Hither he removed his family with a company of Welsh emigrants in 1798. Subsequently he removed from Beulah to Somerset, the county seat of Somerset County, where it is recorded that Thomas Mifflin, Governor of Pennsylvania, appointed him a Justice of the Peace for Quemahoning Township, Somerset County. A little later the same governor appointed him an associate judge in and for Somerset County during good behavior. This commission is dated February 8, 1799. He held this office until January, 1800, when Governor Thomas McKean, who had succeeded Governor Mifflin, appointed him to the more lucrative post of prothonotary, Clerk of the Quarter Sessions, Oyer and Terminer, and Orphan's Court of Wills and Recorder of Deeds for Somerset County. In the midst of his honors and highest usefulness and in the prime of manhood Doctor Rhys died of a sudden attack of pleurisy on December 7, 1804, in the forty-fourth year of his age. His remains are now in the First Baptist Cemetery group (Section 112) in Mt. Moriah Cemetery, at Woodland Avenue and Sixty-second Street, Philadelphia, where there stands a commemorative monument.

My grandmother Murray survived her husband by ten years. Following his death she removed from the parsonage of the First Presbyterian Church to the house, No. 156—now No. 210—West Jersey Street, Elizabeth, in which I was born. It is a substantial wooden house of the type built in that part of the country during the prevalence of the mansard-roof style of architecture, and was surrounded by trees, bushes and in particular a beautiful bed of blue myrtle which has long since disappeared. In the rear of the house and running back across what is now Murray Street was a garden of fruit and vegetables which was a great source of pleasure. The house is still standing substantially as it was in my grandmother's time, having been sold following her death in 1871. She and my grandfather Murray and seven of their ten children are buried in the plot set aside for them by the authorities of the First Presbyterian Church in that churchyard on Broad Street, Elizabeth.

Of the ten children of my grandfather and grandmother Murray, five died in infancy or youth and two died quite early in life. These were Elizabeth, who died of heart disease at twenty-seven and the youngest son, Thomas Chalmers, who died of pneumonia at Baltimore, Md., in 1879, when just twenty-nine years of age. He was by far the most brilliant of the family, having been graduated from Williams College with high honors in 1869. He then pursued the study of theology at the Union Theological Seminary in New York, at Göttingen and Halle, followed by a short residence at the Princeton Theological Seminary. He laid the basis for a really profound oriental scholarship and was snapped up by President Gilman when the Johns Hopkins University was organized, to be the first university teacher of Semitic languages and Orientalia at that institution. His first important course of public lectures was on the Origin and Growth of the Psalms. Immediately following the closing lecture he was stricken with pneumonia and died in a few days, thereby bringing to an untimely end a beautiful character and a life of great promise for American scholarship. These lectures were subsequently published, having been edited by my uncle's friend, Professor Crawford T. Toy, then of Louisville, Kentucky, but later of Harvard University.[1]

Of the ten children my mother was the only one that married. Two others, Rosa and Nicholas, lived to a ripe age. Rosa Murray, born in 1840, was the spoiled child of the family and suffered through most of her life from uncertain health. She was very brilliant and amusing. After my grandmother's death in 1871 she travelled for two years in Europe with her friends, the Evans family of Philadelphia, and thereafter made her home at the house of my father and mother in Paterson until her death in 1913. My uncle, Nicholas Murray, born in 1842, had a splendid mind, a delicate literary sense and a very shy, retiring disposition. He was graduated from Williams College in 1862 and immediately entered the Union Army where he saw service until the end of the war. He then studied law at the Columbia Law School and took his degree with the Class of 1866. Thereafter for five or six years he practised law in the city of New York, when, his health failing as a result of troubles contracted during his military service, he spent three years in Europe. On returning to America he joined my Uncle Chalmers at the Johns Hopkins University where he quickly became the organizer and director of the Johns Hopkins University Press and subsequently librarian of the university. He served with great satisfaction and fidelity in these two important posts until his retirement from active service about 1908. Thereafter he took life easily, travelling a good deal in Europe, South America, Asia and elsewhere. He died at St. Luke's Hospital, New York, on December

[1]Thomas Chalmers Murray, *Origin and Growth of the Psalms,* New York: Charles Scribner's Sons, 1880.

9, 1918, and is buried, as is my Aunt Rosa, in the family plot of my father at Cedar Lawn Cemetery, Paterson, N. J.

From this record it appears that at least three of the four grandparental strains were exceptional by reason of their intellectual characteristics, their religious ardor and their influence among and upon their fellow men. Such a background of inheritance imposes upon those who come after a particularly heavy obligation to try to carry on the record of accomplishment and to do nothing to throw discredit upon it. It is most properly quite customary among us Americans to extol without stint the man who makes much of himself from small beginnings or from no beginnings at all, but surely there is quite equal reason for satisfaction when one can look back upon an ancestral record which abounds in scholarly endeavor, in religious ardor, in patriotic devotion and in public service. All this I can certainly do.

As already pointed out, of the four grandparental strains one is Scottish, one English, one Irish and one Welsh. Since, as the name Murray clearly suggests, that branch of the family too came originally from Scotland, it is evident that the predominant strain is Scottish. Here once more is a source of justifiable pride. Of all modern peoples the little numerous Scots have, beyond all others, done their full share of service to the intellectual life as well as to the government of the British Commonwealth of Nations and to the substantial advancement of the world's progress in its every part and every activity.

There is a delightful story which Mr. Carnegie used to tell with great merriment, of a casual American traveller who found himself for the night at the little inn at Bonar Bridge in Sutherland. It was summer time and after his evening meal he walked out some distance in the light of the long evening to see something of the countryside. He was struck by its attractiveness, but quite as much by the apparent absence of any considerable population. After a bit he saw a Highlander approaching, wearing his characteristic dress. The American visitor being expansive and in search of companionship, hailed the Highlander and said: "Beautiful country, this."

"Ay," replied the Highlander with characteristic taciturnity.

"It is odd that there is no population here," continued the American.

"Naw population?" said the Highlander with surprise.

"No," continued the American. "If there is any population here, where are they?"

"Oh!" exclaimed the Highlander contentedly. "They're all awa' governin' the wurl!"

So far as I have been able to ascertain, there was never in all this long line of known ancestors any accumulation of wealth or indeed any evidence of a desire to become wealthy. The men were either scholars or clergymen or soldiers or sailors, but only in one or two exceptional cases merchants. It is an amusing commentary upon changed conditions that when my grandfather Murray was called to his first pastorate at the Presbyterian Church at Wilkes-Barre, Pa., in the year 1829, his salary was fixed at $600. Even thirty years later, when at the height of his influence and fame, he received a salary of but $1500 as pastor of the First Presbyterian Church at Elizabeth, N. J. Despite this meager economic foundation, he was the father of ten children, five of whom grew to manhood or womanhood.

Our family association with the life of the United States, save in the single case of the Loxley branch, began after the Constitution had been adopted and the government established. The Rhys ancestor came next in 1794, the Murray ancestor in 1818 and the Butler-Buchanan and Lower ancestors in 1835. In their early settlements they were no farther separated than are New York City and Somerset County, Pennsylvania. None of them had any relationship with New England or the South and not until a few years before the War between the States did any of the family connection join the westward movement. Some years before 1860 my grandmother Murray's sister, Mrs. Jackson, removed with her children from Philadelphia, first to Mason City, Iowa, and then to Charles City, Iowa. Her son, James Jackson, served with distinction in the Union army and afterwards became an officer in the regular army of the United States with the rank of colonel, being retired from active service just as the Spanish-American War was about to break out in 1898. He then removed with two of his sisters to Portland, Oregon, and subsequently died there, full of years and held in high consideration by that community. One of my own younger brothers, William Curtis Butler, who was graduated in engineering from Columbia University in 1887, went West immediately thereafter and found professional occupation first at El Paso, Texas, then at Leadville, Colo., next in the Gogebic section of the Michigan peninsula and finally at Everett in the State of Washington on Puget Sound, where he has now lived for more than forty years. Apart from these exceptions, the entire family connection has resided in or about New York, northern New Jersey and Philadelphia.

It is not easy for a son to record with any freedom memories of his father and mother. My father received as good an education as the schools of New York and Paterson afforded a century ago, and at great sacrifice was sent by his mother to the newly established college at Burlington, N. J., which the first Bishop Doane had brought into existence as part of the educational work of the diocese of New Jersey of which he was the head. The institution for the education of girls which he established at the same time still exists, I believe, but the college for young men had a very short existence, since adequate funds for its maintenance were not forthcoming. It is my recollection that but one class was graduated and that it contained four young men. These were William Croswell Doane, later Protestant Episcopal Bishop of Albany, George W. Doane, who became a distinguished Roman Catholic ecclesiastic under the title of Monsignor Doane, both of whom were sons of the then Bishop of New Jersey, George McCulloch Miller, afterward a very prominent New York lawyer and for years President of the Board of Managers of St. Luke's Hospital, and my father.

After leaving Burlington College his mother insisted upon his being apprenticed in one of the Paterson machine shops in order that he might have a trade to fall back upon should that ever become necessary. Instead of entering upon his trade, however, he found employment as a clerk in the linen importing house of James F. White and Company of New York and remained there until he became a partner in the house of Duncan and Butler, who were engaged in the same branch of business. The senior partner was James F. Duncan, a Scotsman, who returned to his native land after the close of the Civil War. My father and mother were married on October 4, 1860, and lived at first with my step-grandfather and grandmother at 27 Clark Street, Paterson, N. J. Within a few months after their marriage Fort Sumter was fired upon and President Lincoln called for volunteers. My father was one of the first young men in Paterson to offer his services, but being a married man he was passed over by the authorities for those who were without the obligation to support a family. He entered earnestly into war work, however, as a civilian and labored hard and long to support President Lincoln and his government. Toward the close of the war his name was drawn in the draft, but at that time he had contracted an illness which made it necessary for him to provide a substitute who served for the few remaining weeks of the conflict.

Following the dissolution of the firm of Duncan and Butler, my father entered into business as a manufacturer with my stepgrandfather, the firm being Meldrum and Butler. They manufactured a printed jute carpet which was my stepgrandfather's invention. The latter did not relinquish his post with Barbour Brothers and the active direction of the manufacturing enterprise was in my father's hands. This business, while never large or highly profitable, was satisfactory and continued until its destruction as a result of the tariff legislation which followed the election of President Cleveland in 1892. Some years earlier my father had also entered upon one branch of the silk business and was engaged in what is known as throwing. This enterprise was never more than moderately successful and eventually my father retired from it entirely.

During his entire life he entered actively into the public life of the city of Paterson and the state of New Jersey as well as into the management of the Republican Party organization. He became a most influential personality in the city and state and for years was President of the Paterson Board of Education. The excellent school system of that city owes no little part of its sound and solid foundation to his devoted and unselfish labor in those early years of its history. He served as delegate to Republican national conventions and as a leader in the work of the city, county and state Republican organization. He was the confidential adviser in respect to New Jersey matters of President Grant, President Hayes and President Garfield, and he was active in shaping party policies and in choosing party candidates. Later in life, at the urgent request of the party leaders, he accepted the post of Supervisor of the State Prison for the purpose of bringing to an end what was said to have been a period of inefficiency and incompetence and of putting the prison administration upon a sound basis. While he held this post he was obliged to go to Trenton, N. J. at least once a week and sometimes oftener, and when his term expired he was happy to be relieved of this rather onerous obligation. He took the keenest interest in the education of his children and followed with affectionate solicitude every step in the early career of each one of them. After a brief illness he died at his home, 175 Hamilton Avenue, Paterson, on September 23, 1904. He with my mother is buried in the family plot at Cedar Lawn Cemetery in Paterson.

A very kind and in most respects accurate review of his life and service may be found in the Paterson *Morning Call* for Saturday, September 24, 1904. Following the sketch of my father's life, the *Morning Call* of that date, speaking editorially, said:

The fact that the familiar face and voice of Henry L. Butler has forever disappeared from the community can hardly be appreciated. He has so long been such a potent factor among us that he has left an indelible impress that will ever remain. He was a born statistician and always able to substantiate his statements by facts and figures. Wherever he stopped and talked there was an interesting group around him. He was a very likeable man, courteous and dignified and yet democratic in character, and altogether charming. He was a walking encyclopedia of the world's events and his study of current doings everywhere was complete. Unusually intelligent, magnetic, fascinating, affable and gentlemanly, he was ever welcome in any society and he made himself agreeable everywhere. He was one of the noted characters of the city, and during his prime was a breathing part and factor of it. He did his work thoroughly and he did not live in vain. His memory will long be cherished, and most fervently by those who knew him the most intimately. When such a prominent personage dies it is hard to conceive that he is really gone—gone just a little ahead of us all—to that bourne toward which we are all traveling never to return.

It is not possible to put on paper what I feel and could say concerning the personality of my mother and that of my grandmother Meldrum. The latter was a typical Englishwoman of the early Victorian period. She was a devout member of the Protestant Episcopal church and a most skillful and devoted housekeeper and homemaker. She was very strait-laced in her judgments as well as in her conduct, and maintained for herself and her family and impressed upon all about her the most rigid standards of personal conduct. Her well-known face and figure as she passed through the streets of Paterson in the days when it was a small town, were recognized by practically every one and she was constantly saluted by those who knew and admired her character and who were impressed by the dignity of her mien and bearing.

My mother's memory is too sacred to be made the subject of record. She bore seven children, two of whom died in infancy while five grew to manhood and womanhood. Of these, all but one are still living. She had received as good an education as was possible for a young woman to have in the days of her youth and kept herself well informed and abreast of the thought and literature of her time by constant and wide reading. She was very fond of music as was my father and they frequently sang together for their own enjoyment and for the entertainment of their family. In my earliest youth my father always read both morning and evening prayer with the entire family assembled.

Later the reading of evening prayer was dropped and finally as the three boys grew toward adolescence the reading of morning prayer was dropped as well. The household was one of great beauty and charm, marked by simplicity and entirely normal relationships. Both the educational work and the sports of the children were followed with keen interest by both parents, who entered into every detail of the life of the family with the utmost zest and helpfulness. This much can perhaps be properly recorded but more may not be said.

Our religious instruction and training were most carefully looked after at home, which is the only place where they can be looked after effectively. One habit which I am sure was of great value was that of spending an hour after supper on each Sunday evening reciting in turn hymns which we had learned by heart. On each successive Sunday evening every member of the family was expected to have learned one additional hymn. The consequence of this practice is that all my life I have known by heart scores of hymns including, of course, the most familiar. This fact has itself been a source of constant satisfaction.

My father was baptized as a member of the Protestant Episcopal church and brought up in that church by his mother and stepfather. The latter was for many years a member of the vestry of St. Paul's Protestant Episcopal Church in Paterson and during the last fifteen or twenty years of his life was a warden of that parish. My mother was, of course, a Presbyterian, trained in the old school of Calvinistic theology both as to faith and practice. She broadened enormously with the years and became by the time my memory begins as catholic and as liberal a spirit as one could imagine. Following their marriage, my father and mother regularly attended the First Presbyterian Church of Paterson, of which the Reverend Doctor

William H. Hornblower was the pastor. He died when I was very young and I have only the dimmest recollection of his personality. His successor was the Reverend Doctor David Magie, whose father, curiously enough, had been pastor of the Second Presbyterian Church of Elizabeth during much of the time that my grandfather was pastor of the First Presbyterian Church in that city. The two families were, therefore, old friends. In 1884 steps were taken to build a new Presbyterian church in the residential portion of the city, to be known as the Church of the Redeemer. Doctor Magie and my own family together with many others transferred their membership at that time from the old church to the new, where Doctor Magie continued as pastor until his resignation in 1907. We children were taken with absolute regularity to the Sunday morning service of the First Presbyterian Church and were also sent to the Sunday school which met early in the afternoon. So far as I can recall, attendance upon the latter was a sheer waste of time, as apparently it almost always is. Unless there can be really effective co-operation and understanding between the home, the school and the church, it is not possible to get very far with any genuine or effective religious training. If these agencies are out of harmony with each other or if any of them be non-existent so far as religious instruction and influence are concerned, then they neutralize each other and the result is apt to be wholly negligible or worse. I do remember having learned the Westminster Shorter Catechism with its 107 questions and answers, all of which I was able to recite from end to end without mistake in March, 1873. This fact is testified to by the inscription on the flyleaf of the copy of a Bible given me at that time and in recognition of that performance by our pastor, the Reverend Doctor David Magie.

Much of the time, particularly after I was twelve or

fourteen years of age, I joined my grandmother and step-grandfather in attendance upon Sunday services at St. Paul's Protestant Episcopal Church. The beauty of the service, particularly the splendid liturgy of the Book of Common Prayer, attracted me strongly and in time sealed my preference for the Protestant Episcopal rather than for the Presbyterian affiliation. Shortly after I was graduated from college, I was confirmed as a member of the Protestant Episcopal church at Calvary Church, Fourth Avenue and Twenty-first Street in the city of New York, by Bishop Horatio Potter. I had been attending that church for some time while residing in New York and had become very fond of the rector, the Reverend Doctor Henry Y. Satterlee, who was afterwards Bishop of Washington.

Partly because of this training and these early experiences, partly, I think, because of my stepgrandfather's influence and his suggestions as to books to read, and partly owing to my philosophical training, I have always had a deep interest in theological literature and theological studies. The writings of Cardinal Newman interested me profoundly and I reread them with great care after I had the honor of meeting him face to face. There were remarkable sermons that I recall by Père Lacordaire which were collected in a stout volume that came into my hands and were read with close attention. During my early visits to England I often went to St. Paul's Cathedral where Canon Liddon, afterwards Dean, used to preach at the afternoon service during the month of August. He was a most extraordinary preacher of vivid eloquence and a spiritual appeal that was both wide and deep. On one Sunday afternoon while taking tea at his house in Dean's Yard after the service, I remarked that having heard him often, I noticed that he never preached less than seventy or seventy-five minutes and asked whether this was accidental or grew out of some definite habit or mode of treating his topic. Doctor Liddon replied with a quizzical smile that any one who had a real idea could not develop it satisfactorily to a congregation in less than an hour's time.

I presume that in all this the inherited traits and associations of the Buchanans, the Murrays and the Rhyses were asserting themselves.

Since my father was an only son and the family name was Buchanan, not Butler, I have never had any Butler relatives save my own brothers and sisters. Similarly, since my mother was the only one of my grandfather Murray's ten children to marry, I have never had any Murray relatives save my own uncles and aunts. The Rhys connection, on the other hand, is numerous but now rather remote. Two members of that family came to occupy posts of exceptional usefulness and public service. One, William J. Rhees, as the name has come to be spelled, a grandson of Morgan John Rhys and the family historian and genealogist, was the able and devoted chief clerk of the Smithsonian Institution at Washington from 1858 to 1907. Another, Rush Rhees, like myself a great-grandson of Morgan John Rhys, made a notable reputation as scholar, theologian and administrator. He was the accomplished President of the University of Rochester for many years. He retired from that post in 1935 and died in 1939.

III

PATERSON: HOME AND SCHOOL
DAYS

DESPITE the fact that all my boyhood associations were with the city of Paterson, I was not born there but at the house of my grandmother Murray which was then 156, now 210, West Jersey Street, Elizabeth, N. J. It appears that my Aunt Rosa, who was a woman of strong sentiment, carried me when hardly more than a few days old up to the highest point in the cupola of the house, accompanied by an American flag, a ten-dollar gold piece and a Bible, the purpose of the excursion being to symbolize patriotism, wealth and piety, to all of which my aunt desired me to be destined. My only personal recollections of this house are some years later and in the very last year or two of my grandmother's life. In May, 1864, my parents moved to the house, 97 Fair Street, Paterson, N. J., which they continued to occupy for eight years. It was a small but comfortable dwelling, standing on a small plot of ground leased by my father from its owner, Thomas W. Hall. During the year 1871 my father, who had purchased property on the west side of Division Street, now Hamilton Avenue, began the building of the house which was our family home for many years. We moved into it in the month of April, 1872, and both of

my sisters were born there. That house is the center of my
boyhood associations and was only a few years ago pulled
down by its owner to make way for a modern apartment
house.

My father died there in 1904, my mother in 1912 and
my Aunt Rosa in 1913. The house stood well back from
the street, and the garden, while not large, supplied ample
fruits and vegetables for household use during a large
portion of the year. At first the house stood quite alone
at the corner of Hamilton Avenue and Auburn Street,
although there were buildings on the northeast and north-
west corners. Speedily, however, that part of the city developed and it was not long before there were no vacant
building sites in the neighborhood.

Among my earliest but distinct recollections are instances connected with the summer holiday season of
1866, including the trip from New York to North Con-
way, N. H., where we spent more than two months at
the Kearsarge House. Similarly, in the summer of 1867
I have a recollection of the trip to Easthampton, L. I.,
and in the summer of 1868 of one to Roslyn, L. I. During
the summer holidays of 1869, 1870 and 1871 I was the
guest of my grandfather and grandmother first at the
Navesink Hotel at the Highlands near Sandy Hook, N. J.,
and later at the Ocean House, Long Branch, N. J. There
are isolated happenings during each one of these summer
visits which still find a place in my memory, but nothing
that is very connected or significant. I do remember that
in the summer of 1870 I was taken to the Lighthouse at
the Highlands to see the conclusion of the trans-Atlantic
yacht race between the English yacht *Cambria* and the
American yacht *Dauntless*. I well recall the great excitement when the English yacht proved to be the winner
by several hours.

The community in New Jersey in which I was brought up was for those days almost ideal—whether speaking socially, economically or politically. Its spirit was thoroughly democratic and we all lived and grew up together and moved about in the life of the town without any signs whatever of that which today disturbs so many persons and which they describe as class-consciousness. This is a particularly artificial product. It need have and should have no possible existence in a democratic society.

In that town every one went to the public schools. In fact, it would have been very difficult to do anything else, since there existed but one small private school for boys and another small private school for girls in that entire community of some fifty thousand or sixty thousand people. My father, who was President of the Board of Education for a number of years, took very great interest in the administration of the school system. He took active part in the selection and promotion of principals and teachers, in the choice of the textbooks and generally in carrying forward the work of the schools in close association with the public opinion of the community.

My school days began early. I was only five and a half years old when I was taken to the school conducted by Miss Elizabeth Calkins in the little building which is still standing on Hamilton Avenue, north of Auburn Street, which was built on the rear of the lot on which stood her father's house. He was Captain Charles Calkins, a veteran of the Civil War and a carpenter and builder who had erected a dwelling for himself and family with shops underneath it on the northeast corner of Hamilton Avenue and Auburn Street. The little schoolhouse was the simplest building possible. It was typical of the ungraded country school, then characteristic of the whole United States and with a value all its own. The elaborate educational machinery which has displaced the ungraded school has, of course, its own excellences, but the ungraded school had merits for which we as a people may well be very grateful. Miss Calkins was the only teacher and she had before her perhaps twenty or thirty children of different ages and stages of advancement, with all of whom she dealt with skill, with kindness and with excellent discipline. She had a great admiration for some of the principles of what was known as the Bell-Lancaster system and in accordance with these, the pupils acted as monitors in turn, each for a half day session. I can see some of us now sitting on the monitor's high stool and looking solemnly out over the little class of busy pupils, charged with a great sense of responsibility because entrusted with a large share of the school's discipline for the moment. With Miss Calkins I spent nearly three years, and the studies pursued must, of course, have been those of the ordinary elementary grades.

In 1870 I was enrolled in one of the upper grammar grades of Public School No. 1 on Van Houten Street, near Washington. This was one of the oldest school buildings of the city and lasted until destroyed by the great fire in 1902. My father was President of the Board of Education at the time and knew intimately the entire teaching and administrative staff of the city school system. The principal of School No. 1 was William J. Rogers, a pedagogue of the old-fashioned type. He was still in service, although at the head of another school, when I myself became President of the Board of Education in 1892. My grade teacher was Mrs. Helen Donkersley, whose family held an important position in the community and who was herself a woman of fine personality and excellent teaching skill.

In the autumn of 1872, when ten and a half years of

age, I was transferred to the high school which was then established in new Public School No. 6 that had just been erected at the corner of Ellison and Summer Streets. It was an excellent building for that time with one rather amusing feature which reflected some current discussions both in medical journals and in the press relative to lighting. The window glass was markedly blue, the purpose being, of course, to admit certain light rays to the schoolrooms and to prevent or minimize the admission of others. My recollections of high-school experiences are very clear and very detailed. The three lower classes were conducted each by a woman teacher, and admirable women they all were. Of the first or D class the teacher was Miss Marion D. Gall; of the C class Miss Frances I. Gilbert; and of the B class Miss Agnes E. Pelser. All were women of the finest type, deeply in earnest in their work and skillful in their conduct of the classroom. Each one of the three was a member of a well-known Paterson family and exercised over her pupils an influence which was not confined, as is so often the case with teachers, to mere instruction, but which covered the whole field of education. To each of these women I owe a debt of personal gratitude which I am glad indeed to record. No one of the three ever married and all have long since passed away.

The first or A class in the high school was conducted by the principal and during my time there were two principals in service. The first was a former Baptist preacher named McIntyre. He was a dreadful person, uncouth, uncultivated, vulgar and violent. What service he could possibly have rendered either to religion or to education passes my comprehension. One of his chief occupations was corporal punishment. For this he used a short, thick and narrow leather strap, toward one end of which were inserted a half dozen brass or bronze rivets. His method of inflicting corporal punishment was to hold the pupil's hand tightly by the fingers and to beat the palm of the hand with the strap. This he did with great violence and, in my case at least, with what seemed like ferocity. The rivets in the strap produced blisters almost at the first blow and subsequent blows broke these blisters and covered the hand with blood. The whole proceeding was revolting quite apart from its painful character, particularly as Principal McIntyre rushed to corporal punishment on the slightest provocation and for the most trivial offenses against discipline. These characteristics of his got him into trouble with public opinion and with the Board of Education. The facts in his case I cannot now clearly recall. My recollection is that he was either removed from office or permitted to resign in order to escape removal.

His successor, William B. Ridenour, was a quite remarkable person. He had a powerful mind that had been particularly well trained in mathematics. He was not a good teacher for the average pupil because he was impatient and rather sarcastic in the presence of stupidity, sluggishness or lack of understanding. For those pupils who were quick and appreciative he was excellent. With them he took the greatest pains and gave them advice and courses of reading which were of great value and helpfulness. My impression is that Mr. Ridenour was also a very shy man. He certainly did not take the public or social position in the community which his post and talents justified. He remained principal of the high school for some years after my graduation and then, if I recollect aright, was connected during the remainder of his life with the work of the Correspondence Schools at Scranton, Pa. Among other kindly acts, I remember his giving me in 1873 with a personal inscription a copy of Dana's

Manual of Geology, telling me that since no science was taught in the high school, I should read this book carefully and, having done so, try to observe in the environs of Paterson and Passaic Falls the rock formations which would illustrate in some degree what I read in Dana's *Manual.*

There has been preserved the record of an examination which I took when a member of D class in the high school, given December, 1872. The subject matter includes arithmetic, grammar, history and geography. The questions, which were apparently dictated, as well as the answers, are in my own handwriting, then very crude and unformed, but the scope of the examination and its character are a very interesting record of the educational practice and method of that time. It may be greatly doubted whether many present-day pupils who are but ten years of age have had the instruction necessary to make any headway whatever with this examination. The answer to each question is rated in the handwriting of Miss Gall and her judgment was: for the arithmetic 96, for the grammar 100, for the history 90 and for the geography 96. She gives the entire paper a rating of 98. It is a pity that more original documents of this kind have not been preserved, since it has become quite customary greatly to underestimate the worth and the character of the public-school training given in this country from 1850 to 1890. In those days teachers were still old-fashioned enough to believe in discipline for the purpose of building both mind and character and in instruction for the purpose of conveying facts which human experience had taught were of value. The present-day notion, that an infant must be permitted and encouraged to explore the universe for himself as if everything were at its beginning and there had been no human experience whatever, had, fortunately, not yet raised its preposterous head. In my time children were really educated.

We had excellent textbooks, some of which I have preserved in my library to this day. Arithmetic and algebra, English grammar and composition, general history and American history together with geography, formed the staple of instruction. Our reading books were old-fashioned collections of carefully chosen material by means of which we were introduced to the best poetry and the noblest prose in the English language. It is all well enough to say, as is now so strongly urged, that a work of literary merit should be read in its entirety, but as a matter of fact for the elementary school and for the secondary school in its earlier stages, the reading-book of carefully selected material has far more educational value. Through its use we were tempted and inspired to read, and did read, both at that time and for years to come, in order to follow up the interest and the information which we gained from the selections brought together by such editors of textbooks as Wilson and McGuffey.

In those simple days no religious complications had developed, at least in that community, and each morning's exercises were opened by the reading of a brief passage from the Bible, by the recitation in chorus of the Lord's Prayer and by the singing of a school song chosen from the book of songs which was adopted for our use by the Board of Education. It was explained to me afterward that the object of the early morning song on the part of the whole school was to give to the entire group of pupils, regardless of class distinction, a sense of unity and solidarity as they began each day's work. This was a very reasonable explanation of an excellent and pleasing custom.

Miss Gall, the teacher of the D class, was particularly

skillful in some of her classroom exercises. I remember as if it were yesterday her method of using the last ten minutes of each morning session. She would call upon the members of the class to rise, to fold their arms behind them and to give close attention. She stood facing the class, with arms folded behind her, and began an exercise in mental arithmetic, the plain purpose of which was to train us to fix our attention and to follow with concentration upon the quick statement of a problem. When all was ready Miss Gall would say something like this: 3 plus 2 minus 1 divided by 2 multiplied by 4 plus 1 divided by 3 plus 2 divided by 5, is how many? The hands would go up of those who had followed and who had the correct answer. This exercise would be repeated with slight variance of the figures used until the bell struck for the close of the morning session. It was not long before Miss Gall had her entire group of perhaps twenty or thirty pupils so well trained that nearly every one of them followed these mental arithmetic exercises with minute attention and was able to give the correct answer when it was asked for.

The weakness of the Paterson High School in those days was that it offered no instruction whatever, even of the most popular kind, in the field of natural science, and nothing whatever in the languages either ancient or modern. As no examination in natural science was then prescribed for admission to the American college, that lack did not affect one's educational advancement, but the same could not be said of the failure to give instruction in the languages either ancient or modern. That was a very grave lack and it was because of this deficiency that when I was graduated from the Paterson High School in 1875, quite prepared to take the examination for college admission in mathematics, in English and in history,

I was without any knowledge whatever of either Greek or Latin, both of which were at that time prescribed subjects. The class of which I was a member was graduated from the high school in 1875 and the public exercises of graduation were held on the evening of June 25 at the Auburn Street Congregational Church which had recently been built at the corner of Auburn and Van Houten Streets. The size of our class had been greatly diminished, as is so often the case, during passage through the high school, so that at graduation our number was but thirteen. Eleven of these were girls and two were boys—Chancy E. French and myself.

In class rank I was given third place, the first going to Nancy Dillistin, a daughter of Alfred Dillistin, grocer, who lived in the First Ward and who was a girl with excellent mind and devoted to her studies, and the second to Mary Graham, a daughter of Archibald Graham, contractor and builder, who lived on what was then York Avenue, now East Eighteenth Street. On June 21, 1924, at the instance of Miss Susan Contesse, who for years occupied a responsible position on the staff of the Paterson *Press-Guardian,* the surviving members of our class were, so far as possible, brought together on the occasion of the laying of the cornerstone of the new high school erected between Market and Willis Streets. It was reported then that only one of the thirteen, Miss Anna Murphy, had died and most of the remaining twelve were present to greet each other and renew old-time associations of fifty years earlier.

My part in the commencement exercises was what was grandiloquently termed an oration, the subject of which was "The Age in Which We Live." I have in my papers the text of this address which is not without personal and historical interest. Its opening sentence, "This is indeed

a wonderful age" was a never-ending subject of teasing
on the part of my father and mother for many years. I
find that I have among my papers two other manuscripts
of about this period, one dealing with the history of
Paterson, which appears to have been written for some
public celebration by the high school, held December 15,
1875. I do not recall what the occasion was but it must
have had something to do with the origin of the Society
for Useful Manufactures, under whose guidance, at the
instance of Alexander Hamilton, Paterson was founded.
Still another manuscript is that of an address by me as
president of the Boys' Musical Club at Paterson, delivered on the occasion of the first public recital by the club.
This was given on April 3, 1877, in the old Sunday school
of the St. Paul's Protestant Episcopal Church which
stood at the corner of Ellison and Church Streets and
was subsequently destroyed by fire. The leader and director of this club was Professor Florian Oborski, an accomplished Pole, who was an excellent teacher of vocal
and instrumental music and who had come from Poland
to Paterson to seek his fortune. Very many years later,
indeed on April 9, 1916, I happened to mention Professor Oborski's name to Mr. Paderewski, who exclaimed
at once that he had known Professor Oborski very well
and had a very high opinion of him as a musician.

Following graduation from the high school, the personal and family problem was how I was to be prepared
for college and to what college was I to go. Our family
associations were with Williams College, where my grandfather Murray had been graduated in 1826 and my
uncles, Nicholas Murray and Thomas Chalmers Murray,
in 1862 and 1869 respectively. On the other hand, Princeton obviously offered strong attractions to a Jerseyman
and for some time we hesitated between the two. Cata-

logues were studied, costs and programs of study compared and every detail of the matter gone into. It was then that my stepgrandfather Meldrum's health caused him to retire from his important post at the Barbour flax spinning works, which fact in turn necessitated a rearrangement of my father's own business plans and responsibilities. As a result the eyes of the family were turned toward Columbia College in the City of New York and inquiries were made as to costs and conditions there. It is a curious coincidence that I was with my father and mother at the Grand Union Hotel, Saratoga Springs, N. Y., in the early summer of 1874 when a great intercollegiate boat race, thirteen crews participating, took place on Saratoga Lake. The colors of the various colleges were hawked about the hotel piazzas and, attracted by the prettiness of the light blue and white button of Columbia, I purchased one and wore it at the race. Sure enough, the Columbia crew won amid great excitement. All this may have been a forecast of what was shortly to come.

The work of college preparation, however, remained to be completed somewhere and somehow. Following my graduation from the high school I returned there in some anomalous capacity for a year of additional work, chiefly in mathematics and in Latin, which Principal Ridenour gave me personally and more or less as a private pupil. For the next two years I studied my classics at home and went for an hour each day to the study of the Reverend Doctor Wyckoff, who maintained a private school for girls in the old Stimson house on Church Street, which was afterward occupied by the Public Library and by the Hamilton Club and subsequently destroyed by fire. Doctor Wyckoff was a true pedagogue of the narrowest type but he heard my daily recitations, corrected my more obvious mistakes and helped me greatly to get ready to pass the dreaded college admission examinations which were looming in front of me for June, 1878. Fortunately, no knowledge of natural science, not even the most elementary, was required for college admission. Had it been, my rejection would have been certain.

Such very elementary scientific knowledge as I was able to gain was derived chiefly from books in my father's library. I well remember my early indebtedness to a little book which he had, entitled Peterson's *Familiar Science*. It was a book which had a literally enormous circulation during the sixties and seventies and which was widely read and used not only by teachers but by and in intelligent households throughout the United States. Modern science was then very little understood and this little book brought together in simple language and in the form of question and answer a vast amount of information of an elementary character, particularly as to physics, chemistry and meteorology. I have since learned that this book was based on an earlier English book of similar form and type which also had a large circulation and whose author was the Reverend Doctor Brewer, headmaster of King's College School, Norwich. In later years I was curious enough to look up these books and found that Peterson's *Familiar Science* was published in 1851 by George G. Evans of 439 Chestnut Street, Philadelphia. A copy of this book, printed in 1860 by that publisher, which was in my father's library, had on its title page "107th thousand." The book by Doctor Brewer was also published in the United States by James Miller, successor to C. S. Francis & Co., 647 Broadway, New York, and later in a revised and enlarged form by A. S. Barnes & Co. A very similar book, but much more elaborate, which I read with pleasure was *The Science of Common Things* by David A.

Wells, which was published by the house of Ivison and Phinney in 1857. It was from Peterson's book that I learned, by counting the seconds until the following thunder was first heard, how to tell the distance at which the electrical discharge which makes lightning took place. This fact interested me because just at that time there was much public interest in the subject of lightning rods and protection against lightning. A boy of curious mind had no difficulty in finding a hundred things to interest him in such a book as Peterson's. Another book of a wholly different character which is remembered for its interest and its contribution to my youthful knowledge is *A Child's History of the United States* by John Bonner which was published by Harper & Brothers in 1855 and which owes its inspiration and its simplicity to Charles Dickens's *Child's History of England.* There were also editions of Defoe's *Robinson Crusoe,* of the *Arabian Nights,* of the *Swiss Family Robinson* and of *English and Scottish Chivalry* by Charles Alfred Maxwell, that were well-thumbed and read many times. Still another favorite book which must not be forgotten was Mrs. Stowe's *Uncle Tom's Cabin,* which was read and reread and from the pages of which, by the way, I got my first knowledge of the existence of the most stately of all mediæval hymns, "Dies Iræ."

The textbooks that I used in preparing to be examined for admission to college in the ancient classics were old-fashioned but excellent. The Vergil, I recollect, was an inheritance from my father's schooldays, some thirty years earlier. It was well printed and helpfully annotated. The prescribed portions of Cæsar, Sallust and Cicero were all contained in one volume entitled Hanson's *Latin Prose,* the editor being, as I recall, a schoolmaster in the State of Maine. The Latin prose composition was studied in a volume whose author or editor was named Arnold. The

Greek grammar of Professor James Hadley of Yale, President Hadley's father, was the one used, and I have forgotten the names of the editors of the *Anabasis* and the *Iliad*. It was necessary in those days to prepare for examination on four books of Cæsar's *Commentaries,* on Sallust's *History,* on six orations of Cicero, on six books of Vergil, on three books of the Iliad and on Xenophon's *Anabasis,* together with Latin and Greek prose composition. The Faculty of Columbia College at that time also insisted on an admission examination in ancient geography. This was the only subject in which I was conditioned and that happened because I was unable, as almost any one however learned would be, to give in order, beginning with Greece and going eastward and northward all the way round to the Euxine, the names both in Latin and in English, first of the capes and then of the rivers of Europe. This very question throws a good deal of light on the very narrow and pedantic character of much of the college instruction of that period.

In preparing for college I was helped somewhat, though very informally, by an odd genius who was a great friend of our family, James D. Donnell. He had been graduated from Amherst College in 1867 in the same class with Professor Burgess of Columbia and had come to Paterson to make his living, partly by teaching and partly in other ways. For a long time he was clerk of the Grand Jury and later was County Superintendent of Schools. No more unprepossessing personality can be imagined than was his, but he was very clever and kindness personified. He helped me over many hard places when I was trying to read the Greek and Latin classics with only such aid as the Reverend Mr. Wyckoff could give me in our daily conferences. There was still another man in Paterson who gave me some instruction although not for a very great length of time nor very systematically. He was a typical German named William Rauchfuss, who taught both the German language and swimming to those young men and young women who desired to learn either. I did not get very far with him and later before going to Germany for the first time took daily lessons in spoken German from Professor Stern in New York whose *Studien und Plaudereien* was very well known as a textbook in those days and who as teacher of a living language had almost uncanny capacity and skill. It was due largely to a very brief training under him that when I went to Berlin as a student I was able to speak the German language and to understand it when spoken.

Looking back on my school days in Paterson, I cannot be grateful enough for the training given by the public schools of that city or for the friendship and instruction of the splendid women in whose classes I successively sat, as well as those of Mr. Ridenour. In fact, the Paterson public-school system of that day was exceptionally excellent and reflected the democratic, and what we are sometimes pleased to call the typical American, character of the town as it then was. The population numbered, if I recollect aright, about 50,000 at the census of 1870 and manufacturing industry was the community's hallmark. In fact, the city of Paterson itself, the history of which is all too little known, is one of the most interesting places in the whole United States and in the days of my childhood was an excellent town in which to live. The population was kindly, progressive and exceptionally intelligent. While the foundations of some large fortunes were beginning to be laid, there was no very great wealth accumulated in a few hands, but there was a great deal of widespread and satisfying comfort. The story of Paterson I have summarized in an address which I delivered on May 30, 1907, at the unveiling of the statue of Alexander Hamilton which stands in front of the City Hall in Paterson.[1] A most impressive and illuminating lesson in economic history and in the relation of population and social welfare to changing industrial conditions can be learned by following the history of Paterson from the time of its establishment in 1791 to the present. The successive waves of changing industry including cotton-spinning, iron and steel, locomotive-building, paper-making and silk manufacture, together with a hundred ancillary undertakings, controlled and conditioned the history of the town and its growth to a city of its present considerable size.

Finally, it is a satisfaction to record the value which conversations at my father's house had in giving me a point of view and a breadth of interest. Often during summer evenings there came to sit for an hour or two on the porch of the Hamilton Avenue house, or in the library when the shorter days and colder weather came, a group of my father's friends who like himself had genuine intellectual and public interests to talk about. These men gossiped not at all or very little about personalities and they were as unconcerned with money as if such a thing did not exist. They talked of books, of ideas, of politics and of the larger happenings in the life of the world. That all this had distinct educational value for a young schoolboy who was privileged to sit and listen cannot be doubted. Among these friends of my father I recall in particular James M. Baldwin, a member of the New York bar and a partner of the late Philo T. Ruggles; George Wurts, for many years editor of the Paterson *Daily Press,* the Republican evening newspaper of the

[1]*Why Should We Change Our Form of Government?,* New York: Charles Scribner's Sons, 1921, pp. 117–136.

town; and Eugene Stevenson, a most brilliant man, member of the bar and later in life a vice-chancellor of the State of New Jersey. There were others, to be sure, but these three stand out not only as the most frequent visitors but as the most sober and solid contributors to the conversations which I so well recall. There are many instruments of education, not all of which are set down in the books, and listening to good conversation is one of the most important of them all.

What I certainly got in those days was a good old-fashioned education.

IV
UNDERGRADUATE DAYS AT COLUMBIA COLLEGE

IN THE life of an American youth going to college is a real event. Certainly it was so in the days when college enrollment was only a small fraction of what it has since become. It was for most of us the first break with home ties and home surroundings, and it meant for all entrance into that larger if indefinable atmosphere which marks off the college from the secondary school.

My own preparation had been entirely adequate in all subjects save those which were then most important, Latin and Greek. The more or less informal and somewhat desultory character of my study of these two languages and the prescribed portions of their literature handicapped me somewhat in comparison with other youths who had come from excellent schools at which Greek and Latin were well taught. What I lacked in technical preparation, however, was perhaps more than made up by a very real and deep interest in both languages and in what they revealed and taught. At all events I had no difficulty with them in college and followed them eagerly throughout the entire four years. As a result I have retained through life not only my interest in the civilizations of Greece and Rome but a reasonable facility in reading their literatures in the original tongues.

The Columbia College of 1878 would not be recognized by those who are familiar only with the Columbia College of the present day. It enrolled fewer than two hundred and fifty students. It had a faculty of but ten or twelve men, and it was conducted on a system long since outgrown and abandoned. Nevertheless, it did its work well and for some reason not easy to understand or explain, the young men who attended Columbia College between 1875 and 1885 carried away a discipline, a range of information and interest and a love for the college itself that have never since been equalled, no matter what or how many improvements in the life and work of the college have been effected. Their number included eight or ten who subsequently rose to a very high plane of productive scholarship and who have left behind them noteworthy reputations as intellectual leaders.

Those who were then undergraduates and who are now approaching the sere and yellow leaf of life have always felt themselves bound closely together through the associations and memories of those particular undergraduate days. The class of which I was a member entered with seventy-eight students. They were, without exception, from New York City or its immediate vicinity. They were drawn from various types, groups and classes, and the old and well-to-do New York families were well represented among them. Perhaps the best prepared for their college studies were the two groups which came, one from St. Paul's School, Concord, N. H., and the other from the private school of Doctor Everson in New York City. On the whole, the standard of scholarship of the class was excellent and their interest in their daily work must have been satisfactory to their teachers.

The prescribed college program consisted of fifteen academic exercises a week, three each day from Monday to Friday, inclusive. The classes were held at 10, 11 and 12 o'clock and continued for fifty-five minutes. They were preceded by compulsory chapel exercises, for which the bell rang at 9:30. Prayers according to the prescribed form chosen from the Book of Common Prayer were read by the chaplain, who was then the Reverend Doctor Cornelius R. Duffie. A hymn was sung, and any announcements which the President had to make followed the chaplain's benediction. My recollection is that these chapel exercises were more or less of a farce. Compulsory chapel attendance lasted until 1891.

During freshman year our attention was concentrated upon the subjects of Greek, Latin and Mathematics. In addition to these there were two hours weekly given to Rhetoric and English Composition under the direction of Doctor John D. Quackenbos, who was much more of a secondary school than a college teacher, but whose insistence upon the avoidance of certain familiar solecisms and vulgarities and whose fondness for precision in the choice of words were wholly commendable and excellent in their effect. He never permitted us to confuse *farther*, relating to distance in time or space, with *further*, relating to inference. He used to insist that only a circle had a center and that a road, for example, had a middle but not a center. He was particularly insistent that we should avoid the split infinitive, as well as never make the very common error of saying *replace with* or *by* when the correct phrase was *displace for* or *by*. He told us that this very common use of the word *replace* was due to the mistranslation of the French *remplacer*. During sophomore year we carried on with Greek, Latin and Mathematics and in addition heard one lecture a week on general Chemistry by Professor Chandler, attended two exercises a week in English Literature under Professor

Charles Murray Nairne and were required by some curious freak of faculty unwisdom to study the Anglo-Saxon language and its very meager literature under the doubtless scholarly but certainly tactless guidance of Doctor C. P. G. Scott. During sophomore year there was inserted in the program of studies what on looking back one may see was the thin edge of the coming academic revolution. This was the study of the constitutional history of England, using the stout volume by Stubbs as a textbook, with Professor Richmond Mayo Smith, a most competent and learned young scholar whom Professor Burgess had brought back with him from Germany, as the instructor in charge. Beyond the weekly lecture on Chemistry given by Doctor Chandler in sophomore year, the two lectures weekly on Physics given by Professor Rood in junior year and the lectures on Astronomy given by Professor William G. Peck in senior year, we had no study of natural science as that is now everywhere carried on. If one happened to be a student of engineering, he had ample opportunity for laboratory work in Chemistry but otherwise the knowledge of science which he then obtained at Columbia College was only such as could be given by descriptive lectures. Both Professor Chandler and Professor Rood were quite admirable in this respect and I would not for a moment undervalue either the information which they conveyed or the effect which their teaching produced.

My distinct recollection is that the teaching of the classics in those days was almost wholly of that dry-as-dust type which has pretty nearly killed classical study in the United States. Professor Drisler, who was then the Jay Professor, was a man of remarkable elevation of character and of mind as well as a sound and thorough scholar. He was, however, so given to insistence upon the minutest details of grammar that our eyes were kept closely fixed

on the ground and we hardly ever caught any glimpse of
the beauty and larger significance of the great works upon
which we were engaged. For example, I recall that during the first term of the sophomore year we were to read
with Doctor Drisler the *Medea* of Euripides and that
when the term came to an end we had completed but
246 lines. In other words, we never came to know what
the *Medea* was all about or to see either the significance
of the story or the quality of its literary art. The Adjunct
Professor of Greek, Doctor Augustus C. Merriam, was a
scholar and teacher of a different type. He invited those
of us who were specially interested in Greek literature
to join what he called a βουλή, or voluntary class, which
met with him once or twice a week outside of the hours
set apart for the prescribed program of studies. In this
βουλή our little group read the entire *Iliad* and the entire *Odyssey*. We quickly became so facile that we were
able to read at sight, with occasional aid from Professor
Merriam, who enjoyed as much as we did the notable
experience of getting the swing and the sweep of the
story as it was unfolded in the noble verse of Homer. Professor Merriam unhappily lived but a few years, since he
died of pneumonia contracted while spending a year at
Athens in service as Director of the newly established
American School of Classical Studies there.

In Latin Professor Charles Short was a pedant if ever
there was one. He gloried in nice and fine distinctions
and in surprises, but whether he was dealing with Horace,
with Juvenal or with Tacitus, he was always attending
to the less important matters which the study of these
authors suggested. He had just collaborated with Doctor
Charlton T. Lewis in the editing of a new Latin lexicon
and constantly reminded us as an evidence of his thoroughness in scholarship that he had done the letter A,

while his colleague, Doctor Lewis, had done all the letters from B to Z, inclusive, in the same time that he, Doctor Short, had taken with a single letter.

In those days the towering personality for freshmen and sophomores was Professor John Howard Van Amringe, afterwards Dean of Columbia College. With his drooping gray mustache and square military shoulders, he loved to assume an air of terrifying fierceness, but as a matter of fact he was the kindest and most tender-hearted of men. During freshman year he came once weekly into our classroom and conducted the exercise, whether in advanced algebra or in solid geometry. During sophomore year he had personal charge of our instruction in mathematics. He made it his business to know every student before him and all about him. He treated each one and taught each one as a separate individual and yet never lost his grip on the class as a whole. Professor Van Amringe was in no sense a great mathematician, for the higher reaches of modern mathematics were quite unfamiliar to him. But for the clear, orderly and illuminating presentation of mathematical studies as included in secondary school and college programs, he was a teacher of the highest order of excellence. Over and above that, he quickly became a personal friend and counsellor.

Just as I entered college there arrived and was added to the faculty a young and most earnest scholar, Archibald Alexander, who had been graduated from Princeton College with the Class of 1875. He had then spent some two years or more in the study of philosophy and psychology at the German and Austrian universities. He came of a well-known family of scholars and teachers and brought an entirely new element, both personal and intellectual, into the faculty of the college. He taught us

Logic and Psychology in junior year and the History of Philosophy in senior year. Since these were, together with the classics, my favorite subjects of study, I came to know him very well and indeed immediately upon graduation became his assistant and during his frequent illnesses his substitute.

The revelation of Columbia College for me, however, and its greatest service were to be found in the teaching of Professor John W. Burgess, who in senior year gave four lectures weekly during the first term on the constitutional history of Europe and a like number during the second term on the constitutional history of the United States. His junior associate and protégé, Professor Richmond Mayo-Smith, was at the same time giving us two lectures weekly on the economic basis of the modern state. If any more remarkable instruction than this was ever offered in an American college, I do not know of it. To hear these lectures was like setting out on a voyage for the discovery of new lands and for the study of new languages, new literatures and new institutions. Professor Burgess's scholarship was not only profound, but in highest degree practical. He made the story of the development of political and social institutions so vivid and so real that it has never been even dimmed, much less forgotten. It was from these lectures that I first learned the distinction between the sphere of government and the sphere of liberty, and that distinction has controlled my thinking and my public activity during my entire life. I believe it to be the fundamental thought in all that relates to the social, economic and political associations and undertakings of men. It offers a sure foundation for the true philosophy of democracy, and it puts government in the place where it belongs, namely, that of subordination to the liberty which called it into existence to serve

JOHN W. BURGESS
[1844–1931]

Professor of Political Science and Constitutional Law in Columbia
University, 1876–1912

and to protect liberty. If I were to put my finger on any one person or any one series of ideas that has most profoundly influenced my thinking, that person would be Professor Burgess and that series of ideas would be those which he expounded in his lectures to the senior class in Columbia College during the academic year 1881–82. The lectures by Professor Richmond Mayo-Smith on the economic basis of the modern state were also singularly illuminating and informing. I took elaborate notes of these but unhappily during the years they have been lost and I found on inquiring of Professor Mayo-Smith's family after his death that he had apparently preserved no copy of the manuscript which he used in these lectures. I fancy they were drawn from lectures which he had heard while a student at the German universities, but they were nonetheless remarkable on that account.

The lectures by Professor Archibald Alexander on the history of philosophy lacked form, consecutiveness and adequate interpretation, yet the subject with which they dealt was to me so fascinating that I was drawn powerfully toward it. Professor Alexander's health was very fitful and uncertain, and he was obliged to omit a very considerable proportion of his stated academic exercises. So troublesome did this state of affairs become that, at the suggestion of President Barnard, Professor Alexander requested me, while still a senior, to act as substitute for him in giving instruction in Logic and Psychology to the junior class if he himself were detained by illness.

President Barnard was a most extraordinary figure. He belonged to a physical type that is no longer common and to an intellectual type which is always very rare. When I knew him his moderately tall form was invariably clad in a long black frock coat and black trousers, which were in sharp contrast to his snow-white hair and beard. He was exceedingly deaf and carried an instrument through which it was necessary to address to him even the most casual or uninteresting remarks. He had had an extraordinary career. Born in Connecticut of a well-known family and graduated from Yale College with the Class of 1828, he had, after those early experiences which are set out in the volume by Doctor John Fulton[1] which describes his life, sought his career in the South and was chief executive of the University of Mississippi and professor of mathematics and natural philosophy and later of chemistry and natural history at the University of Alabama. His active mind concerned itself not only with education but also with politics. He became the chief editorial writer for the local Whig newspaper, and an amusing incident is related of him in that connection.

His colleague, the editor of the local weekly Democrat newspaper, was obliged to be away for a time, and he requested Doctor Barnard to do his editorial work for him. During the absence of this editor Doctor Barnard conducted a lively political debate with himself, writing one week a Whig editorial and replying to it the following week with a Democrat editorial, as much to the mystification, one would think, as to the amusement of the reader of the two sharply opposed newspaper policies.

When the Civil War was impending, Doctor Barnard resigned his post, being a loyal defender of the Union, and came to Washington in very poor circumstances indeed. He obtained employment on the Coast Survey and it is reported that his remuneration was only $600 a year. How he came to be elected tenth President of Columbia College is a story of dramatic interest. The incumbent of the chair of physics, apparently not a very eminent

[1]John Fulton, *Memoirs of Frederick A. P. Barnard, 10th President of Columbia College in the City of New York.* New York and London: Macmillan, 1896, 485 pages.

FREDERICK A. P. BARNARD
[1809–1889]

Tenth President of Columbia College, 1864–1889

man, Professor McCulloh, left his post to join the Confederate forces and in 1863 his chair was declared vacant by the trustees. The choice of his successor was hotly contested, the two candidates most strongly urged being Doctor Frederick A. P. Barnard, then with the United States Coast Survey at Washington and one of the organizers of the National Academy of Sciences, and Ogden N. Rood, who after a very thorough preparation in modern physical science at the German universities was then at Troy, N. Y., as a member of the faculty of the institution there which it was hoped would be built into a genuine university. Through the support of Lewis M. Rutherfurd, who was then one of the most influential trustees of Columbia College and who was himself deeply interested in science, being an astronomer of no mean competence, the choice fell upon Professor Rood by the margin of a single vote. At just about this time President Charles King resigned his office because of ill health and sailed for Europe to spend the few remaining years of his life in Rome. His two daughters, Mrs. Eugene Schuyler and Madame Waddington of Paris, were both acquaintances of mine in later years and they had much that was interesting to say of their father's personality and peculiarities.

What the trustees had learned of Doctor Barnard during the contest over the vacant chair of Physics had impressed them so greatly that, the presidency of the college being vacant and Doctor Barnard having had a useful career at two universities in the South, they asked themselves what better could they do than to choose the rejected candidate for the chair of Physics to be tenth President of Columbia College. This they did on May 18, 1864, and thereby opened the way to pretty much everything that has happened since. What may be called the Barnard epoch was assuredly something new in the history of Columbia and marked one of those silent but complete revolutions which now and then manifest themselves in the institutional life of man.

In my student days Doctor Barnard's contacts with the students were few and far between. He addressed us from time to time at morning chapel on some matter of immediate interest, and of course on stated occasions such as the annual Commencements. It was his habit now and then to visit a classroom, apparently for no particular purpose since he could not hear what was going on. On such occasions we always rose in salute and remained standing until the President had left the room. For some reason or other which I cannot describe or recall, President Barnard took an interest in me and occasionally summoned me to his office during the afternoon to question me about various things or to offer me advice of one kind or another. It was on one of these occasions that my future career and dominating life interest were determined. This happened some time after the middle of junior year. Doctor Barnard sent for me one afternoon and, after a few preliminary words, asked me bluntly what I intended to do upon graduation. As a matter of fact, I had not given very much thought to this matter at that time, but I answered rather conventionally that I expected to study law, to take an interest in politics and to do the usual things that went with those interests and occupations. Doctor Barnard, after hearing this statement, replied crisply and somewhat bluntly: "That would be a great mistake. Any one can do that sort of thing and in fact hundreds do it every year. Why not do something distinctive, something that is really worth while, something new and constructive?" He enlarged upon these questions of his by plunging into a really eloquent exposition of the subject of education and of the place which the study of education and its problems should and might occupy in the intellectual and political life of the American people. He pointed out how the study of this subject had been overlooked in this country and that the way was open for some one who would make this topic his own, to have an almost clear field and to perform a really great constructive service, both for the intellectual life and for the American people. I listened with growing interest but without much understanding. Education I had always thought of as a mere process involving the teacher and the taught. To look upon it as a great social institution having a philosophical basis and a moral purpose and ideal was something that had never entered my mind.

President Barnard was quick to see my lack of understanding, but with kindly patience asked me to think over what he had said before coming to any decision as to my career. Meanwhile he added: "Read this book carefully and you will get some notion of what this subject is that I am talking about. Bring it back to me when you have read it and let me know how it impresses you." With this he dismissed me, having placed in my hands a little volume entitled *German Letters on English Education*,[1] which set forth in excellently clear fashion the observations of the author, a German public official, on education as conducted in England, with acute philosophical criticisms and admirable explanations and illustrations. Having read the book through once or twice, I returned it to President Barnard in due time with the statement that it interested me very much indeed and had opened up an entirely new field of study and reflection. The good doctor smiled and saw that he was making headway. Not long

[1] Ludwig Adolf Wiese, *German Letters on English Education,* tr. and ed. by Leonhard Schmitz. London: W. Collins, 1877, 296 pages.

after this he gave me to read during the summer holidays the stout *Geschichte der Pädagogik* by von Raumer,[1] which I discovered was the classic book on this subject in the German language.

My German was pretty poor, since I had had only such casual instruction as Mr. Rauchfuss had given me in Paterson and such very unsatisfactory teaching as I was getting by attending a voluntary class at Columbia, where, under the guidance of Professor Schmidt, a few of us were stumbling through Schiller's *Der Geisterseher*. In fact, one of the greatest deficiencies of the Columbia College of that day was the utter lack of instruction in the modern European languages. Of French we heard absolutely nothing, and the same was true of Italian and of Spanish. In German no stated instruction of any kind was offered, but those who were so minded might out of regular hours and without any academic credit meet Professor Schmidt twice a week for the study of this language in its elements. All this was changed with a rush when President Barnard succeeded in having the Trustees, by resolution adopted June 7, 1880, make complete and excellent provision for instruction in all the principal languages of continental Europe, including the French, the German, the Italian, the Spanish and the Scandinavian tongues. Nevertheless, I stumbled through von Raumer with the aid of a dictionary and discovered to my surprise that this subject of education of which President Barnard was speaking had a long and famous history and had really played a profoundly important part in shaping the current of civilization as well as in being shaped by that current.

The result of all this was that I became an enthusiastic

[1]Karl Georg von Raumer, *Geschichte der Pädagogik* . . . Gutersloh: C. Bertelsmann, 1877–80. 3 vols.

convert to President Barnard's ideas and hopes for me, and straightway resolved to abandon all thought of the study of law and its accompaniments and to give my life to an academic career for the express purpose of understanding, promoting, developing and applying the subject of education, both as an intellectual discipline and as a human institution. It was only a little later that I caught sight of the ideal of a modern university and quickly intertwined these two conceptions and purposes, the one with the other.

The College in those days, particularly during our first two years of residence, was a very simple and naïve sort of place. In not a few of its characteristics it differed little from a secondary school. A most curious marking system prevailed and was rigidly enforced. The monthly maximum for each class was obtained by multiplying twenty by the number of times the class attended in that course or department. Therefore, as there were fifteen normal exercises a week, the monthly maximum mark was 300. These marks were recorded with precision and were publicly posted each month. Our class was divided into two sections of approximately equal size, the line being drawn through its membership at about the middle of the alphabet. In our several classroom exercises we were seated in alphabetical order. For four years I had on my left Drayton Burrill, a delightful fellow who afterward became a prominent stockbroker in New York, and on my right Robert S. Carlin from Brooklyn, a very earnest and devoted student who subsequently entered the General Theological Seminary and became a priest of the Protestant Episcopal Church. Unfortunately, he died at an early age. All these queer academic habits and traits were marks of an era that had existed for some forty or fifty years but which was now approaching its end.

On the surface there were no signs of the upheavals that were about to take place and which did take place beginning in the year 1880. Trustees and members of the faculty, some of them at least, probably appreciated the extent and character of the forces that were at work making for change and progress, but the students were quite oblivious of it all. The main factor was, of course, President Barnard, who, despite his years, his infirmity and his increasing feebleness, was an intellectual force of great vigor and effectiveness. His Annual Reports were the first of their kind to contain discussions of large questions of educational theory and educational policy, but they were usually so far in advance of contemporary opinion that they failed of immediate effect. President Eliot once told me that it was President Barnard's Report of 1866, in which he pointed out that college attendance in the United States was falling off in proportion to the population, which turned his attention to questions affecting the attractiveness and adequacy of the conventional college curriculum of those days and which led him shortly thereafter to his vigorous advocacy of the elective system of college studies.

These Reports, particularly those for 1877 and the following years, contained discussions and expositions some of which proved to be prophetic and all of which have become classic. The Report for 1879 created a panic by advocating the admission of women to Columbia College, a recommendation which was continued with renewed vigor in the reports for 1880 and 1881. It is the latter Report that contains the exposition of education as a science, which was undoubtedly in the President's mind when he was discussing this subject with me at just about the time when he must have been at work upon the preparation of this document. No more admirable or complete exposition of this subject has ever been made by any one. The Report for the year of my graduation, 1882, included a careful and elaborate presentation of the argument for the development of Columbia College into a university. Copies of these Reports were given me by President Barnard upon their appearance, and their reading and study were part and parcel of the influences which controlled and shaped my choice of a life career.

In his official relations President Barnard had a rather hard time. By reason of his restless intellectual activity and his wealth of fertile ideas for the improvement and development of Columbia College as it then was, he ran counter to the prejudices and conventions both of the faculty and of the trustees. Every member of the faculty and every trustee had the greatest possible respect for President Barnard and held him in highest esteem, but they did not on that account accept his views and recommendations, far less give him that undivided and cordial support without which a leader in any cause is hopelessly handicapped. Time and time again I have seen President Barnard come from the monthly meeting of the trustees, face flushed and muttering to himself, as a result of some recommendation which he thought important having been either pigeon-holed or negatived.

In those days the trustees really administered the College in all its details, leaving practically no authority or initiative to the faculty, and to the President only such as he could acquire and command by reason of his personality and arguments. The trustees had formed the unfortunate habit of interfering with every detail of college administration, no matter how small. The result was always delay, misunderstanding and too often incompetence. Meeting as they did for two or three hours on one afternoon each month from October until June, the trustees required every act or recommendation, no matter how minute, to come before them for consideration and action. A famous case had reference to the request of Professor Quackenbos that there be placed in his lecture room a small wooden box with a locked door, into which students in Rhetoric and English Composition might drop their papers at prescribed times, all this being for the convenience of Professor Quackenbos himself. This recommendation went to the trustees and was by them referred to the Committee on the Course and Statutes to inquire and report as to whether such an addition to the educational equipment was expedient. The trustees on receiving a favorable report from this Committee, then referred the proposal to their so-called Standing Committee to ascertain whether the proposed construction was practicable. When this Committee reported in the affirmative, another reference was made, this time to the Treasurer for consideration as to whether an appropriation could and should be made to meet the cost, estimated at $4.50. In due time the Treasurer reported favorably and the box was put in place on the wall of the lecture room occupied by Professor Quackenbos. Meanwhile, however, an academic year had passed and more or less of the energies of some twenty men had been drawn upon to secure a determination of this great question.

The letters of Hamilton Fish, who was an active and influential trustee from 1840 to 1849 and from 1851 to 1893, and the diary of the Reverend Doctor Morgan Dix, who was an equally active trustee from 1862 to 1908, and that of George T. Strong, who played a leading part in the work of the trustees from 1853 to 1875, all of which are still unpublished but to be found in the Columbia University library, contain abundant and very detailed evidence of the way in which the trustees of that time passed upon questions of most minute detail. Indeed, it is plain that in the opinion of the distinguished Rector of Trinity Church, the business cared for by the trustees at their stated meetings was a good deal of a bore. Of the meeting held on November 6, 1879, Doctor Dix writes: "Of all the bores of my life, those meetings are the greatest." On March 6, 1882, referring to the consideration that was being given to the choice of a new professor of English Literature, Doctor Dix recorded this opinion on his return from the meeting of the trustees:

The state of mind of the trustees on the subject of the Professorship is simply chaotic; no one is sure of any candidate, and no one person can be said to be prominent in any way.

All appointments were made by the trustees without any reference whatever to faculty opinion and with only minor consideration of the recommendations of the President. The trustees invited and secured from all sorts of persons not connected with Columbia College applications for appointment and recommendations of candidates. In connection with one important vacancy I remember seeing a printed list of the names proposed for appointment, together with a summary of the academic records of each and the names of their endorsers. The list contained some twelve or fifteen names, and the endorsers were almost without exception persons not connected with the teaching staff of Columbia College.

It must be said for the trustees of that day that as individuals they were an exceedingly strong body of men. A board that commanded not only the service but the willing and devoted service of such men as Hamilton Fish, Samuel B. Ruggles, William Betts, Lewis M. Rutherfurd, William C. Schermerhorn, the Reverend Doctor Morgan

Dix, Stephen P. Nash, Joseph W. Harper, Jr., and Doctor Cornelius R. Agnew, was a board with which few other like bodies in the country could be compared, save unfavorably. The changes that were to revolutionize the relation of the trustees to the work of the College began at about the same time as did the intellectual and educational revolution which took place in the College itself. This was marked by the election as trustees during my undergraduate years of Edward Mitchell, W. Bayard Cutting and Seth Low, who were the first of the group which was to guide and control the institution during the two epoch-marking decades that followed. They were all still trustees at the time of my own election to be President of the University.

Of course it goes without saying that such an administrative system as then prevailed at Columbia College was quite preposterous. To have trustees as individuals participate in and interfere with the daily administration of the educational work of the institution was in violation not only of all wise academic procedure, but of common sense itself. Nevertheless, this habit of participation and interference on the part of the trustees had been so thoroughly formed that it was very difficult to break, and it was not until it was broken that the faculty began to be what it should have become much earlier, and that the President acquired the opportunity and power of leadership which belonged to that office. In one notable instance the trustees went so far as to decline to permit President Barnard to print, without their previous censorship, one of his Annual Reports because of the vigorous arguments it contained in support of his recommendation that women be admitted to Columbia College on equal terms with men.

In the relation of the trustees to the College there was during the quarter century which preceded the year 1885 one especially unfortunate circumstance. The Treasurer of the Corporation was Gouverneur M. Ogden, and in his hands rested the management of the corporate finances, including the oversight of the leasehold properties which constitute the so-called Lower and Upper Estates. Mr. Ogden was a trustee and during much or all of this time was also Comptroller of Trinity Parish. He was able, devoted and most conscientious, but his whole conception of the College was as a property-owning and property-developing corporation. To spend money for the precise purpose for which it had been given to the trustees seemed to him most reprehensible. His every instinct was to save, to acquire and to what he described as "plow in." Being a trustee, his incumbency of the office of Treasurer gave him a commanding position and for many years he was not only a thorn in the side of President Barnard but, despite his ability and devotion, a most unfortunate influence in all that affected the relation of Columbia College to the City of New York. It was by reason of his point of view and activities that the legend came into existence and gained ground that Columbia was so rich that it needed no new gifts. That legend has not died away even now and during its half century or more of continuance has done infinite harm. In the light of this situation the trustees became very restless and the passing years made them increasingly conscious of the harm which Mr. Ogden's policy was doing. Therefore when Mr. Ogden died in 1885 they postponed the election of his successor as Treasurer until they had amended the By-Laws of the Corporation so as to provide that thereafter the Treasurer should not be a trustee. Having accomplished this, they thereupon elected as Mr. Ogden's successor John McLean Nash of the class of 1868, whose father, Stephen P. Nash, was a most influential trustee. Mr. Nash served with loyal devotion and complete unselfishness in this important office until his death in 1916.

There is another story which ought to be recorded, since it illustrates perfectly the point of view and the attitude toward the public of the trustees of that day. On one occasion shortly before my undergraduate years, and before the erection of the building known as Hamilton Hall which stood on Madison Avenue between Forty-ninth and Fiftieth Streets, the Corporation was officially notified by the Regents of the University of the State of New York that on a given day and at an hour named the Regents would make an official visitation to Columbia University, being represented for that purpose by their Chancellor, Mr. Pruyn, and two of his associate Regents. At the hour fixed for the visit a carriage containing the three Regents drove up to the entrance to the old campus on Forty-ninth Street, just east of Madison Avenue. The iron gates to the Campus were closed, and standing on the pavement to greet the visitors were the chairman of the trustees, Mr. Hamilton Fish, Mr. Samuel B. Ruggles and Mr. Gouverneur M. Ogden, Treasurer of the Corporation. Greeting the official visitors and bowing with that punctilious and splendid manner which Mr. Fish always had, he said to Mr. Pruyn: "Mr. Chancellor, we are most happy to welcome you here this morning. It is my duty to say to you, however, that if you come as Regents to make an official visitation to Columbia College, as a matter of right, then the gates behind me are closed. If, on the other hand, you come as citizens of the State of New York interested in education, to see our work and our equipment, then everything that we have is freely at your service." Mr. Pruyn hesitated a moment and then accepted Mr. Fish's invitation to visit the College. The gates were thrown open and the episode ended.

The purpose of Mr. Fish, Mr. Ruggles and Mr. Ogden was to indicate with perfect clearness to the Regents of the University of the State of New York that the Regents had no legal authority over Columbia College, which was in existence before their own body came into being. It was an odd happening and thoroughly characteristic not only of the trustees of that time, but of Mr. Fish himself. He was the highest and finest type of American gentleman of the old school, but he never yielded any point of law or of what he conceived to be of right.

Something ought to be said of the social life of the undergraduates of that time. There was no provision for residence in college and there had been none since the removal in 1857 from the old and original site on the Queen's Farm at Church and Murray Streets. Nevertheless, the undergraduates had voluntary social organizations of their own that were numerous, interesting and in many respects of good influence. The Greek letter societies played an important part, and the best known among them, Delta Kappa Epsilon, Delta Phi, Delta Psi and Psi Upsilon, attracted to their membership pretty much of all that was best in each class of that period. There were two old literary societies which divided the allegiance of the students, the Philolexian Society, founded in 1802, and the Peithologian Society, founded in 1806. These two societies held weekly meetings for the reading of essays, the delivery of orations and the carrying on of formal debates. They were entirely under student control and were admirable in every way. A few years earlier some undergraduate schism had led to the foundation of a third literary society named for President Barnard, but while it flourished for a few years this society never had anything like the importance or the influence of the two old and historic organizations. The Philolexia and Peithologia, as they were familiarly called, represented that same movement among American college students which is marked at Princeton by the American Whig and the Cliosophic Societies and at the University of North Carolina by the two like societies there. All four of these go back to the eighteenth century and so indicate that in the years which preceded and attended the foundation of the government of the United States, American undergraduates were busily engaged in practising the arts of oratory and of debate.

There were student publications of various sorts. The *Acta Columbiana,* which appeared at intervals of three weeks, was a combination of college newspaper and magazine. Of this I became an editor during freshman year and was editor-in-chief for a year or two following. Just before I entered college the *Columbia Spectator* had been established by a group of clever young men who combined literary and artistic skill. Each year the junior class published a volume which was more or less a summary record of undergraduate organizations and happenings. This was known as the *Columbiad.* For the *Columbiad* of my class I was editor-in-chief and the author of the nonsensical pseudo-drama with which the volume opened entitled "A Glimpse of Hell or an Hour with the Anglo-Saxons." This was an attempt to describe in undergraduate fashion the happenings in the classroom of Doctor Scott, who had charge of the course in Anglo-Saxon then prescribed for sophomores. That estimable gentleman was greatly offended by the publication and began vigorous proceedings to have the entire board of editors disciplined. The only real sufferer in the matter was Robert Arrowsmith, my intimate friend and chum, whose devotion to Columbia lasted until his death a few years ago. He, as business manager of the publication, was summoned before the faculty for examination and possible punishment. His account of the episode was always most amusing, since as a matter of fact several members of the faculty, including Professors William G. Peck and Van Amringe, entirely sympathized with the fun-making of the students at the expense of Doctor Scott. They probably felt, however, that they could not yield to their sympathies in this respect and joined in a more or less formal and meaningless rebuke of Arrowsmith. What they did do, however, was to forbid the circulation of that *Columbiad*. Such copies as were still in the hands of Arrowsmith were turned over to the faculty and destroyed by burning. Very few copies remained. One of these found its way into the University Library for permanent preservation and one I have in my own personal collection of undergraduate material.

In those days athletics flourished with some difficulty. There was no athletic practice ground or field belonging to Columbia, and those who would play football or baseball or who would participate in track athletics had to go by train to Harlem to find opportunity for training and exercise. The crew had a boat house on the Harlem River and, despite obstacles, made some excellent records. Indeed, one of my first exhibitions of college loyalty after receiving notice of my admission to the freshman class was on a hot summer night in July, 1878, to parade up Fifth Avenue with a shouting group of students and alumni offering welcome to the Columbia crew which had just returned from their victory on the Thames at Henley. This was a notable occurrence in the history of American college athletics, to say nothing of the commotion which it made in Columbia College itself.

I was rejected both as a candidate for the class crew and for the football team because of insufficient weight, but I did play cricket and enjoyed it greatly. At that time cricket was played at Columbia, at Harvard, at the University of Pennsylvania and at Haverford, and there were intercollegiate matches almost every spring or autumn between teams chosen from the student bodies of these colleges. I was a member of the Columbia cricket team for two years.

A markedly weak point in the equipment of Columbia College in those days was the Library. It contained only a few thousand volumes and was housed in one fairly large room above the Chapel. It was open for a very limited number of hours and on very restricted terms. One of the student jokes was that no books were bought save such as the librarian had time to read before they were placed on the shelves. At a time when the annual appropriation for the support of the Library was $1500, the librarian infuriated Professor Burgess by stating in his annual report that he was happy to say that he had expended but $300 of this amount. Professor Burgess, in turn, scandalized not only the librarian but the trustees by placing an order in London for a complete set of *Hansard's Parliamentary Debates* in order that his students in constitutional history might have this material available for reference and study. His action in so doing was regarded as little short of scandalous, which only shows what a long distance we have come in the relatively few years between that time and this. So far as the books on philosophy are concerned, I can testify that almost every book now in the University Library in that field, other than the *Bampton Lectures* and Sir William Hamilton's *Lectures on Logic* and on *Metaphysics,* was bought by myself or by those who have succeeded me in the administration of the Department of Philosophy.

There was one characteristic in the life and work of

the Columbia College of those days which has long since passed and does not command the attention which it deserves. In the year 1859, presumably following the stirring up which attended the famous report, prepared a year or two earlier by a committee of trustees, on the state of the College and ways and means of developing it into a university, the faculty ordained that the five students of each graduating class who stood highest as shown by the records of their conduct and scholarship during their whole course of four years were to be known as honor men and their names published in the annual catalogues. A few years later this rule was amended so as to provide for the publication only of those who stood in what was described as the first class of honor. These were students whose average rating over the whole four years was 95 or higher, the maximum being 100. The names of these first honor men, beginning with the Class of 1859, were regularly published in the annual catalogue for thirty years, when the system was discontinued. An examination of that printed list will show that it contains a very large number of names of men who subsequently became useful, important or even famous, either in letters or in science or in public service or in the church or in the world of practical affairs. This list, covering as it does some thirty years, establishes conclusively the fact that there is a direct relationship between high academic standing and achievement in later life. It is a very remarkable list and would well repay republication and comment now. It will be found in full in my Annual Report for 1937.

The graduation exercises of our class were held, as was then customary, at the old Academy of Music on Irving Place and Fourteenth Street early in the month of June. Professor William G. Peck, who had a magnificent military bearing, having been graduated from West Point, as he took much pride in reminding us, as head of the class which was graduated one year earlier than that in which the future General Ulysses S. Grant ranked No. 21, acted as chief marshal. In his queer, squeaky voice he called the roll of dignitaries who were entitled to places in the procession, beginning with the President of the United States and coming down through a long list of national, state and city officials until he finally reached some one who was in attendance. The exercises were of the old-fashioned sort and opened after prayer with a Greek salutatory oration which had been assigned to me. To this day I can remember the first line of it but absolutely nothing more. That line was this:

Ἤματι τῷδε πάλιν, νεαροὶ φίλοι ἠδὲ γέροντες

There were two or three English orations, music, the award of prizes and finally a valedictory address by a member of the class. Each man received his diploma from the hands of the President, and when the procession had retreated and disbanded, undergraduate days were at an end and the stern business of everyday life had to be faced.

My financial experience as an undergraduate is rather interesting. When I entered college the annual tuition fee was $100, raised a year or two later to $150. From that day to this the last money ever given me by any one, which I have not myself earned, was my father's check for $100 to the order of the Treasurer of Columbia College, with which I paid my tuition fee for the freshman year. From that time on I had no difficulty in earning, by teaching and by journalistic work, such modest sums as were needed to pay my college bills and to meet my ordinary personal expenses. The latter were reduced by the fact that for nearly the whole of the first two years I resided with my stepgrandfather and grandmother in Brooklyn and was thereby saved the cost of board and lodging. I did more or less writing for the old *New York Tribune* and taught both in the very smart school for girls conducted by Mrs. Sylvanus Reed and in the private school for boys conducted by Frank Drisler, son of our own Professor Drisler, who was himself a Tutor in Mathematics when our class entered college. In those days there were several money prizes given, with a value of $100 each, following special examinations at the close of freshman, sophomore and junior years. During my undergraduate course I was awarded several of these and was to that extent assisted financially in meeting my own expenses. When I was graduated from college I had paid all my college bills and incidental expenses, including three summer trips to the West, except tuition for freshman year, and had about $1000 in the bank.

During its progress through college our class, as so often happens, suffered greatly in numbers. While about a hundred offered themselves for the admission examinations in June, 1878, only seventy-eight passed those examinations and were enrolled with the freshman class in the following October. When we came to graduation there were but forty-nine names on the roll. A few of these had been added by transfer from other colleges after the Class of 1882 had entered college, so that probably more than half of those who were enrolled as freshmen disappeared before graduation day came around. The class was one of average ability, of average social composition and has been one of average achievement in later life.

It is clear that my choice of Columbia College was providential. Had I gone either to Williams or to Princeton, as was at one time contemplated, the whole course of my life would certainly have been very different. There would then have been no President Barnard and no Professor Burgess. Williams College was at that time in a state of intellectual torpor, the period of Mark Hopkins having closed and no new and powerful stimulus to the intellectual life having yet been developed. More than that, Williams College, excellent institution as it is, lies isolated and remote in the Berkshire Hills and is quite apart from that busy life of man, intellectual, social and political, which has always had for me a most powerful attraction. At Princeton conditions were quite different. The extraordinary and unique personality of President McCosh was shaking up the dry bones of an institution which had been little more than a country high school in New Jersey. Intense and narrow, restless and persistent, impatient and abounding in new suggestions and ideas, Doctor McCosh brought about at Princeton a veritable revolution. This revolution was under full headway at the time when I should have been an undergraduate had I gone there. To realize what sort of service Doctor McCosh rendered, one has only to recall the names of West, Alexander, Scott, Osborn, Ormond, McCay, Magie, Wilson, Fine, Armstrong and Hibben to appreciate that he spurred into intellectual performance a most distinguished group of young men who brought honor to themselves and fame to Princeton by their service to scholarship and to science through long years of productive activity. For me, however, Columbia College with its historic background, its urban environment and its new era just ready to begin was, as the event proved, the happy and fitting place to receive my fundamental intellectual discipline as well as the stimulus and the ideals of a lifetime. Two priceless possessions I certainly gained from those four undergraduate years. One was the constant companionship of ideas and ideals and the second was a profound respect for scholarship and for scientific method. Surely, to have given these two possessions to a company of American youth is an achievement sufficient to counterbalance any number of idiosyncrasies and shortcomings.

V
THE YEARS OF GRADUATE STUDY

AN ACADEMIC career having been decided upon, with the philosophic study of education as its cornerstone and university building as its foundation, the obvious steps following graduation from college were to make the necessary and adequate preparation. My father was reluctant to give up his hope that I would choose a career that would make possible official participation in the political life of the country, but he was good enough to be greatly interested in my hopes and plans and to follow them with affectionate and intimate attention. For such a task as I had in mind it was desirable to pursue without delay advanced courses of graduate study both at home and abroad, and if possible to obtain the higher university degrees. On graduation I had been awarded the Fellowship in Letters, which with a like Fellowship in Science was given each year to those members of the graduating class who it was thought would be able to profit by graduate study and training in research. This fellowship had a value of $500 a year and was tenable for three years. Professor Alexander, who naturally had charge of my advanced work in philosophy, gave me most excellent counsel for which I shall always be very grateful. He told me to postpone my period of study at foreign universities until I had first taken at Columbia the degree of doctor of philosophy; since, as he pointed out, the requirements for this degree in Germany were so very minute and so very technical that the time and effort necessary to comply with them would be largely wasted and would prevent my getting those greater benefits which a period of free and untrammeled university study in Germany and France would certainly bring. When I contrast my own experience with that of other young American students who were without this sound advice, I am doubly grateful to Professor Alexander.

He put me to work upon the philosophy of Kant, and subsequently guided me through the entire development of nineteenth-century German philosophy including Fichte, Schelling, Hegel, Schopenhauer and von Hartmann. Since I had already come to know Doctor William T. Harris of St. Louis and was following his papers printed in *The Journal of Speculative Philosophy* and elsewhere, this entire experience was most illuminating and abundant in intellectual stimulus. For a week or two during one summer vacation I attended the sessions of the Concord School of Philosophy, where the venerable A. Bronson Alcott and Doctor Harris were the presiding geniuses. As a topic for my dissertation I took "An Outline of the History of Logical Doctrine," and went to work upon it most assiduously. The choice of this topic was influenced by the fact that although but a young graduate student I was teaching logic to the junior class with considerable regularity, since Professor Alexander's uncertain health made him quite ready to turn this task over to me when he found that I was willing to do it and could carry it on to his satisfaction. As a matter of fact the combination of advanced study and teaching was wholly admirable. The practical work of teaching constantly raised new queries, and the opportunity for systematic graduate study provided the ways and means of answering these. At that time candidates for the degree of doctor of philosophy were not required to print their dissertations but to deposit a manuscript copy in the college library. I distinctly recall complying with this regulation, but in these later years have not been able to find my dissertation anywhere. I assume that, perhaps with other unimportant material of like character, it was lost or destroyed when the university was moved from the Forty-ninth Street site up Morningside Heights. In addition to my graduate study of philosophy I continued my work in Greek and Latin, getting some glorious experiences from the study of Plato but finding little benefit from the work given me by Professor Short. How unimportant his work was for my particular intellectual interest may be seen from a very technical philological paper which I contributed at Professor Gildersleeve's request to the *American Journal of Philology* in October, 1885, with the title "The Post-Positive *Et* in Propertius."

Both my graduate study in philosophy and my teaching were more or less hampered by the paucity of the college library as it then was. Something had to be done to put pressure upon the authorities to provide us with books and periodicals. President Barnard had just succeeded in carrying out another of his projects and had brought Melvil Dewey to be librarian in place of the antiquated gentleman who had held that title for a number of years preceding. Mr. Dewey was a revolutionist in every sense of the word, and before we knew it the college library, from being almost non-existent, blossomed out into the most interesting, the most rapidly advancing and the most useful part of the whole college administration. Mr. Dewey can never be thanked enough for what he did as librarian in those days. He was part and parcel of what I have always called the Barnard-Burgess-Dewey revolution. Had it not been for him, no one can say how long it would have taken Columbia to get such a magnificent and well-administered library as it has possessed these many years. We younger men, together with the new faculty members who had been appointed to chairs in the modern languages and in political science, whole-heartedly supported every proposal for the expansion and improvement of the library. Unfortunately Mr. Dewey went so far and so fast that, to use a familiar phrase, he sawed off the limb upon which he was sitting. The less progressive element among the trustees viewed him and his policies with unconcealed alarm and they put no obstacles in his way when Mr. Whitelaw Reid, then an influential regent of the University of the State of New York, invited Mr. Dewey to go to Albany as the executive officer of that body.

While it was to be some years before there was any recognition of education as a subject of graduate study, yet, at this time, through the kindly counsel of President Barnard, I was becoming familiar with the literature of education and with classic works on the subject in English, in French and in German. His own cousin, Henry Barnard of Connecticut, who had been, together with Horace Mann of Massachusetts, one of the earliest moving forces in the building of the American common-school system, used to visit President Barnard occasionally, and I had the pleasure and satisfaction of making the old gentleman's acquaintance. His career was then drawing to an end, but there was opportunity for me to form great admiration for his personality and public service and for his literally stupendous accomplishment in planning and publishing his *American Journal of Education*. From all this it was but a short step to the study of Horace Mann's reports and then to an examination of the forces that were then at work to promote the advancement of education in the United States. One of these was obviously the National Education Association, which I joined in 1885 and to which I gave vigorous and enthusiastic service for some twenty years. Then that organization, from being a body of genuine educational leaders who were dealing with ideas and institutions, degenerated into a large popular assembly which quickly fell into the hands of a very inferior class of teachers and school officials whose main object appeared to be personal glorification and personal advancement. So it passed out of the picture.

During this period of graduate study, the ferment in the trustees and in the faculty was steadily increasing. The newer accessions to the trustees were more amenable to the progressive ideas that were in the air than were their elders, while Professor Burgess was persistent, persuasive and untiring in presenting his conception of university development and university work. It was at that time that he wrote his remarkable paper entitled, *The American University: When Shall It Be? Where Shall It Be? What Shall It Be?*[1] which put into a few thousand words the gist of the argument which was so soon to carry conviction in places of authority. He used to tell this story which illustrates perfectly conditions as they then existed.

In his Annual Report for 1880, President Barnard commented with ill-concealed sadness and disappointment upon the fact that the year had brought no final consideration and approval of certain propositions pending before the trustees, which would, if adopted, constitute a new departure in the educational system of Columbia. It so happened, however, that at the very meeting at

[1]Boston: Ginn, Heath and Company, 1884.

which this Report was submitted, resolutions were adopted approving both arrangements for a wholly new and ambitious program of instruction and advanced study in the modern European languages and the establishment, as a first step toward the development of a university system, of a School of Political Science precisely as planned and advocated by Professor Burgess. The latter had left New York some weeks earlier to visit European universities and to consult with the small group of really remarkable young men whom he had selected to be his colleagues and associates in the new enterprise. These men were Richmond Mayo-Smith and Edmund Munroe Smith, not in any way related, both graduates of Amherst College and former pupils of Professor Burgess, who were shortly to become at Columbia the distinguished representatives of economics and statistics and of Roman law and comparative jurisprudence, respectively; together with Clifford R. Bateman of Illinois, also a graduate of Amherst and a former pupil, whom Professor Burgess had selected to develop the subject of administrative law. Unhappily, Mr. Bateman died almost as soon as he entered upon his work at Columbia. He was succeeded as representative of administrative law by Frank J. Goodnow, another Amherst man, who served with distinction as a member of the faculty of Columbia University until he went to be president of Johns Hopkins University in 1914. During a bright summer day, early in June, 1880, Professor Burgess was stretched at length on the sunny slopes of the Rigi, talking over his plans with the two Smiths and Bateman, when a messenger boy handed him a cable dispatch from New York signed by Samuel B. Ruggles. The message read: "Resolution authorizing School of Political Science adopted today. Thank God the university is born."

This rather striking episode is an illustration of the keenness with which Professor Burgess, on the one hand, and his allies among the trustees, chief of whom was Mr. Ruggles, on the other, were pursuing their ideal. President Barnard was with them heart and soul and supported them by every means within his power. Despite his infirmity and the passing years, his mind was as keen, as fresh and as open to new ideas as if he were fifty years younger. President Barnard grew old in body but he never grew old in mind.

It was my good fortune to be in close touch with all this through President Barnard and Professor Burgess, to follow their arguments with admiration and with sympathy, and to read all the reports, even those that were confidential, which accompanied and recorded the discussions that were going on. It was a liberal education to have had that relationship in those days.

In addition to carrying on my graduate study, I was all this time teaching and writing in order to earn the income necessary to meet my expenses. I did some journalistic work for the old *New York Tribune* and for the Paterson, N. J., *Daily Press*. From Harry Thurston Peck, the brilliant scholar of the Class of 1881, I took over the task of trying to make it possible for the younger son of Mrs. Brockholst Cutting to pass the examinations for admission to Columbia College. This young man had many amusing and interesting characteristics, but love of study and capacity for learning were not among them. After two years the task was given up as hopeless with the consent of all concerned. At the same time I was getting some personal experience of the administration of public business and earning a little additional income by serving for a time as secretary to the Board of State Prison Inspectors of the State of New Jersey and as secretary to the New

Jersey Commission on State Water Supply. My father was a member of each of these bodies and my selection was, of course, due to him. These posts, while in nowise important, did give rather exceptional opportunity to come in contact with some matters of large public importance and social significance. Some of the things I learned from conversation with prisoners, and much that I learned through hearing the discussions as to the impounding and distribution of potable waters, have stood me in good stead these many years.

It was through this service in connection with the administration of the New Jersey State Prison at Trenton that I met Samuel Gompers, and I joined him in doing all that I could to improve the conditions of prison labor. Gompers was a very remarkable man. I came to know him well and worked in close co-operation with him for a number of years in the endeavor to improve labor conditions of various sorts and kinds. It also proved to be possible to use the summer holidays to begin that acquaintance with our western country which has been so intimate, so full of enjoyment, and so helpful in many ways. There is hardly any part of the continental United States that I did not visit either then or in the years shortly following. In addition I made a journey to Alaska in 1887 when that territory seemed much farther away than it does now. Fortunately, I reached the western country before the frontier life had entirely disappeared.[1] It was still to be seen in the Black Hills, in some of the mining camps of Colorado, in Arizona and in Nevada. The settlements and camps whose life and interests then filled with amazement the mind of a curious youth, have long since passed into sedate and conventional communities. As a result of all this, before I was thirty years of age, I

[1]See Volume II, *That Amazing West of Ours.*

had spoken either on education or in political campaigns in every State and territory of the United States. There was no community of any considerable size in which I did not have at least an acquaintance, and in hundreds of cities and towns there were men and women whom I could justly call friends and companions. The importance of these contacts and associations in broadening my horizon and in giving me a real knowledge of the American people and of our entire country cannot be overestimated.

The examinations for the degree of master of arts were in nowise difficult, and were quickly passed at the close of the academic year 1882–83. Those for the degree of doctor of philosophy were a quite different matter. Professor Alexander, who had me in charge, subjected me to a series of discussions and questions which lasted the better part of a week. These took place at Castle Stevens, at Castle Point, Hoboken, where Professor Alexander then lived, he having married the daughter of the house. We discussed and debated for two hours or more each morning, and then after luncheon he resumed the grilling, which ended only late in the afternoon. Not only was I required to be familiar with the general history of philosophy, but to have a very intimate and detailed knowledge of modern philosophical literature since the seventeenth century. The whole theory and practice of logic from the time of Aristotle, and the literature of that subject, including the new theories just then being brought forward in England and France, particularly by Keynes and Jevons, were also part of the ground covered. Finally my dissertation was accepted, my examinations pronounced satisfactory and the degree was awarded at the commencement of 1884. The time had then come for my first trip abroad.

To meet the cost of this, I had accumulated something

more than $2500, and my University Fellowship had one more year to run. Having taken my degree, I gained permission from the trustees, through President Barnard, to spend the third year of the Fellowship abroad. I came within an ace of missing this opportunity owing to the embarrassment of the Second National Bank in which my money was deposited. By great good fortune, and after standing in line for several hours, I was able to draw out my balance just before the bank temporarily closed its doors. My passage was booked by the Cunard Steamer *Servia*, then the newest and best of the transatlantic ships. With her 8500 tons and her very restricted accommodation when contrasted with the great transatlantic liners of today, it is difficult to see how we were able to look upon her, as we did, as a model of comfort and luxury. My passage ticket from New York to Liverpool in the first cabin, where I shared an inside stateroom with another man, cost eighty-five dollars. The crossing was uneventful, but my new and marvellous experiences began as soon as I touched the landing stage at Liverpool on the eighth day after leaving New York.

It has never been, and is not now, possible for me to land in England, or to be on English, or rather British, soil without a feeling of exaltation. It must be the ancestral blood which manifests itself in instinct and emotion, but England and Scotland are in my case the old homeland where everything seems familiar and upon which everything that has happened in the world for hundreds of years seems chiefly to be built. The French are the Greeks of the modern world, while the English are the ancient Romans. The French have all the Greek intellectual precision, artistic perception and sense of detachment, and have cast these in a mold and in forms of expression purely their own. The English, on the other hand, despite the marked intellectuality of their leaders generation after generation, and despite their massive contributions to literature and to science, are distinguished above all else by their practical capacity to govern themselves and other peoples, by their steady common sense and by their ability to solve the most serious problems, not with the instruments of formal logic, but with those of reasonableness and of practical-mindedness. What has been said of England, what has been said in her praise by authors and by poets, quickly finds and has always found a responsive echo in my own mind and heart. There are some lines of Kipling which stir the blood of any one who loves England as I do, and it is a keen pleasure to read over and over again those stately and well-known passages of English prose which record and extol the English achievement and the English spirit.

From Liverpool it was a short journey to Chester, which, by reason of its old buildings and its walls, had peculiar attraction for a young student from America who saw it for the first time. My first Sunday in England was spent at the village of Kirkheaton, near Huddersfield, at the home of Mr. Hefford Ainley, whose brother-in-law, John Shaw by name, had been my father's neighbor in Paterson and had made him executor of his will. In this way, I had come to know the Ainleys, and they were good enough to ask me to stop with them as soon as possible after reaching England. The younger son of the family, Joseph H. Ainley, who died in 1938 at Harrogate, became my good friend and remained so throughout his life. Unhappily a very grave form of illness seized him while still a young man and he was never able either really to enjoy life or to continue in any active occupation. It was he who took me on my first visit to York Minster and who pointed out every architectural beauty and every historic spot in that wonderful cathedral. It would interest no one but myself to record the experiences of the next few weeks, striking and absorbing as they were. A crowded visit to London, where my first personal contacts with men and women of importance were established, primarily through Lord Coleridge, whose mother was a daughter of the Reverend Doctor Gilbert Buchanan of Woodman-sterne and therefore my father's aunt, was followed by visits to half a dozen cathedral cities, to Stratford-on-Avon, to Oxford and to Cambridge, and then to Scotland. There I had opportunity to visit at St. Andrews my step-grandfather's family, the Meldrums, and at Rohallion, in the valley of the Tay, between Perth and Dunkeld, Mr. John Bett, an old-time friend of my father's. Mr. Bett was a Scotsman who had spent some fifteen or twenty years in New York in business, and having acquired a substantial fortune returned home to spend the rest of his life in comfort and ease. Rohallion was a revelation to me, since, while I had often read of such places, I had, of course, never seen, much less visited, one. It was a stately old-fashioned house, surrounded by hundreds of acres of shooting. It was Mr. Bett's great pleasure to take me up on one of the hills of Rohallion and to point out to me both Birnam Wood and Dunsinane, in order that I might see how accurate was Shakespeare's well-known line.

After this came a hurried visit to Belgium and to Holland, a trip up the Rhine by boat, two weeks in Paris, and then by train to Berlin to settle down to the winter's work. What followed is told, as fully as I can remember it, in the next chapter, "A Voyage of Discovery." Many of the experiences of the year that followed are burned so deeply into my consciousness that even today they are as keen and as vivid as though they had but just taken place.

In Berlin I lived at a pension kept by Frau Doktor Jüngling at 48 Mohrenstrasse, and was as comfortable there as the climatic conditions of Berlin in winter would permit. Then sun used to rise, nominally at least, about nine o'clock in the morning and to set somewhere about three o'clock in the afternoon. As the sky was overcast substantially every hour of the time from November until March, one could work or read only with lighted lamps. The son of the house was an odd person of middle age, Paul Jüngling, who wrote literary and dramatic criticism for the *Vossische Zeitung* or "Tante Voss," as it was popularly called. He was very critical, indeed contemptuous, of America and Americans, but a good deal of the advice he gave as to books to read and plays to see was sound and useful. Having been freed through Professor Alexander's sound counsel from the duty of making technical preparation for the degree of doctor of philosophy, I was able to spend my time in whatever way seemed most profitable and most enjoyable, as well as most likely to help me fulfill the purposes for which I had come to Europe.

A great advantage and opportunity which the university student in Berlin had in those days came from the privilege which he enjoyed of admission both to the Royal Opera House and to the Royal Theatre for a merely nominal sum on presentation of his student's card. My recollection is that one paid a mark, about twenty-five cents, to be admitted on a student's card to the upper gallery. It may well be believed, that with this abundant opportunity at hand, it was possible to acquire a liberal education both in the opera and in the classic drama. The artists were, of course, of the highest class, and the resulting enjoyment and benefit were great indeed. In fact, it may truthfully be said that the informal and inci-

dental advantages which came from student residence
in Berlin at that time were quite as great as those which
resulted from formal academic relationships, if not greater.
The distinguished scholars, men of letters, and artists
whom one constantly met were themselves powerful instruments in a liberal education. Imagine what it meant
to an American youth who was planning to devote his
life to scholarship and to university service, to come face
to face with Mommsen, the historian of Rome, with Ernst
Curtius, master of Greek archæology, with Wundt of
Leipzig, who was revolutionizing psychology, with Klein
of the same university, who had a notable group of young
American mathematicians in his seminar, and to hear
Vahlen at Berlin conduct his seminar in Latin! My impressions of Zeller and Paulsen, valued and indispensable
teachers, are recorded in the chapter to which reference
has been made. I also found it possible to hear lectures by du Bois-Reymond, whose pamphlet entitled *Die
sieben Welträthsel* was just then being read by every one
and eagerly discussed; by von Treitschke, whose fiery eloquence seemed more amusing than important; by Gneist,
who had made himself a chief authority in the field of
English constitutional history; and by Pfleiderer, the eminent theologian.

There was one incident of that winter which impressed
me deeply, since it illustrated the human kindliness of a
powerful monarch. The social season in Berlin opened
with the court ball given in the Royal Opera House early
in January. Invitations were naturally limited to the
court circle, and were exceedingly difficult to get, particularly for foreigners. To my great delight, I was invited by Frau von Schaack to be her escort on that occasion. This lady had been born of a noble family, and in
childhood was a playmate of the Crown Prince, after-

ward Emperor Frederick III. She had made an unfortunate marriage and had not been able to maintain her
personal and social position. Indeed, her husband had
gone to America and left her without support. Oddly
enough, some time later, I came upon him as an inspector
of customs at the Port of New York. Although Frau von
Schaack was no longer able to maintain her social position, and indeed was keeping a pension at 203 Friedrich-
strasse, she had not been lost sight of by the old emperor
and his family. The court ball was a most brilliant sight,
since Germany was then at the very height of its power
under Bismarck, and the men whose names were associated with the war of 1870-71 were for the most part
still living. The brilliant and distinguished company, with
breasts covered by orders and ribbons of every conceivable sort, made a very gay and impressive scene. At about
ten o'clock trumpets sounded and the emperor began his
slow march about the room, the crowd falling back to
make a lane through which he and his following company
might pass. The emperor bowed now and then from left
to right as he recognized faces, his blue eyes shining under
his shaggy reddish eyebrows. On his arm was the Empress
Augusta, this being what proved to be her last public
appearance. Following behind were the Crown Prince
and his wife, and after them Prince William of Prussia,
afterwards Emperor William II, and his recently wedded
wife, and behind these some twenty or thirty personalities
of the greatest distinction. Among them were the very
beautiful Princess Friedrich Karl, Bismarck, von Moltke,
von Roon and others. It is not easy to describe the sensa-
tions of an American student at finding himself face to
face with this truly great company of men and women.
The point of the story which I wish to record is that, as
the line was formed to allow the royal party to pass, Frau

von Schaack found herself in the front row of the company. As the old emperor came to where she was standing, he stopped for an instant, bowed and took her hand. She was the only person in the entire company whom he greeted in this personal way, and it was plain to me that his act was intended to mark the fact that, although her lot in life had not been what it once promised to be, he did not propose to overlook the old relationships or her personal merits. It was a very touching and a very charming incident, and Frau von Schaack went home that night literally walking on air.

Experiences and conditions in Paris were quite similar to those in Berlin. In Paris, while following courses of lectures at the Sorbonne and familiarizing myself with the city and its life, I lived at 85 Rue La Boétie with the family of Madame d'Harmenon. She was a very able woman in middle life, with a large circle of acquaintances among men of letters, artists and musicians, with all of which Paris abounds. Her husband was a quiet little man, somewhat older than herself, who was a professor in the Lycée Condorcet. Madame d'Harmenon had gone to England during the troubled period of 1870–71 and had maintained herself by giving French lessons in Bristol. She spoke English well and had a greater knowledge of English ways and customs than was or is usual for French women of her class. The conversations at table in the Rue La Boétie and the small informal evening gatherings were both highly interesting and often amusing. Time and again there would come for déjeuner or for dinner or for the evening some celebrated musician or some well-known man of letters. All of this was full of advantage for one who, like myself, was keen to go beneath that more or less formal surface of things which is all that the usual American traveller sees when he goes to Europe.

From Rue La Boëtie to the Sorbonne was a distance of some two or three miles, which I traversed on foot regularly every morning. Sometimes I would go by one street and sometimes by another, with the result that before long I had a fairly intimate knowledge of the central and older part of Paris with its local markings, its shops and its monuments. Gambetta unfortunately had died before my first visit to France and, therefore, I never saw or heard him. At that time, however, his name was still on almost every lip, and his career was being discussed constantly in the press. A powerful political figure just then was Jules Ferry, and by a piece of good fortune I happened to be in the gallery of the Chamber of Deputies on the afternoon that his ministry fell in the division over the Tonking episode. In those days, however, I saw less of the politicians and public men than of the intellectual leaders of France, concerning whom I have recorded my impressions in the following chapter.

My intimate relationship with France and its leaders which began in 1885 has been continued with increasing strength to the present day. As Member of the Academy of Moral and Political Science, and therefore of the Institute of France, I enjoy an invaluable association which is as abundant in pleasure as it is full of honor. In student days I heard lectures by Taine and Renan and found myself in social circles where were Daudet and Zola, Brunetière and Gaston Boissier, Gaston Paris and Fustel de Coulanges, as well as Henri Poincaré, the very eminent mathematician. In later years and through the generous and kindly offices of my intimate friend and associate, Baron d'Estournelles de Constant, I came to number among my acquaintances and friends almost every important man in France. It will suffice to name M. Briand, for whom I had the greatest possible admiration. M.

Poincaré, whose mind, while formal and legalistic, was very powerful, M. Léon Bourgeois, who declined almost as many high honors as he accepted, and M. Hanotaux, whose rapid-fire criticisms and judgments and whose literary skill make him always a most stimulating companion.

That student visit to Europe ended with a few weeks in London during which I spent not a little time in trying to familiarize myself with the collections of the British Museum and the best methods of using these for my purposes. I lived right under the shadow of the museum at 6 Montague Street, Russell Square, where the new buildings of the University of London have since been built.

Probably twelve months could not have been spent by me to better advantage in preparation for what I planned to do than were the months between June, 1884, and June, 1885. This was my first and, so far as I could then forecast, probably my only visit to Europe, and I hungrily made the most of it. Little did I think then that I should cross the Atlantic more than fivescore times, and that the life of London and of Paris, of Berlin, Vienna and Rome, would become as well known to me as that of New York, and that the nooks and corners of western and central Europe were to be as familiar as those of my own United States.

The cost of this period of travel and study was grotesquely small when judged by present standards. There is still in my possession the account book in which I recorded every item of expenditure, whether large or small, during these twelve months. Including the two voyages across the Atlantic, the expense of travel through Great Britain, Holland, Belgium, Germany, Switzerland and France, as well as the cost of living and the academic fees at Berlin and Paris, amounted in American money to

almost exactly $1750. By the American students at Berlin
I was looked upon as unduly extravagant because I paid
for my room and board in Mohrenstrasse the princely sum
of 140 marks or $35 a month. In Paris the cost of room
and board in the Rue La Boétie was 40 francs or $8
a week. It must be said that in both cases full return was
given for the money paid.

VI

A VOYAGE OF DISCOVERY

WHEN, in 1807, the philosopher Hegel published his *Phänomenologie des Geistes*—a work
which seems to me one of the most note-
worthy in all the literature of philosophy—he referred to
it as a voyage of discovery. He gave the work this inviting name because in it he undertook to trace the history
of consciousness in its growth from the first stages of culture up to those theoretical and practical convictions
which underlie modern civilization and constitute its basis
and foundation. I am using the term in an analogous but
far less ambitious sense. What I have in mind is to state
as simply and as directly as I can, and as correctly as
may be possible after the passage of fifty years, the impressions and reflections of a young American who, like
so many others of his day, took ship a generation ago to
seek instruction and inspiration at the universities of a
foreign land.

So rapidly have our American universities progressed
during the past generation that it is only with some effort
that we can think ourselves back and reconstruct the
academic life, organization, and methods of fifty years
ago. At that time a visiting European would have been
able to discover no universities whatever in the United
States. He would have found Mr. Eliot in the midst of his
severe task at Cambridge, reorganizing Harvard College

and its attendant professional schools, giving new ideas to their governing boards, leading in the reconstruction of their programs of study, and exerting a wide influence on the thought and policies of academic teachers in all parts of the United States. He would have found Doctor McCosh growing old at Princeton, but full of zeal and abounding in vision, and so stirring the imagination and appealing to the ambition of a group of young students that he created by his own efforts an exceptionally talented company of productive scholars, though few in number. He would have found a small Columbia College in the City of New York, with President Barnard calling aloud for the means with which to make progress and to seize the opportunity that he saw so clearly, while here and there a younger scholar was planning plans and dreaming dreams of what might some day be brought about on that ancient foundation. He would have seen vigorous intellectual life at Philadelphia, at New Haven, at Ithaca, at Ann Arbor, at Madison, at Berkeley, and at Charlottesville, but at no one of them would he have found a university. On reaching Baltimore he would have opened his eyes a little wider. For here, still young and still taking on form, was the promise of a real university. Here had been brought together by the genius of President Gilman a company of really advanced scholars and a small group of really inspiring and productive university teachers. Everything was being subordinated to the university ideals of inquiry, of productive scholarship, and of publication. The beginnings were yet small but they were highly promising.

The fact that these were the conditions then existing in the United States was one of the reasons why the more ambitious and energetic of those American college graduates of that day who looked forward to scholarship as a career hastened across the Atlantic as soon as means could be found, to Oxford and to Paris, to Berlin and to Vienna, to Leipzig and to Göttingen. To come under the influence of a European university, particularly of a German university, was then the height of academic ambition.

For half a century the German universities had been drawing to their libraries, lecture-rooms, and laboratories an increasing number of American youth. These had been received with great hospitality, and they had repaid the welcome tendered to them by assiduous study and by grateful recollection and appreciation of one, two, or three years of scholarly companionship, intellectual stimulus and careful discipline. As the young American of the scholarly type reached the close of his college course, or perhaps after he had passed a year or two in graduate studies at his alma mater, he possessed himself of a *Universitäts-Kalender,* and began to inform himself regarding the leading German scholars, the lectures that were to be given during the following semester, and conditions and cost of life in a German university town. Every scrap that had been printed on any of these subjects was read with avidity, and questions, definite and precise, were asked right and left of those older scholars who had already been enrolled at a German university. The processes and ceremonies attendant upon reporting to the local police, upon matriculating at the university, upon securing the signature of the proper professors to the student's *Anmeldungs-Buch* were inquired into, and suggestions as to procuring suitable lodgings were eagerly sought. It must be confessed that when all these questions, necessary and unnecessary, were answered the undertaking still seemed to be a venturesome journey into a strange and quite unknown land. The little German and French that were then taught in college would not bear the weight of the necessities of daily conversation and must be quickly supplemented by practical instruction in both languages. Financial arrangements had to be made, and the cost carefully counted. Finally, the plunge was taken and the shores of America faded from sight for the first time.

One can never be young but once, and one can never make the first trip to Europe a second time. There is something quite unique in the anticipation with which one first approaches the Old World in the endeavor to make its acquaintance. From history and from literature in both prose and verse, as well as from anecdote and books of travel, the whole scene is intellectually familiar, or at least it seems to be so. Contact with it, however, dispels this illusion and reveals for the first time real Europe, whose heart is beating underneath the surface with the blood-flow of centuries in a way that cannot be recorded and described on the printed page. Then, as now, too many Americans went abroad without ever getting to Europe at all. They got to hotels where only Americans went; they got to banking houses where only American newspapers were on file; they got to summer resorts where Americans predominated; but too rarely did they get beneath the surface of Europe to come in contact with the rich, fine, cultivated life of the people. The student bent upon getting the best that a European university had to give was more fortunate. He was literally forced beneath the surface of Europe, and was compelled to enter into the familiar and institutional life of England, of Germany or of France, just as an Englishman, a German or a Frenchman would do. In Germany, to be sure, he was apt to want to live on a little higher plane than the usual German student. He wished for somewhat better food and was satisfied with somewhat less beer. He liked a better-warmed room during the cold days and nights of a north European winter and he could not subsist without some measure of that ventilation which the Continental European regards as one of the most mischievous manifestations of the Evil One.

Nevertheless, the American student, particularly in Germany, was able in those days to come very close to the life of the people, to enter into their joys and their anxieties, to read their newspapers and their books, to go to their concerts and their theatres and to hear their reflections upon the world at large, and particularly upon that new world from which the student himself had come. At that time there was more migration from Germany to America than is now the case, and there were somewhat more and stronger immediate personal ties between households in the Fatherland and households on this side of the Atlantic. Nevertheless, the lack of understanding of America was complete. The fact that some persons had been lynched in New York during the draft riots of 1863 had developed into a conviction that lynching was a favorite New York pastime, and that delicate women were exposed to the disagreeable sight of victims of the lynchers hanging from an occasional lamp-post. Any public disorder or dereliction, or any unusual or discreditable occurrence which the newspapers had made much of, was magnified into a habit or an institution. There were no American institutions of higher learning; there was no American literature; American art was not existent and American science was a negligible quantity.

All this was a great shock for the young voyager, who had set out with a quite different impression of his own country's importance and achievements. He found now that it was regarded, good-naturedly enough, as an overgrown and irresponsible child, rich no doubt and likely to grow richer, but not able to make any contribution to the higher life of the world. Argument on any one of these points was of little avail. The minds of men and women, even those of more than usual intelligence and wide reading, were closed. The result was frequently vexation of spirit and loss of temper, but the discipline was useful. This sort of reception was well suited to reduce the bumptiousness of the young American, and to make him understand for perhaps the first time how old and how large the world was and how set were its ways of thinking and of appreciating the newer peoples.

The winter of 1884–85 was a particularly interesting time to be in Berlin owing to the Socialist agitation then in active progress. The city was in what was technically termed a minor state of siege. This was a rather toplofty term to describe a situation in which police regulations as to domicile, public meetings, processions and the like were particularly stringent. At that time Berlin was much less than one-third its present size. The population was probably 1,200,000, and as there were some 20,000 soldiers stationed in and about Berlin, one who had never seen a military officer in his life, except in a parade of the militia on Decoration Day, met these gayly uniformed gentlemen at every turn, in the streets, in the cafés, and in all places of public resort, with no little surprise. This experience of itself induced reflection. What were all these officers and soldiers doing? Why were they withdrawn from productive industry? Why were they so quickly deferred to by the civilian population? Such questions as these the young American asked, and he received replies that revealed to him, again for the first time, a different view of the state and of government from any that he had come in contact with at home.

New and interesting experiences awaited him at every turn. Emperor William I, *der alte Kaiser,* as he was affectionately called by the populace, was to be seen every morning in the window of his working-room at the palace, at the corner of what was then called the Opern Platz. It was the custom of His Majesty to return by a gracious gesture every greeting from one who might pass his window, and to rise in his place and formally salute whenever a body of troops, however small, passed by. The Crown Prince, who was after a few years to succeed to the throne for three months as Emperor Friedrich III, was the very ideal of manly dignity and beauty, and seemed to incarnate in his own person the attributes and traditions of royalty. His eldest son, who succeeded to the throne until his reign was ended by the Great War, was then an officer of the garrison. He was frequently seen driving or riding about the city, and came into familiar converse with a considerable group of young men, among whom occasionally an American student was included. The daily sight of royalty and of the imperial trappings and ceremonies gave to the institution a reality that it had never before had in the American's mind. To him Emperors and Kings had always seemed far-away personalities, recorded in history and worthy of a place beside the demigods and heroes of the ancient mythology. Now he was to find that these royal personages were very real, terribly human, quite visible to the naked eye and ready to enjoy and to enter into all the pleasures and satisfactions of life.

Naturally the university itself was the first place to be sought out after the great Friedrich Strasse Bahnhof had been left behind and lodgings chosen and occupied. So this was the great University of Berlin! On either side of the court sat in marble state the two Humboldts, Alexander and Wilhelm. The low, well-proportioned building, built of brick and covered with stucco, had a curious attraction. In and out of its doors and across this court had walked for seventy-five years some of the great men of the world. What would one not have given to see Hegel cross the garden behind the university building, making his way toward the Platz which now bears his name and which contains his effigy; or to see Schleiermacher turn his steps toward home at the end of one of his great lectures on religious feeling to the students of theology! Imagination could even see the magnetic personality of Fichte himself moving about in these halls and streets. Trendelenburg, Harms and Droysen had recently died, but von Ranke was still there as a link with the past, although he was nearly ninety years of age, and opposite his name in the announcement for the semester were printed the significant words *liest nicht*. It was a great occasion for the young American when he first put his foot inside that academic building. Every hallway and every lecture-room seemed to echo with the footsteps and with the voices of great scholars who had shaken or moulded the world of thought. The bulletin-boards were covered with curiously written notices of one sort or another. Every notice was eagerly spelled out in order to gain some information of student customs and of academic life. Then the offices of dean and of questor were hunted up, in order that when the time came for the formal ceremony of matriculation one might know where to go.

The next step was to buckle down to a better mastery of the German language. Hours each day were devoted to poring over German grammars and reading books; to conversation in lodgings, on the streets, and in the Thiergarten with companions who were chosen for the purpose; in reading the daily newspapers and in attending

The University of Berlin, 1884–1885

the theatre. Of all these devices perhaps the two most useful were the daily conversations on the streets and in the Thiergarten with chosen companions and the nightly visit to the theatre, where precise enunciation and correct pronunciation seemed to make German so easy to understand.

A letter from Professor Chandler to Hofmann, the great Berlin chemist, was the occasion of some concern, for it proved that Hofmann was at the moment rector magnificus of the University of Berlin, and how to approach so exalted a personage required both preparation and advice. The preparation took the form of a solemn suit of black and a silk hat. Advice took the form of pointing out the hour of the day when the eminent personage should be sought at his own home. This proved to be a simple little house on Dorotheen Strasse, not far from the university buildings; but the formal preparations seemed to have been made in vain, when the rector magnificus opened the door himself and took his frightened and awed visitor by the hand for a most friendly and kindly conversation. This visit broke the ice. If the rector magnificus was so easy to approach, then to meet the professors, both ordinary and extraordinary, to say nothing of the Privat-Docenten, must be a very simple matter indeed. So in most cases it proved.

As the particular subject of study in this case was to be philosophy and educational theory, the steps of the newcomer were naturally directed first to the apartment of Eduard Zeller. This apartment would be as easy to find today as it was fifty odd years ago. Professor Zeller and his charming wife, the daughter of Ferdinand Christian Baur, the founder of the so-called Tübingen School of Theology, lived at 4 Magdeburger Strasse, III Treppen, and thither the young inquirer climbed. Zeller's personality is not likely ever to be forgotten. He was then seventy years of age, slight and spare of build and frame, with a massive forehead and the kindest of kind dark eyes. While at work in his study he usually wore a long dressing-gown fastened at the waist by a cord, and he stood at a high desk like a bookkeeper, with his notes and books of reference spread about him in orderly fashion. Here was the greatest living authority on Greek philosophy, and the man whose patient industry had brought to a conclusion the *Philosophie der Griechen*, an almost final authority in its field. Never was great scholar kinder to the youngest and most callow of apprentices, and never were more pains taken to give a youth an insight into the life and thought of the Greeks and their meaning for all time. Moreover, Professor Zeller saw to it that his pupil had opportunity on Sunday evenings to meet, under his roof, some of the most charming and cultivated men and women who then adorned and represented the intellectual life of Berlin. After all these years one can see now the quick-moving figure of du Bois-Reymond, the physiologist, whose pamphlet entitled *Die sieben Welträthsel* was then being widely discussed and attacked; or the graceful gentleness of Goldschmidt, who had no superior as a master of commercial law, and whose conversation moved easily over both legal and practical topics. On these Sunday evenings, too, there occasionally came Gneist, who was particularly interesting as the chief authority on English public law; Vahlen, whose spoken Latin in his seminar on Lucretius was as delightful as it was novel to hear; and Ernst Curtius, who can still be seen in the eye of memory sitting at the base of a statue in the Neues Museum, placidly describing to a group of students, notebook in hand, the characteristics and significance of the works of ancient art by which they were surrounded. On

EDUARD ZELLER
[1814–1908]

Professor of Philosophy at the University of Berlin, 1872–1895

two of these Sunday evenings Bismarck joined the company unannounced and sat smoking his pipe as unconcernedly and talking as freely as if he were an ordinary citizen instead of the ruling power of a great nation. Those were truly noteworthy evenings, and on looking back it would seem as if they were perhaps of more and more lasting educational value than the laboriously attended lectures that extended over so many months.

One's first experience in a German university lecture-room is interesting in the extreme. At that time there was nothing like it in America. In order to be officially permitted to attend a course of lectures it was necessary to seek out the given professor in his private consultation-room and to secure his signature in the *Anmeldungs-Buch.* On request he would assign a specific seat in the lecture-hall, particularly if the student were a foreigner and anxious to be placed where he could hear clearly. In one particular *Anmeldungs-Buch* it is still possible to spell out the signatures of Zeller, for his course on the general history of philosophy; of Paulsen, for his courses on the introduction to philosophy and on educational theory, as well as for his seminar on Kant's *Kritik der reinen Vernunft;* of Dilthey, for his course on logic and theory of knowledge; of Rehmke, afterwards professor at Greifswald, for his practical exercises on Kant's *Prolegomena;* and of Doctor Lasson—who lived to be more than eighty-five years of age—for his course on fundamental philosophical problems.

These great scholars differed widely in their method of presenting their several subjects. On Zeller's own recommendation very few notes were taken of his lectures. The young American having possessed himself of a copy of the professor's *Grundriss der Geschichte der griechischen Philosophie,* followed closely his exposition, book open in hand, and wrote out his impressions of what had been said on returning to his lodgings. Dilthey, on the other hand, was very insistent that precise notes should be taken. To this end he divided his daily lecture into two parts. It was his custom to speak for about twenty-five minutes in a general way in exposition of the subject under immediate consideration, and then for twenty minutes to dictate, with painstaking accuracy and reiteration, precisely what he wished the student to put down. It would have been so easy for Professor Dilthey to print this material in a pamphlet that his practice was always resented as more or less of a reflection on the art of printing.

Few lecturers were more persuasive, illuminating and delightful than Friedrich Paulsen.[1] This extraordinary man was then just coming into his fame and reputation. While his classrooms were crowded and his influence very great indeed, he was still but a *professor extraordinarius*. The reason popularly assigned for this in the university was that Paulsen was somewhat too progressive and radical in his views to command the full approval of the ruling powers at the Cultus Ministerium. He was thirty-nine years of age, and his swarthy complexion, flashing eye and eloquent voice made an impression that no lapse of time will ever weaken or destroy. In his lectures on educational theory he opened up what was to the young American a wholly new and unknown field of inquiry. The notion that the great activity and human interest called education might be subjected to scientific examination and analysis and might be shown to rest upon definite philosophical principles was nothing short of a revelation. In America education had always seemed to be—well, just education! In Paulsen's crowded lecture-room, on the

[1] *Friedrich Paulsen: An Autobiography.* Translated and edited by Theodor Lorenz. New York: Columbia University Press, 1938.

other hand, it was a most fascinating subject of study. In his seminar on Kant, Paulsen came in very close touch with the fundamentals of his subject and with the select company of students who were admitted to his companionship, there to receive the severest and most searching criticism both of the methods and of the results of their work. Twenty years afterward, when Paulsen had come fully to his own and when his influence not only in Germany but outside of it was literally enormous, and when the years had turned his coal-black hair into a most becoming iron-gray, he, seated either in his study or in the garden of his home at Steglitz, used to laugh over the experiences of long ago and to recall with that American student, who remained to the end his close and intimate friend and correspondent, much that had happened in the interval both in Europe and across the Atlantic. Paulsen was much touched by the appreciation accorded him in America, and when Professor Frank Thilly, then of the University of Missouri, translated his more important books into English he was as much pleased as a young girl on going to her first ball.

There are other impressions and memories, too, no less vivid and no less inspiring. There were the evening popular lectures of du Bois-Reymond, who reflected the curiously divergent influences of Johannes Müller and of Neander, in which he expounded and interpreted in masterly fashion the developing progress of modern science and the significance of its controlling principles and its most far-reaching results. There were also the early lectures in what soon proved to be a far too technical course to follow, by von Helmholtz on *die Wellentheorie*, in which he connected together by a single formula and brought under the dominance of a single law, wave-motion of every sort, whether manifested in the realm of matter, in that of mind, or in that of social organization. Then there were the Monday evening popular discourses by von Treitschke, who was at the very height of his influence and power. To listen to these discourses was, for the first few moments, distinctly disagreeable, since von Treitschke's deafness left him without any power to control his voice. In consequence it was frequently almost painful to listen to his utterance. It was not long, however, before one forgot the utterance in the vividness and vigor of what the man was saying. That at the end of a generation his social and political philosophy was to shake the whole world with the evidences of its power was little dreamed of in those days. True, von Treitschke's attacks on England, and on America as well, seemed even then to be very bitter and very frequent. But they proceeded so plainly from a complete misconception of the Anglo-Saxon character and temperament that they did not seem likely to be practically influential. Treitschke's favorite complaint against both Englishmen and Americans was that they were hypocrites and nations of mere shop-keepers making pretense to the possession of cultivation. More than once he said, with the most astonishing emphasis, that England and Englishmen were lost to all idealism and that they possessed no national vigor. Interesting as this was, it was not long before the basis on which it rested made itself plain. Treitschke could not understand how any nation or people could prefer common sense to logical perfection, and so, when the Anglo-Saxons, deterred by common sense, failed to carry out to their logical conclusions certain professed principles of conduct, he accused them of hypocrisy.

Then there was Pfleiderer, who represented what was left of Hegelian influence in the faculty of theology. There was Kirchhoff the Hellenist and Kirchhoff the physicist.

FRIEDRICH PAULSEN
[1846–1908]

Professor of Philosophy at the University of Berlin, 1878–1908

Brunner was teaching German legal history, and Dern-burg was painfully expounding the Pandects to students of law. Bernhard Weiss, who lived to a great age, had classes of considerable size in the theology of the New Testament and the life of Christ, while Dillmann lectured on Old Testament theology. Waldeyer, the great anat-omist, whose name long stood at the head of the list of the medical faculty, was leading the world in his partic-ular branch of knowledge, as was Virchow in his, although he found time to engage in politics and to stand as a candidate for the Reichstag. Robert Koch was a member of the medical faculty, but his greatest fame was yet to come. Mommsen was nearly seventy years of age and quite the most picturesque figure in the whole university group. His spare, keen face, with his long, white hair and sharp black eyes and bent shoulders, were so familiar to the people of Berlin that as he passed through the streets hats were lifted as to royalty, for every Berliner under-stood that in Mommsen Berlin and Germany had one of their chiefest treasures. That young American well re-members having heard Mommsen say, at one of Zeller's Sunday evening gatherings, that the reason why he had never continued his *Römische Geschichte* through the imperial period was that he had never been able to make up his mind as to what it was that brought about the collapse of the Roman Empire and the downfall of Roman civilization.

The list of those whose lectures might then be heard, and whom this young American did hear at least once, usually out of sheer curiosity, is too long to be recounted. There were those of Weierstrass in mathematics; of Schmoller and Wagner in economics; of Weber, in San-skrit and Indian lore; of Kiepert, the geographer; of Förster, whose charm of personality gave him much

greater influence than would naturally attach to a professor of a subject so little followed as astronomy; of
Delbrück, who was already teaching history; and of Diels,
who though only a *professor extraordinarius* in those days,
was already marked out for the unusual distinction that
he gained later on. In ethics there was the exceptionally
interesting personality of von Gizycki, who was but thirty-
four years of age and destined to a life all too short.

The freedom which made it possible to hear and to
meet all these men was gained by following the advice
of Professor Archibald Alexander. As I have said, he had
enjoined fulfilling all the conditions for the degree of doctor of philosophy and taking that degree before leaving
America. This left the young American with no technical
and time-consuming requirements to meet in Berlin, but
set him free to get all that he could, and as he could, from
the great scholars there assembled.

Of the men who were later the chief representatives
of the University of Berlin, many were at that time still
winning their spurs elsewhere. Harnack, who was so long
the chief ornament of the theological faculty, was then
but thirty-three years of age and a professor at Giessen.
The great Hellenist, von Wilamowitz-Möllendorff, son-in-
law of Mommsen, was less than forty years of age and a
professor at Göttingen. Emil Fischer, the chemist, was but
little more than thirty and had a chair at Erlangen. Benno
Erdmann was about the same age and a member of the
faculty of philosophy at Breslau. Eduard Meyer was at
that same university, while Delitzsch was at Leipzig. Schie-
mann had at that time no university connection.

Important as the German universities, particularly Berlin, were in after years, it is probable that they occupied a higher relative rank from 1830 to about 1890 than
they have since enjoyed. Truly, there were academic

giants in Berlin sixty years ago, and each one of them
had his share in making over and in building up the intellectual fabric of that young American student. Zeller
and Paulsen were naturally by far the most influential,
for association with them was constant and intimate, and
the subjects of which they were masters were the young
student's chosen field of study. But each great scholar
whose lecture-room was entered, if it were only for a
single visit, left an ineffaceable impression of what scholarship meant, of what a university was and of what a long
road higher education in America had to travel before it
could hope to reach a plane of equal elevation. From
Zeller was learned the true meaning of the Greek spirit
and the real significance of the embryology of Western
thought as contained in the noble records of the Greek
philosophers. It was Zeller who made real beyond peradventure the truth afterward expressed so compactly by
Sir Henry Maine, that everything that lives and moves
in the Western world, save only the blind forces of nature,
is Greek in its origin. When it came time to leave Berlin
the old teacher gave to his young American pupil a copy
of the latest edition of his *Grundriss,* in which he inscribed
as a farewell message of friendship and of counsel the well-
known saying of Solon, Γηράσκω δ'ἀιεὶ πολλά διδασκόμενος.
What Solon said of himself was equally true of Zeller, and
must always remain true of those whom Zeller influenced.
All alike grow old constantly learning many new things.

From Paulsen was learned the lesson that Kant came
to teach, namely, that without a critical examination of
the process of knowing it is quite useless to attempt to
discuss knowledge. Paulsen's exposition of Kant's critical
method and his discipline in its applications made it impossible ever again to fall a victim to any of the varied
forms of sheer assumption in which uncritical and dog-

matical philosophy presents itself. From Paulsen there was learned, too, the lesson that the process of education rests primarily on the training of the will, the building of character, and that it should give to conduct a social aim or purpose. If ever two great teachers produced a lasting influence on the mind and thought of a pupil, Zeller and Paulsen produced that influence on the mind and the thought of their young American student.

In Berlin every hour of the day and of the evening was an educational influence. Not only lecture-rooms, but personal visits, the theatre, concerts, the opera, the many delightful opportunities for social intercourse, all combined to give an atmosphere and to provide a stimulus. This was really education. This was really contact with great personalities and with sources and standards of power—intellectual, moral, æsthetic. Where else in the world could the narrow means of a student have admitted him for a mark to hear rendered one of the great operas—German, Italian or French—or on any Wednesday evening for half a mark to the Bilse Koncert-Halle on Leipziger-strasse, to listen to a complete symphony by Beethoven, by Mozart, by Brahms, or by Raff, superbly rendered by one of the best orchestras in the world? Where else could one have had opportunity for a mere trifle to hear Shakespeare superbly acted or to see the classic German drama put upon the stage with every possible aid to its complete understanding and appreciation?

Opportunities to study the political life of the new and rapidly developing German Empire were not lacking. There were vigorous debates in the Reichstag just then, and a kindly word from a university professor gained for the young American opportunity to hear, under the best auspices, a stirring debate between Bismarck and Lieb-knecht, the forceful leader of the Social Democrats. A fascinating figure in the Reichstag was Doctor Windthorst, known familiarly as *die kleine Excellenz,* who was exerting enormous influence as parliamentary leader of the Center, or Catholic, party. His fellow Hanoverian, Benningsen, was the spokesman of the National Liberals. In addition to this striking group of parliamentary leaders, there was the spare and grim form of Moltke himself, who occasionally had a very brief word to say on matters of military organization and policy.

Surely this was a real voyage of discovery, and the discoverer often staggered under the load that he was called upon to carry. Indeed, it took the better part of a subsequent generation to enable him to digest and to assimilate it all.

After Berlin came Paris, and the American student who has missed that sequence has lost one of the great opportunities of the intellectual life.

In 1885 the Third Republic was still regarded as frankly experimental, and every type of republicanism was contending for the mastery in its public life. Royalists of one type or another were as plentiful as strawberries, and it was not at all unusual to hear a discussion after dinner as to which of the various claimants of the overturned throne of France was the most likely to gain possession of it. Sainte-Beuve, Baudelaire and Flaubert had, indeed, been dead for some years, but they were still the oracles of the more cultivated youth of France, and it was their names that came oftenest to the lips of the student of literature or of the ambitious aspirant for literary fame. Edmond Scherer was writing in the columns of *Le Temps,* and Jules Simon, well on in years but vigorous, was doing the same in *Le Matin.* Daudet, who gained almost everything that he wanted except election to the Academy,

was to be met not infrequently, as was Zola, who although
not so famous as he became later, was writing at a great
rate. Brunetière was then only sub-editor of the *Revue des
Deux Mondes,* and his principal work remained to be
done; but, nevertheless, he was decidedly a person of
weight and intellectual circumstance. At the Sorbonne,
Gréard was ruling with benignant capacity and assiduity.
The first climb up the slow slope of what remained of
Mont St. Geneviève called up in imagination the days
of Abelard and William of Champeaux and the great
philosophical discussions which then divided the intellectual world of Europe.

Then there were the scholars whom it was a joy and a
privilege to meet. There was Gaston Boissier, who made
Horace and Cicero, Vergil and Tacitus seem like old
friends, and who brought before the mind's eye with the
utmost vividness the life of Pompeii and of Rome and the
happenings in Roman Africa. There was Gaston Paris,
the mediævalist, without an equal. There was Fustel de
Coulanges, whose *Cité antique* had already exercised its
strange fascination on this particular American. There
was Henri Poincaré, who, though often suffering in body,
had one of the most penetrating of modern minds. Naturally a central object of interest and almost of pilgrimage
was Louis Pasteur. Renouvier one might know from his
books, but the man himself lived too much withdrawn
from other men to make possible a meeting in the flesh.
Paul Janet, who, while neither original nor constructive,
was one of the most agreeable and lucid of philosophical
lecturers, was at his best.

Almost every stone in Paris seemed to cry out with the
voice of a great man. Here both history and literature
seemed to have been made. Over yonder was the tower
from out whose bells rang the signal for the massacre of

St. Bartholomew. Not far away was the place where stood the Bastille, symbol and token of an old and dead order. Beyond, at the edge of what was now the Place de la Concorde, had stood the guillotine, under whose knife were beheaded good and bad alike. One wandered about the bewitching streets of the Quartier Latin as in a trance, expecting to meet at every turn a figure walking out of the pages of Balzac or of Dumas or of Eugène Sue. It was not easy in tracing out the lines of the Paris of history, of the Paris of the Revolution and of the Paris of that day to keep back the manifest evidences of emotion and excitement that sought to find expression. For the first time the Latin spirit came to have definite meaning and reality. It was so different from the Anglo-Saxon spirit as revealed in America and so different from the Teutonic spirit as revealed in Berlin. Somehow it seemed subtler and more refined, more delicate and more highly civilized than either. As the young student moved about in the social and intellectual life of Paris and breathed the spirit of the place, he began to feel himself in companionship with the Greeks of modern times, the one truly civilized people in the world. It became so much more easy than it ever had been to understand the impatience of the French with other and less favored peoples than themselves. They knew and had passed through so much that others had still to learn and to come to know. Of all Europe, France alone had passed through the baptism of a revolution. Quasi-revolutions and attempts at revolution had marked the history of other lands, but France, and France alone, had passed out from under the old rule, tried as if by fire, and had preserved in the fulness of the modern spirit and with the richness of an age-long cultivation the true and high standards of judgment in things of the mind. Evidence of this multiplied day by day as the young American made his daily pilgrimage all the way from modest lodgings in the Rue La Boëtie to the Sorbonne. Sometimes his steps would follow one course and sometimes another, but always and everywhere the evidences of cultivation and of civilization abounded. Paris revealed itself as the only place in the world where conversation was a fine art and where the publication of a new book by a writer of note was hailed as an event of social importance.

And so it went. On every side and at every hour the young student found impressions, ideas, judgments, opinions, experiences pouring in upon him with a richness that was truly overwhelming. He began to see that Paris was the one place to which to go to file down and to polish a student's mind that had been forged and hewn out in the rough in Germany. The two civilizations, the two national and racial spirits, the two universities seemed in no sense antagonistic, but rather highly and wonderfully complementary. This again was real education. Men of light and leading, men who knew what standards were and who insisted on applying them, were close companions, instructors, and guides. What young student from across the Atlantic would not find his mind enriched and inspired by experience such as that?

The French political life was even more interesting than that of Germany, for it seemed to be in closer touch with the realities of politics. Gambetta had been dead for three years, but his spirit and his influence were very much alive. Jules Ferry fell from power on a dismal March day in 1885 with a roar that shook even the quiet precincts of the Sorbonne. Of radical and of socialist oratory there was an abundance to hear, and the semi-comic, semi-tragic figure of General Boulanger was still troubling the political waters.

The American student who has never been to the

University of Paris has missed something which no German university could ever give him. But he should come to Paris after having studied at Berlin, or Leipzig or Munich. The reason is that the highly artistic and very subtle method of the French savant is a perfect complement to the patient and plodding meticulousness of the German *Gelehrter*. The artistry of the French was manifested in their exposition of every subject. Whether one was listening to Renan on the history of the Semitic peoples, or to Taine on the philosophy of art or to Caro on Goethe, he could not fail to see the national and racial characteristics manifesting themselves in splendid and compelling fashion. To end an intellectual voyage of discovery at the University of Paris is to put a frame on a picture that would be imperfect without it. The drill, the discipline and the training in patient thoroughness one got in those days in Germany as he could not get it in America, in England, or in France. But a point of view, a sense of proportion, the meaning of the intellectual life and standards of taste in judgment and appreciation were taught at the Sorbonne and in Paris as nowhere else in the world.

If ever there was a true Voyage of Discovery, this was it!

VII
BUILDING A UNIVERSITY

DURING my residence abroad, I kept in touch with happenings at Columbia through letters from President Barnard, Professor Burgess and Professor Alexander. When I returned in the autumn of 1885 to Columbia, my fellowship had expired, but I was made Assistant in Philosophy and my term of academic service, therefore, remained unbroken. At Columbia itself there were mighty stirrings. President Barnard and Professor Burgess were eagerly urging their views, and the trustees were becoming steadily more sympathetic. A scheme of instruction for graduates, of which I myself had been one of the first to take advantage, had been adopted in June, 1880, and at the same time the undergraduate course of study was broadened and liberalized. In the spring of 1883 the trustees so far departed from their traditional policy of secretiveness and aloofness as to issue a pamphlet on "The Financial Condition and Present Needs of Columbia College." The statement contained in this pamphlet had been formally adopted by the trustees on April 2, 1883. It set out that the revenue of the corporation at that time was some $336,000, of which more than one-third was provided by the fees of students, while the expenditures were some $299,000. This statement by the trustees called for an additional endowment of $4,350,000 in order to provide an annual revenue of $217,500, the

amount estimated to be necessary to carry out the plans
as then formulated. It is interesting to observe that among
the items of proposed new expenditure contained in this
pamphlet are $25,000 annually for the library and $7500
annually for the history, philosophy and art of education,
this being the particular field which President Barnard
desired me to cultivate. Shortly thereafter in 1891 and
1892 the statutes of the college were revised, largely under
the influence of George L. Rives and John B. Pine, who
had become trustees in 1882 and 1890 respectively. The
first steps were then taken toward the establishment of a
new administrative system in which the faculty would
have the authority properly belonging to it. From that
time on things happened with increasing rapidity and the
attention of the trustees was divided between the important problems relating to the reorganization of the
college and its development into a university and those
growing out of the renewals of leases on the Upper Estate,
which were then to be made. On March 7, 1887, the
trustees had appointed a special committee of their number on the Elevation of the Course of Instruction, which
committee consisted of William C. Schermerhorn, Reverend Doctor Morgan Dix, Stephen P. Nash, F. Augustus
Schermerhorn, and Charles M. Da Costa. It is from the
appointment and work of this committee that there date
the final and positive steps which brought into existence
the Columbia University of today with the historic Columbia College as its foundation. At the instance of President Barnard and Professor Burgess the question was then
discussed as to whether the old Columbia College with
its undergraduate program of study should be continued
or brought to an end in order to focus all the energies
and all the resources of the corporation upon the new
program of university work. This question was vigorously

debated and finally answered in favor of the retention of the college because of the strong views to that effect held by a majority of the faculty as well as by the Columbia alumni.

Fortunately I collected and have kept all the documents which bore upon these discussions and developments, and they are bound together in my volume entitled *Columbia University: Miscellaneous Documents, 1880–1896, Volume I.* In view of the fact that these papers and reports were printed in small editions, and that, as Columbia was then administered, there was no official whose business it was to collect and to preserve them, it may be that my collection is the only one in existence.

The committee of trustees on the Elevation of the Course of Instruction addressed a letter under date of April 10, 1888, to each of the existing faculties, asking their opinion on four specific matters. These were: first, the expediency of retaining the School of Arts, as the undergraduate department was then called, as part of the College; second, the expediency of removing the School of Arts to other buildings within or without the city limits; third, the expediency of so modifying, extending and elevating the courses of instruction that the instruction hereafter to be given should be confined to what are known as post-graduate studies; and fourth, the best methods of so modifying the courses of instruction that the entire system of education should be placed upon a higher plane. These matters were hotly debated for some months, and then answered by the faculties of Columbia College, of the School of Mines, of the School of Law and of the School of Political Science. These reports have great historical interest and reflect accurately the state of opinion as it then existed among the teaching scholars of Columbia University.

It was plain that the crux of the whole matter was to be found in the question as to what should be the future of the undergraduate department, then known as the School of Arts. A few were frankly in favor of its discontinuance despite its long and honorable history and the great body of sentiment which clustered about it. Another few were in favor of maintaining the status quo, while the larger body of opinion favored some sort of university development, retaining the School of Arts, but so altering and adjusting its relationship to the more advanced and professional work that a wholly new situation would be created. It was nearly the end of the year 1888 before replies were received from all the faculties. A number of individual professors, among them Professor William G. Peck, Professor John S. Newberry, Professor Charles Sprague Smith, Professor Thomas R. Price, and Mr. Frederick W. Whitridge, then a member of the Faculty of Political Science, took advantage of the opportunity afforded them and made separate replies to the questions of the trustees. Some of these replies were of great consequence. This is particularly true of the letter written by Mr. Whitridge under date of January 11, 1889. Subsquently, having been appointed Adjunct Professor of Philosophy, Ethics and Psychology, I was myself invited to write a similar letter, and did so under date of April 5, 1889. This letter was accompanied by a diagram which was intended to illustrate my conception of the university organization which I then advocated and the relation of its various parts to each other. This letter is here printed in full.

COLUMBIA COLLEGE, April 5, 1889.

Charles M. Da Costa, Esq., Secretary,
 29 Nassau St., New York City.

MY DEAR SIR:—In response to your letter of invitation dated March 18, 1889, I beg to submit for the consideration of the

Committee on the Elevation of the Course the following statement of my individual views with reference to the modification, extension and elevation of the course of instruction in Columbia College.

The questions as to the desirability of retaining the School of Arts and as to the extension and elevation of the course of instruction are entirely distinct. In the present condition of American education an undergraduate department is not a detriment to a university, but rather a source of strength. Furthermore, our own School of Arts has justified its existence in a long and honorable history. It is deeply rooted in the affections of a numerous and enthusiastic body of Alumni. It is today in a position to do admirable educational work of a disciplinary character. It is doubtless true that undergraduate students will never flock in large numbers to a college situated in the heart of a great city, where many of the pleasantest and most attractive features of student life must always be lacking. But it is also true that the oldest and only well-equipped college in the metropolis may reasonably be expected to attract from three to five hundred students in the immediate future, if its curriculum is so modified as to appeal more strongly than it now does to students of varied tastes and inclinations.

But the time has fully come when the work of Columbia College can no longer be confined to the old channels even though those channels be broadened and deepened. The problem of superior or university education is awaiting its solution in the United States, and Columbia College may fairly be called upon to take a leading part in working out that solution. Situated as it is in the metropolis, with its libraries, its museums, its art galleries, and its busy intellectual life, that Columbia College with its resources and its opportunities should develop into a University is as necessary as it is natural. In planning for such development it must be borne in mind that a university can hardly be legislated into existence nor will it be constituted by a mere change of name. Those conceptions of a university which identify it with a group of technical or professional schools, or with a college in which all or most of the courses of study are elective, are equally to be avoided. A true university exists today, as it has always existed, by virtue of the methods of instruction which it employs and the privileges which it offers. In the university *Lehrfreiheit* and *Lernfreiheit* exist side by side. The teaching is no longer disciplinary and formative, but free and suggestive.

The distinction between the College and the University being thus established, two practical questions present themselves: (1) where, in the existing organization, shall the line between the College and the University be drawn; and (2) what form of university organization is desirable.

That the line between the work of the College and that peculiar to a university should be drawn at the close of the present junior year seems clear. The average age of those students at Columbia who enter the senior class is more than twenty years. The Columbia senior is therefore at least a year older than the average German student who enters the university. These students of the senior year are amply qualified both by their age, by their average ability, and by their previous training to enter upon university work. In fact, the present senior year is in its composition and character a university year. Again, the universal experience of American colleges points to the close of the junior year as marking a point of departure in the student's intellectual life. Even those institutions that have most strenuously resisted the extension of the system of elective studies in the undergraduate course have given it some place in the curriculum of their senior year, and thus have impliedly recognized the distinction that is now advocated.

There is still another and a very potent reason for concluding the purely disciplinary work with the junior year. The present tendency is to consider the baccalaureate degree as the sign of a completed education. This is an error of grave importance and without any warrant in university history. The degree of Bachelor was conferred by the early universities as a mark of apprenticeship, and signified not that the holder had completed any course whatever, but that he had entered upon the course of training which led to the degree of Master or Doctor. If now, we return to the ancient practice and confer the baccalaureate as a university degree after a four years' course of study, the last year of which is the first year of a three years' university course, the student will be led to look upon his education not as completed, but as only begun when he receives his degree of A.B. The result of this will be that a larger number of men will see the value and importance of continuing their studies through the full university curriculum.

In our own School of Political Science, where the custom now advocated for the whole university has prevailed for some years, it has had precisely the effect indicated. Those American colleges which have added a graduate department to a four years' undergraduate course made up entirely of disciplinary studies have not succeeded in attracting many students to the former, for the reason that the undergraduates, having no experience of university methods and no proper conception of university work, have found no inducement to pursue a course of higher and more special study.

Finally, it cannot be argued that a division between disciplinary and university studies at the close of the present junior year would destroy the School of Arts. It would, on the contrary, strengthen and develop that school; for by thus increasing very largely the number and variety of the elective courses offered to the senior class, students would be attracted to the School of Arts in larger numbers than at present, and its influence and usefulness would be materially increased.

In deciding upon a proper and efficient plan of university organization, we can derive considerable assistance from the experience of foreign countries, but even more from the conditions which have gradually been developed here. Inasmuch as we already possess two university faculties in full operation—those of Law and Political Science,—and the nuclei of two more in the Faculty of the School of Mines and in the body of teachers giving graduate instruction in the School of Arts, the line of future development seems plain. The Faculty of the School of Mines should be taken to represent a university Faculty of Natural Science. This would involve no change whatever in the School of Mines itself, nor in the present absolute control of the faculty over the work of that school. This university·Faculty of Natural Science should then be requested to prepare a course of study covering three years and leading to the degree of Doctor of Philosophy. The first year of this course should be open to all students who have satisfactorily completed the junior year in any college of equal standing with Columbia, and should be offered as an elective course to members of the senior class in Columbia College.

The three great groups of Law, Political Science and Natural Science being thus organized, it remains to provide a university faculty for the philosophical, philological, and literary studies. In accordance with the university usage which applies the name Philosophy, despite its more dignified traditions, to the subjects which remain after all other faculties have been provided for, this faculty would be called the University Faculty of Philosophy and the course under its control and supervision would be the School of Philosophy. The Faculty of Philosophy would consist then of the professors and adjunct professors giving advanced instruction in the history of philosophy, ethics, and psychology, in classical and comparative philology and literature, and in the modern languages and literatures. At the present time seven professors would be eligible for this faculty. If this faculty is organized, chairs of general history, comparative philology, archæology, belles-lettres, pedagogy and geography should be speedily established and their incumbents added to it.

It may conceivably be objected that a philosophical faculty organized on this basis is without precedent, and that it is an injudicious innovation to separate the natural and political sciences from the philosophical faculty and from each other. This objection is, however, not well taken. For, on the one hand, the organization of a faculty of philosophy as indicated above involves less disturbance of existing conditions than any other plan yet proposed for such a faculty, and on the other it is entirely in accord with the most recent and progressive developments in the European universities. When the University of Strassburg was reorganized in 1872, Roggenbach with all the experience of the other German universities to guide him, yet untrammeled by any of their conservative traditions, provided for a faculty of philosophy in which only the chairs of philosophy, philology, and literature were represented. The political sciences were added to the law faculty, and mathematics and the natural sciences were organized separately, precisely as has been recommended above. At Munich the political sciences have a faculty of their own, and since 1873 the philosophical faculty has been divided into two sections, one for philosophy, philology, and literature and one for mathematics and the natural sciences. It need hardly be pointed out that these sections are but the forerunners of separate faculties. At Tübingen there are separate faculties of philosophy, of political science, and of natural sciences. At Würzburg the division of the old philosophical faculty has begun, and at the Swiss universities an all-inclusive faculty of philosophy is now almost unknown. In France, too, the distinction between the Faculty of Science and the Faculty of Letters is one of long standing. Recent precedent is therefore not only not opposed to such a scheme of university organization as that herein indicated, but is clearly in its favor.

This Faculty of Philosophy should, when thus organized, prepare a three years' course of study leading to the degree of Doctor of Philosophy, and the first year of this course should be offered as elective to members of the senior class, and also thrown open to students who have completed the junior year in other colleges, on the same terms as those specified for the courses in Law, Political Science, and Natural Science.

It should be permissible for any university student not desiring to be confined to the course presented by a single faculty, to make such combination of the courses offered by the several faculties as may meet with the approval of the University Senate. There would thus be combined with great freedom of individual choice, an authoritative body to decide what limits to such choice must be set. The practical effect of this provision would be to substitute for the present system of absolutely free election in senior year, a system of elective courses of great scope and variety.

These four university faculties would suffice for many years to come, and until it might seem advisable to establish closer relations with the School of Medicine and reciprocity between Columbia and the two great theological seminaries of this city. These faculties would afford the intending student abundant opportunity to perfect himself in a great number of subjects of human knowledge, and would constitute a university in fact as well as in name. By the creation of four faculties on the lines indicated, every professor engaged in university work would be a member of one faculty only and would have one vote, and only one vote, on matters of university concern.

As the professors are grouped together in faculties, so should the faculties come together, in the persons of their chosen representatives, in the University Senate. This body should consist of the president of the university and three delegates chosen from and by each faculty. The Senate should exercise a general supervision and control over the entire university, confer all degrees, decide all questions involving two or more faculties, or the relation of the university faculties to the School of Arts, and prescribe the curriculum of the freshman, sophomore and junior years. The degrees of Bachelor, Master, and Doctor would thus be university degrees, to be conferred after one, two or three years, respectively, of university work, by the Senate upon such candidates as the several faculties might recommend.

The School of Arts Faculty would naturally be composed of officers giving instruction to the freshman, sophomore, and junior classes, and would have control of the details of the instruction given to those classes, and of the discipline of their members. For some time to come it is quite possible that members of some one or more of the university faculties might be entitled to seats in the Faculty of Arts, but this would involve neither confusion nor injustice, since the latter body, not being a university faculty, would not be entitled to representation in the Senate.

I venture to believe that a scheme of university organization and development, such as is briefly outlined above, is that best warranted by Columbia's past and most full of promise for her future. By the adoption of this plan the College of the past and its traditions will be preserved, but out of it and above it will rise an institution worthy of our highest ideals of American education, an institution able and willing to foster learning and to promote progress—the University of Columbia College.

The accompanying diagram is intended to show at a glance how the proposed university faculties will be related to the School of Arts and to each other.

Very respectfully submitted,
NICHOLAS MURRAY BUTLER

The views expressed in this letter and the academic relationships set out on the accompanying diagram were, with a few minor modifications, accepted by the trustees and became the basis of the plan adopted shortly thereafter for the organization of an institution which is the Columbia University of today.

One of the most interesting papers in my possession is a printed copy of this letter of mine which I had sent to President Eliot of Harvard with a request for his suggestions and criticisms. He returned it under date of February

28, 1890, with his pencilled comments. For me this is a most precious paper and one of exceptional interest for the student of the history of higher education in the United States. The differences between what may be called the Harvard plan and the Columbia plan of university building are implicit in President Eliot's incisive and illuminating comments on my proposals. He never cared much for what has come to be known as the graduate school. He had in mind creating a university out of the historic American college by elevating the standard of admission to the latter, by making its program of study wholly elective and by strengthening and liberalizing that program in every way. He held the opinion, and frequently expressed it, that it mattered little what subject one studied, but that it mattered much how he studied it. President Eliot met the argument that there was a strong tendency in this country unduly and unwisely to postpone the entrance of young men upon the active duties of life by frankly proposing to reduce the period of college study from the conventional four years to three years. This plan, if and when carried out, would assimilate the organization of higher education in the United States to that organization as it exists on the continent of Europe. The gymnasium and the university in Germany or the lycée and the university in France, and the corresponding institutions in Italy, in Spain, in Belgium and in the Scandinavian countries, would be represented in the United States by the secondary school and the college would be transformed and called university.

The system of organization which I had in mind and advocated, and which has widely prevailed throughout this country, was quite different. It was based upon a principle which I derived in part from the close observations of actual educational conditions, both at home and

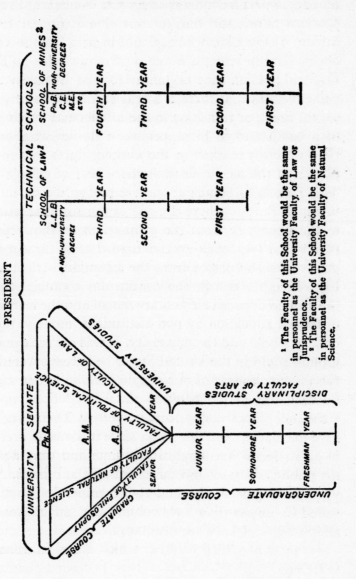

abroad, in part from the writings and counsels of President Barnard, Professor Burgess and President Andrew D. White of Cornell University, and in part from some psychological observations which were made to me by Doctor G. Stanley Hall, then at Johns Hopkins University. This principle was that there is a real and not a merely theoretical break or transition in the intellectual development of a youth and in his appropriate studies at about the time which is marked in the United States by the completion of the second or sophomore year of college work. This fact, in substance at least, is recognized on the continent of Europe where the age of the students who pass to the university from the gymnasium or the lycée was then about two years greater than that of the American youth when he passed from the secondary school to college. In other words, the continental countries covered the ground between elementary school and the completion of formal education by two institutions, namely, the secondary school and the university. It was my idea that this ground could in the United States be better covered, and the practical needs of our people here be better met, by dividing this period between three institutions, namely, secondary school, college, and university. There is no need here to enlarge upon this point, since it has been presented in all its forms and applications time and time again in my public addresses and published official reports. As the years have passed, the underlying principles of this so-called Columbia plan have commended themselves more and more, and have received application in a variety of ways, most of which could not have been foreseen fifty years ago.

It would not be easy to convey to the reader of today an adequate conception of the extraordinary ferment which was then going on in Columbia College. Indeed, the whole educational atmosphere was charged with the electrical effects of what was being said, written and done, particularly at Columbia and by President Eliot of Harvard, President White of Cornell and President Gilman of Johns Hopkins. A little later President Harper of the University of Chicago came upon the scene with his amazing vigor of mind and body and his sheaf of fertile ideas. These powerful personalities, while differing sharply on many matters of detail, were entirely at one in insisting that the American university must somehow or other be brought into being and adequately supported, not only to crown and to cap the nation's educational system and its scholarly endeavor, but to serve as an instrument for the constant discovery and interpretation of new truth in every field. Truly there were giants in those days, and the interplay of influence between men and ideas in Germany, in France, in Great Britain and in the United States was as constant as it was extraordinary. Before long almost every institution of higher education in the United States was, so to speak, feeling its pulse and taking its temperature as a means of diagnosing its actual condition and prospects in the midst of all this.

Almost without exception, the separate and individual colleges that are usually but incorrectly described as the small colleges, quickly accepted the distinction between college and university, and settled back into the conviction that the wise policy for them was to continue to be colleges and to do college work, but to do it better than ever before and with a much more liberal and elastic program than had hitherto prevailed. The tax-supported state universities of the West were, however, in a different situation. In many cases they rested upon a basis of financial support that could readily be made adequate to permit the development of a program of advanced scholarly and professional work. In several states, the example of what was happening at Columbia, at Harvard and at Johns Hopkins served to stimulate action and to hasten endeavors at true university building.

A general survey of this entire movement is recorded in a statement which I made to the University Council on February 15, 1921. I there summarized the various steps taken to build and to develop Columbia University, and indicated their relationship to what was going on in other parts of the country.

One unforeseen and unexpected by-product of all this was to involve me in some temporary problems and embarrassments due to the repeated and very tempting invitations which reached me to accept administrative posts in other parts of the country. Since my mind was entirely clear as to what I wished to do and as to how and where I wished to do it, these very flattering invitations never really shook my purpose in the least. Nevertheless, it was a problem how to deal with them with the appreciation and respect that were their due, particularly since, in almost every case, they carried with them a financial reward several times as great as then seemed likely to attach to any possible future at Columbia. At one time or another, in the years between 1886 and 1899, I was approached either formally by committees of governing boards or informally by individual members of such boards, with the request that I permit myself to be proposed for president of the state universities of Ohio, Indiana, Illinois, Wisconsin, Iowa, Colorado, Washington and California, the latter with great insistence and on two separate occasions. In addition Governor Stanford did his best to get me to become the first president of Stanford University in 1891.

Of these invitations there were three that took prece-

The Author as junior member of the Faculty
of Columbia College, 1889

The Author as junior member of the Faculty
of Columbia College, 1889

dence of all the others, and as to each of which a few words may be said. In the planning of Stanford University, Governor and Mrs. Stanford were really very naïve. One recalls the story of their visit to Cambridge and their inspection of Harvard University under the guidance of President Eliot. While crossing the Yard, Governor Stanford stopped, and with a wide sweep of his arm, said to President Eliot:

"How much would it cost to duplicate all this?"

President Eliot naturally demurred at giving a quick or specific reply, and called attention to the fact that the larger value of Harvard University was to be found not in its grounds, its buildings, and its material equipment, but in its traditions, its history, its achievements, its influence.

"Oh, yes, I know," responded Governor Stanford impatiently, "but how much money would it take to duplicate this campus and all these buildings?"

With some hesitation, President Eliot replied that it might take as much as fifteen million dollars. Thereupon, Mrs. Stanford, who had been listening carefully, cried out gleefully, "We can do it, Leland." And their walk across the Yard proceeded.

So far as I could see, Governor Stanford's whole conception of university building was purely material. He thought that money could buy anything and could do anything, and was both chagrined and surprised when he found sometimes that it could not. Two of these occasions for surprise and chagrin happened in this wise. The governor's original choice for the first president of the new university at Palo Alto was undoubtedly Doctor Andrew D. White of Cornell with whom he had advised intimately as to his plans and for whom he had the greatest admiration. When Doctor White, after making a special visit to

Palo Alto, explained why he could not accept the great
honor which Governor Stanford tendered him, it was
General Francis A. Walker, the distinguished economist,
administrator and man of affairs who then presided with
so great brilliance over the Massachusetts Institute of
Technology, to whom Governor Stanford turned. No better choice could have been made, and had General Walker
felt able and willing to accept the invitation to go to California, the whole future of Stanford University and its
authority would have been assured from the outset. As I
recall, General Walker then received a salary of $6000, to-
gether with the occupancy of a modest house on Beacon
Street, not very far from the buildings of the Institute.
Either from President White or President Eliot Governor
Stanford had learned that General Walker was the best
man to be entrusted with the planning of the new institution in California, and that his salary was some $6000.
General Walker himself is my authority for the anecdote
which follows. Governor Stanford called upon him at his
house in Boston, and after briefly outlining his plans and
hopes for the new university, bluntly invited General
Walker to become its first president at an annual salary of
$10,000, together with the occupancy of an official resi-
dence to be erected on the campus of the new university.
Having made what he regarded as a munificent proposal,
Governor Stanford settled back in his chair, his face plainly
expressing his conviction that the financial temptation was
too great for General Walker to resist. To his astonishment,
the latter politely but firmly pointed out that he was well on
in middle life, that he was settled most comfortably and in a
post that was greatly to his liking, and that it would be
too great a revolution in his whole personal life to change
his home now from Massachusetts to California, even
under the most attractive and inviting conditions which

Governor Stanford had described. The latter, unable to escape the conviction that there was really nothing at stake save money, repeated his invitation most urgently, first at a proposed salary of $15,000, then of $20,000, and finally of $25,000. That any man in General Walker's position should be so lacking in good sense as to refuse an offer of that kind was beyond Governor Stanford's comprehension. Nevertheless, General Walker did just that thing. Governor Stanford was deeply disappointed, and never understood to his dying day why General Walker was not willing to become the first president of Stanford University.

Having failed to secure General Walker, Governor Stanford then asked the General to suggest some one who seemed to him suitable for the new post. General Walker assented gladly, and described the type of man who he thought should be selected. He laid emphasis upon the fact that, as the whole university movement was beginning to take on new forms and new vigor and that since the proposed institution would be able to begin at the beginning, free of all the limitations of convention and local custom, and since it was to be placed in a comparatively new part of the country, its first president should be a young man with his life before him, with everything to gain and nothing to lose by putting his hand to this task. If possible, he added, one who was already associated with the university movement that was under way should be chosen. General Walker then indicated that he knew a young man of this type whom he strongly recommended and who he thought could probably be had. He paid me the very great honor and compliment of giving my name to Governor Stanford, with a short statement of what he thought were my qualifications for the new post. Without knowing anything of what has just been written,

I found myself summoned to an interview one evening in March, 1891, at the Hotel Brunswick, on Fifth Avenue and Twenty-sixth Street, with Governor and Mrs. Stanford. They were most agreeable and most interesting. For perhaps a half-hour they engaged me in conversation, telling of their visits to various university towns and recounting their observations. They then outlined rather finely what they had in mind as a memorial to their son, and after a talk of nearly an hour ended by inviting me to become the first president of Stanford University at an annual salary of $10,000. It goes without saying that my breath was taken away, since I had only recently been advanced at Columbia from an instructorship at $1200 to an adjunct professorship at $3500, and was immersed not only in my studies and teaching, but in my administrative tasks, both at Columbia and at the College for the Training of Teachers, which I had brought into existence four years earlier. Strong as was the financial temptation and inviting as was the prospect of planning and building an American university from the ground up, I felt so sure of the correctness of my earlier choice and of my constant persistence in it, that I was able with entire kindness and politeness to make Governor Stanford the same reply which General Walker had made shortly before. As in the case of General Walker, Governor Stanford repeated his invitation several times and went up the same scale of salary with me as with General Walker. My strong conviction is that he thought I was a lunatic when his fine and most inviting offer was declined. After that was over we talked for some time more and I ventured to suggest to Governor Stanford that he consult President White of Cornell and ask him to suggest a suitable person to be the first president of Stanford University. I was not then aware of the fact that Governor

Stanford knew President White intimately and had made him the first offer of the new presidency. President White always seemed to me to be a real statesman in education. He had large scholarship, broad views, a progressive mind and a wide acquaintance. I afterwards learned that Governor Stanford did consult President White again and that it was he who suggested the name of David Starr Jordan, an early graduate of Cornell and just then president of the University of Indiana, for the post to which he was shortly afterward invited by Governor Stanford and which he held with so much distinction.

My experience in respect to the presidency of the University of Illinois and of California was somewhat similar. The University of Illinois began its career as the Illinois Industrial University, and it was not until 1885 that its name was changed to its present form. In 1891 Doctor Peabody, who had been Regent—the name then given to the chief administrative officer—of the university for eleven or twelve years, either died or resigned. Mr. Francis C. McKay, a principal of one of the public schools in the city of Chicago and a most earnest and devoted trustee of the state university, promptly came to New York to see me. He said that he was authorized, following an informal conference of the trustees, to offer me the presidency of the state university which it was intended to develop into an institution fully worthy of that name with the whole power and wealth of the State of Illinois behind it. The invitation was a most honorable one and flattering in the extreme, but for the same reasons which led to my decision in the case of Stanford University, I declined it. At that time an acting Regent was chosen, and after three years Mr. McKay came to see me again, insisting with great emphasis upon the chance the University of Illinois offered to its president to make a national reputation and to perform a national service. My convictions and intentions remained unchanged, however, and I pointed out to him the advantages of choosing the very able educational administrator who had been displaced for political reasons as Superintendent of Public Instruction in the State of New York and was just then Superintendent of Schools at Cleveland, Ohio. This was Andrew S. Draper, who was shortly thereafter elected president of the University of Illinois and served with great distinction and acceptability for ten years.

The invitation to the University of California was twice repeated with great urgency and was undeniably attractive from many points of view. The first invitation came to me in 1890 at the hands of Horace Davis, who was then president of the University of California and who desired to be relieved of that office. Mr. Davis was primarily a man of affairs and had served acceptably in the Congress of the United States. He was most kind and complimentary in all his allusions and in the form of his invitation in which he was supported by a man of great force and energy; Arthur Rodgers, who was a Regent of the university, profoundly interested in its welfare and development. Following my declination, Doctor Martin Kellogg was chosen president and served for some eight or nine years. Then pressure upon me was renewed, Mr. Rodgers coming all the way across the continent to urge acceptance of the invitation and painting its attractiveness with undeniable force and eloquence. Once again I had the pleasure of suggesting an appointment which proved to be of great value. Professor Benjamin Ide Wheeler, although easily the most popular and one of the most distinguished professors at Cornell University, was not wholly happy there, largely owing to his disappointment at not having been chosen president of the university at the time Doctor Schurman was elected. I suggested his name to Mr. Rodgers, who promptly journeyed up to Ithaca to see him. Within a few months Doctor Wheeler was elected president of the University of California and served until his retirement twenty years later.

These happenings are set down in part for their personal interest and importance, and in part to illustrate the fact that substantially one and the same impulse toward university development and university building was manifesting itself throughout the whole United States during those busy years.

President Barnard's epoch-marking administration came to an end shortly before his death in May, 1889, in the eightieth year of his age. His lifelong infirmity and his failing strength led him to ask relief and retirement from active service at the close of the academic year 1888–89. The Trustees graciously retired him on full salary and with the privilege of occupying the President's House during the remainder of his life. On assuming the presidency of Columbia College, Seth Low purchased the house, No. 30 East Sixty-fourth Street, which then stood at the corner of Madison Avenue, and lived there during his entire term of office. There was no other President's House until the present building was constructed in 1912.

When President Barnard could no longer attend to the daily duties of his office, Doctor Henry Drisler, Jay Professor of Greek and the senior member of the faculty in service, was designated by the trustees to be acting president until a permanent successor might be chosen. During the last two or three years of his life, President Barnard busied himself, *more suo,* with the question of his successor. His first choice was General Francis A. Walker of the Massachusetts Institute of Technology, but his name had to be passed over because he was not a communicant of the Protestant Episcopal Church, as was made a condition in the grant to Columbia by Trinity Parish of the property known as the Lower Estate. The validity of this condition has been much disputed, but it has always had very great sentimental importance. There are letters in existence which indicate that President Barnard canvassed the possibilities pretty widely and passed in review the names of all sorts and conditions of men. One of these was William B. Potter, then living at St. Louis, Mo., who had been graduated from the Columbia School of Mines in 1868. He was a member of the well-known Potter family of New York, and Bishop Henry C. Potter was his brother. The argument in his favor was that he was a graduate of Columbia who, by his training and experience, was in sympathy with the new scientific movement in education and would bring to the administration of the institution a broader point of view than would most others whose names were mentioned. His name was urgently pressed by a certain group among whom were many prominent graduates of the School of Mines. Finally, however, after some months of consideration and consultation, the choice of the trustees fell upon Seth Low, himself a graduate of the college with highest honors in the class of 1870 and a trustee since 1881. Mr. Low had gained the confidence and respect of his fellow trustees both by his public career and by his active and effective participation in the task of renewing the leases of the property included in the Upper Estate which were then falling due. Mr. Low had plunged into active political work shortly after leaving college, and had been elected Mayor of Brooklyn at a very early age in 1881 and again in 1883, as a candidate committed to municipal reform. In commenting upon Mr. Low's name as that of a possible successor, President Barnard, in a letter addressed to Mr. Stephen P. Nash, made a comment which proved to be as well justified as it was shrewd. He said, in effect, that Mr. Low's predominant interest was in politics and in public life and that, were he now to become president of Columbia, he would not be able long to resist the temptation to return to his first and chief love. Precisely this happened.

The conflict between Mr. Low's academic service and his political ambitions quickly became evident and it is common knowledge that the trustees were greatly disturbed in consequence. As early as 1894 President Low invited a group of trustees to gather at his house to advise him as to his acceptance or rejection of the nomination to the mayoralty, which then seemed very probable. The trustees were sharply divided and as a result Mr. Low wrote a letter stating that he could not accept the nomination for Mayor of New York. To this statement, however, he added that if it should appear that he was the only one on whom all opponents of Tammany Hall could unite, he should feel bound in conscience to accept the nomination and run for Mayor. Fortunately for the developing university, not Mr. Low but William L. Strong became the anti-Tammany nominee for Mayor and was elected. Three years later, however, Mr. Low accepted a nomination for Mayor against the wishes of the trustees and tendered his resignation as President of the University. Consideration of this resignation was postponed until the result of the election should be made known.

The Reverend Doctor Morgan Dix in his unpublished diary records that on November 3, 1897, "we 'sat on the remains' of Seth Low at the office in Wall Street until 3 P.M." Doctor Dix states that Mr. Low was looking very much worn and appeared surprised and displeased when the trustees decided to discuss the situation in his absence and to delay bringing any report for the present. After

Mr. Low had left the trustees agreed that he should have leave to withdraw his resignation, but also that he must receive a distinct intimation that the trustees did not wish him in future to have anything whatever to do with political affairs. It was this frank and definite expression of opinion which led Mr. Low to resign the presidency in October, 1901, following his nomination for the mayoralty during the month preceding.

The election of Mr. Low in October, 1889, brought to a head the studies and discussions of the whole problem of university organization. He did not assume office until February, 1890, and then quickly assembled the entire faculty membership for a series of evening discussions in the building which had been in Doctor Barnard's time the President's House, but which was now to be used for administrative offices. These discussions were held in order to come to a conclusion as to the policies to be adopted in organizing the University. President Low followed what he called the military order in calling upon faculty members to participate in these discussions and to give answers to the specific questions that were proposed. Being myself the youngest and most recently appointed faculty member, my name was called first, and I had the great advantage of presenting my views and supporting arguments before any one else spoke. My letter of April 5, 1889, to which reference has already been made, was, of course, my text. Shortly thereafter Mr. Low summed up his findings and recommendations in a report to the trustees, and the revised statutes of 1890, 1891 and 1892, the drafting of which was chiefly done by Mr. John B. Pine, Clerk of the Trustees, were the quick result. These statutes brought the new university organization into being.

Meanwhile, I had been busily engaged in developing

advanced courses in philosophy for graduate students, and was drawing into them small groups of devoted and conscientious men almost every one of whom became not only markedly useful, but distinguished in later life. In President Barnard's Annual Report for 1883, there will be found mention by Professor Alexander[1] of one graduate student, this being myself. A second and fuller reference is made by Professor Alexander in his report for the year 1884.[2] He there describes the beginnings of a philosophical society which I had organized as part of our new undertaking, and which for a number of years was a useful and flourishing agency in developing graduate studies and in leading to a wider acquaintance with contemporary philosophic literature. This society was the beginning of all the graduate work in philosophy and related subjects which afterward became so extensive and so intensive.

In his report for 1886, President Barnard discusses at length[3] the work of the Department of Philosophy and its program for the future, and mentions with great kindness my own relation to it. In the same report[4] is recorded the success of the first series of public lectures on education, which lectures, as I shall point out later, laid the foundation for the organization of Teachers College and for all the stupendous activity of Columbia in that field during the following fifty years. During the academic year 1885–86 Professor Alexander was absent through illness substantially the entire year, and I was put in charge of the department. My report on the work of the year is printed with President Barnard's report for 1886.[5]

[1]Frederick A. P. Barnard, Annual Report to the Trustees of Columbia University, 1883, p. 73.
[2]Ibid., p. 52.
[3]Frederick A. P. Barnard, Report for 1886, pp. 39–43.
[4]Ibid., pp. 55 ff.   [5]Ibid., pp. 83–85.

President Barnard's report for 1887[1] records my appointment to give instruction with the rank of Fellow, and later[2] records the success of the course of public lectures which it was my good fortune to organize and which was the forerunner and prophecy of the vast work in University Extension which has multiplied the influence of Columbia and its service manyfold. During this year Professor Alexander returned to service for part of the time, and his report on the work of the department, together with a supplementary report of my own, will be found in the President's Annual Report for that year.[3] It is this same report which records the beginnings of systematic group instruction for graduate students, which paved the way to the establishment of the Faculty of Philosophy three years later. The President's Annual Report for 1888[4] records my promotion to the rank of Tutor, with a salary of $1200. Again Professor Alexander's report and my own supplement thereto deal with the development of group instruction in philosophy as it was then proceeding.[5] This was the last report written by President Barnard himself, that for 1889 being written by Doctor Drisler as acting president. This report records my appointment to be Adjunct Professor, the salary of which post was then $3500.[6] From that time on I was in full charge of the Department of Philosophy owing to Professor Alexander's continued ill health and subsequent resignation in 1889.

The new university statutes of 1890 made provision for

[1]Frederick A. P. Barnard, Report for 1887, p. 8.
[2]*Ibid.*, pp. 39 ff.
[3]*Ibid.*, pp. 90–91.
[4]Frederick A. P. Barnard, Report for 1888, p. 9.
[5]*Ibid.*, pp. 58–60.
[6]Henry Drisler, Annual Report to the Trustees of Columbia University as Acting President, 1889, p. 21.

the Faculty of Philosophy precisely as I had outlined and urged it. At the first meeting of this faculty on May 9, 1890, I was chosen to be its Dean. The period of laying foundations was over and that of building the super-structure had begun.

What has happened since that time is fully reported in the twelve Annual Reports of President Low and in the thirty-eight Annual Reports which I have submitted to the trustees. The story is truly a fascinating one. The ends in view were clearly conceived and progress toward their achievement depended entirely upon securing the means with which to proceed to their accomplishment. This problem of university building presented itself in a four-fold aspect. There was, first, the need of securing groups of outstanding scholars and leaders in research in order to give to at least half a dozen departments of learning a distinction which the whole academic world would recognize. Then there was the problem of the permanent home and physical equipment of the new University, which was so serious and so pressing that its solution could not be long postponed. Next there was the aim of public service to be realized through an organized Summer Session, well-planned University Extension with special reference to adult education and a University Press for publication of works of scholarship and inspiration as the University's contribution to the literature of the time. Then, finally, in recognition of the worldwide and international char-acter of scholarship and intellectual service, there was the aim of bringing to the new University a succession of out-standing scholars from universities in other lands and having our scholars in turn visit foreign universities so often as occasion might offer.

The first of these tasks was a most inspiring one. The title of my professorship was Philosophy, Ethics and Psy-

chology, which led Professor Burgess to remark that what
the trustees had given me was not a chair but a settee!
So soon as President Low took office I brought this matter
to his attention, pointing out that my own special interest
was Philosophy and that I should like to be permitted to
bring to the faculty two new men specially devoted to
Ethics and Psychology, respectively. When this request
was granted, I went at once to Baltimore to consult President Gilman and Professor G. Stanley Hall. As a result
Professor James H. Hyslop was brought to Columbia
from Bucknell University, Pennsylvania, to be Professor of
Logic and Ethics, and Professor James McKeen Cattell
was brought from the University of Pennsylvania to be
Professor of Experimental Psychology. Both men had been
University Fellows at Johns Hopkins. Professor Hyslop
I had not known, but he rendered admirable scholarly
service until his forced retirement through ill health in
1902. Professor Cattell, who was just then an important
personality in the new movement in the field of psychology, I had met while he was a pupil at Leipzig working in the laboratory of Professor Wundt. He quickly
became the leading spirit in the new psychological movement and has played a very large part in it from that
day to this. He was in service at Columbia from 1890 to
1917. In the most important field of zoology practically
nothing had been done, and when we called Henry Fairfield Osborn from Princeton, Edmund B. Wilson and
Thomas Hunt Morgan from Bryn Mawr and added Bash-
ford Dean and Calkins, the most distinguished group of
teachers and research workers in that field was brought
into existence. It seemed to us important that in the field
of English literature the University should have the inspiration and service of men of letters who were not primarily academic teachers. To that end we brought George

Edward Woodberry from Boston, together with Brander Matthews, George Rice Carpenter and William P. Trent. These men formed a most inspiring group who attracted and guided the thought and literary work of a long generation of ambitious students. In physics there was Pupin; in chemistry, Chandler and later, Bogert and Sherman; in sociology, Giddings; in music, MacDowell; in geology, Kemp; in civil engineering, Burr; in botany, Britton and Underwood; in anatomy, Huntington; in pathology, Prudden; in mathematics, Fiske, Cole and Woodward; in architecture, Ware; in Indo-Iranian languages, Jackson; in modern European languages, Charles Sprague Smith, H. H. Boyesen, Calvin Thomas, Todd and later John Dyneley Prince; in law, Keener, Burdick and Canfield and, in international law, John Bassett Moore; in economics, John B. Clark and Seligman; in history, Sloane, Osgood, Dunning and Robinson; in Latin, Harry Thurston Peck, Egbert and Nelson G. McCrea; in Greek, Perry and Wheeler; and in philosophy, a little later, Woodbridge. These men were, each and all, of the highest type of intellectual leaders and scholars of university equipment and rank, and they, together with their associates and successors, were the true builders of Columbia University as a world center of teaching and research.

The Faculty of Political Science had already come into existence and with Burgess, Mayo-Smith, Munroe Smith and Goodnow, was without a peer. It was necessary to make over the Faculty of Law, to alter its course of instruction and to inspire it with University ambition as a substitute for professional zeal. The College of Physicians and Surgeons had likewise to be reconstructed both in theory and in practice; and Doctor Bard's vision, a century and a quarter earlier, of a Medical Center carried toward realization, however slowly. The School of Mines was in excellent condition and needed only normal development. All these undertakings, which were of highest importance, took time and their accomplishment meant that the University must have greatly increased financial resources.

Then came the question of where the University's permanent home should be found. When the old College was driven by the march of events from its first site on the King's Farm, it had been the intention to place it on the Upper Estate which was then remote indeed from business buildings or even from residences. Renwick, the architect of Saint Patrick's Cathedral, drew a plan for a new Columbia College building, perhaps the largest build-ing which had then been proposed in this country, to stand on the west side of Fifth Avenue and to extend almost from what is now Forty-ninth Street to what is now Fifty-first Street. It was placed back from Fifth Avenue and was shown in grounds charmingly laid out and sur-rounded by trees. It is of record that Saint Patrick's Cathe-dral was placed where it is so that it might always face the quiet gardens of Columbia College!

When removal from the King's Farm became urgent and funds were not at hand with which to build the new structure planned for the Upper Estate, the trustees leased that property and purchased the block bounded by Madi-son Avenue, Fourth Avenue, Forty-ninth Street and Fif-tieth Street, then occupied by the Institution for the Deaf and Dumb. This was intended to be but a temporary site while a permanent home for the College was being chosen farther north, since there were already signs that the Upper Estate would not long remain remote both from business buildings and from residences. Before anything could be done, however, the Civil War came, the financial situation of the College became more acute and so it was that a site intended to be temporary was occupied for forty years.

Meanwhile the search for a permanent location farther up the Island had never been abandoned. Various individuals took part in it from time to time, but nothing was accomplished. Indeed, just before Henry Villard built the stately brownstone houses on the block north of the College site, it was seriously proposed that Columbia should itself acquire that block and look forward to remaining in that situation permanently. Fortunately, that plan was frustrated, and the search for another and permanent home continued.

During the closing years of the administration of President Barnard, the College was in a great state of ferment and turmoil. New ideas and new projects were being brought forward year by year and almost week by week. While the rentals from the Upper Estate had improved, they were not yet, by any means, adequate or sufficient to give the trustees a free hand in dealing with other problems. During all this period—indeed, from 1754—the College had received but an insignificant number of gifts or bequests, and these uniformly of small amount. The great tide of benefaction which was shortly to begin was not then in evidence or even suspected.

This was the background when John B. Pine, the youngest and most vigorous of the trustees, asked me to join him in the search for a new site. On many successive Sunday afternoons in the autumn of 1890, I went with Mr. Pine all about the upper part of Manhattan Island, searching for a site to be urged upon the trustees as the permanent home of Columbia University. Any proposed site south of 110th Street was rejected, it seeming certain that the march of progress would soon make such a site unsuitable, no matter what attractions it might present at the moment. This applied to property, which was carefully examined, west of the south end of Central Park along what is now Central Park West, and also to several blocks on the east side of Riverside Drive bounded on the south by West Seventy-second Street. The matter soon resolved itself into a choice between three high points on Manhattan Island: Morningside Heights, then generally known as Bloomingdale; a height of land near Audubon Park where the American Academy of Arts and Letters, the American Geographical Society and the Hispanic Society now are; and the high point on what is today Fort Washington Avenue which is now the site of The Cloisters and the very attractive Fort Tryon Park.

Having in mind protection from possible developments in the future, accessibility from east and from west as well as from north and from south, and comparative isolation, we finally settled on Morningside Heights as our choice. The prompt purchase of this property was urged upon President Low and the trustees. It was my fortune to spend several evenings with Mr. William C. Schermerhorn, then Chairman of the Trustees, at his home, 49 West Twenty-third Street, going over maps and discussing future possibilities and developments. Mr. Schermerhorn, who was himself greatly interested in real-estate holdings, followed closely every detail of the suggestions that were made. It was then my urgent proposal, which Mr. Pine shared in theory but thought wholly impracticable, that the trustees should at that time acquire the entire body of land between Morningside Drive on the east and Riverside Drive on the west and between West 110th Street on the south and West 122d Street on the north, except such part of it as had already been acquired by the Cathedral of St. John the Divine and by

St. Luke's Hospital. It seemed to me that since the trustees had had long and successful experience in leasehold property, and since their purchase of any part of this land as a home for the College would greatly and at once increase the value of all the rest of it, they should themselves get this benefit for the College and its future endowment by acquiring and leasing for twenty-one-year periods such parts of the property as they did not or could not immediately use for academic buildings and their surroundings. I remember pointing out that this property was practically an island, since Morningside Park protected it on the east and the Hudson River on the west, while 110th and 122d Streets were both boulevards under the control and maintenance of the Park Department.

At that time this entire tract could have been purchased for a relatively modest sum compared with later values. Had this been done, the future endowment of Columbia would have been made secure through its own foresight and its own act. It must be remembered that there were then no houses or improvements anywhere in the neighborhood, that the Bloomingdale Insane Asylum of the New York Hospital stood in comfortable isolation on a height surrounded by grass and trees, and that the city lots, each twenty-five by one hundred feet, existed only on the map. At that time these lots were thought to be worth from $1600 to $2000. On the day following the announcement of Columbia's purchase of part of this property, their price advanced to $4000 and within two years some of them were being sold at $20,000 to $22,000 each. All this enormous increase in value was given, in effect, to casual holders and to speculators, when a reasonable amount of foresight and courage would have brought it to the coffers of the University.

The first purchase by the University, on which an

option was taken in December 1891 and the purchase finally completed in 1892, included that portion of the property between Amsterdam Avenue and Broadway, 116th Street and 120th Street. South Field was acquired in 1903 and East Field in 1910–14 at steadily increasing prices. For each of these purchases the amount paid was several times that for which they might have been acquired in the period from 1892 to 1894.

George W. Vanderbilt had become very much interested in the development of the New York College for the Training of Teachers, now Teachers College, and while this search for a new site for Columbia was going on, I took Mr. Vanderbilt into our confidence and suggested his acquiring for Teachers College the property adjoining whatever land the College might decide to buy. Up to that time Mr. Vanderbilt and I had been looking at the block between Broadway and Central Park West, Sixty-second and Sixty-third Streets, which then seemed very far out in the country. On making his first visit to Morningside, Mr. Vanderbilt's judgment concurred with that of Mr. Pine, that the Morningside Heights site was to be preferred. When the time came, therefore, he was ready to purchase and did purchase for Teachers College the property on the north side of West 120th Street between Amsterdam Avenue and Broadway, to which that institution was moved in 1893 from its original home at 9 University Place.

The acreage which was purchased then and subsequently for the University has long since been outgrown. In particular, the School of Law and the Schools of Engineering have for several years past required greatly increased facilities and accommodation. What was done, however, proved to be of extraordinary significance. It placed the University on one of the highest points of

Manhattan Island, protected on either side and away from the chief marts of trade and commerce. It made possible the building of what will some day be regarded, perhaps, as an American twentieth-century Mont St. Geneviève.

The University took possession of that portion of the present site on Morningside Heights which it had then acquired, on October 1, 1894, and at once proceeded to study how it might best be developed. In order to secure legislative action to prevent cutting this site to pieces by opening streets across it, the trustees ceded to the city forty feet of land between Amsterdam Avenue and Broadway in order to give 120th Street a width of one hundred feet. They likewise conveyed to the city a property which was one-half of the present width of 116th Street between Broadway and Amsterdam Avenue. These steps made the unity of the new site secure. The trustees selected three outstanding architects, Richard M. Hunt, Charles C. Haight and Charles F. McKim, to study how the architectural development of the new site might best be planned. Their several projects were carefully studied and then passed upon by the head of the Department of Architecture, Professor William R. Ware, and by Frederick Law Olmsted of Boston. The Gothic architecture of Mr. Haight was rejected as unsuitable. The reasons were that the cost of the ground made it necessary to erect high buildings and that Gothic windows would not provide adequate light for libraries and laboratories under modern conditions in New York City. It is interesting to recall that one of these architectural projects made the University face to the east, another made it face to the west, while that of McKim, which was finally chosen, made it face to the south. When McKim was asked why he had done this, his answer was most characteristic: "So that

Columbia University may always look the City of New
York straight in the face!"

The Morningside Heights site was formally dedicated
with most impressive ceremonies on May 2, 1896, at
which time Abram S. Hewitt, of the Class of 1842, delivered a memorable commemorative oration. Adequate
provision by way of buildings was made in time to permit
the transfer of the University's educational work from the
Forty-ninth Street site on October 1, 1897. "No university," wrote President Low, "has a nobler site; no city
has a greater opportunity."

The Summer Session, the work in University Extension
and that of the Columbia University Press which has now
become one of the most important publishing undertakings in the country, went forward by leaps and bounds,
and a position of leadership in the whole movement for
adult education was quickly gained. As other institutions
and agencies developed in later years the work in this
field, it became less important for Columbia University
to devote as much energy and financial support to it as
had been needed at first.

Finally, the stream of visiting scholars from European
and South American countries grew steadily greater and
more impressive. Were a list of these visiting scholars to
be printed, it would look almost like a directory of the
world's learning in that period. Among those of outstanding reputation who came to the new University in the
first few years following its organization were Professor
Hermann Helmholtz of the University of Berlin; Bishop
Barry, formerly Primate of Australia and afterwards
Bishop of Rochester and Canon of Windsor; Professor
Robert Y. Tyrrell, Regius Professor of Greek in the University of Dublin; Professor Wilhelm Dörpfeld, distinguished German archæologist; and from London, Doctor

T. W. Rhys-Davids, the Orientalist, of University College, and T. Humphry Ward. It was the visit of M. René Doumic of the Académie Française which brought forth the following witty limerick from the pen of Professor Edward Delavan Perry, the well-known Columbia Hellenist:

> Monsieur René Doumic-a
> 'E cannot-a speak-a
> Any of ze An-glay;
> So I say to eem-a
> Je vous estime-a-
> Ve get on ver-a well zat-a-way.

It was also a great pleasure to see to it that professorships were named for some of the great scholars who had adorned the early history of King's College and Columbia College as well as for some of the personalities who had contributed so much to the guidance of the corporation's work, in order that these men should not be overlooked or forgotten in the university development of the twentieth century. So it was that chairs were named for Bard and Hosack, for Dalton and Valentine Mott, for Renwick and Vinton and Newberry, for John Jay and Gouverneur Morris, for Da Ponte and Lieber, for MacVickar, Gebhard and Anthon, for Torrey and Rutherfurd and Ruggles, for Kent and Dwight, for Davies and Betts and Hamilton Fish.

During the half-century universities have greatly changed in many respects. The German universities have, through obvious causes, lost their leadership and their distinction. The Italian universities produce and have produced a number of most important scholars and scientific leaders, while those of France have gone their way in quiet pursuit of their historic aims. In England, Oxford and Cambridge are, in a sense, more powerful than they have ever been and have adapted themselves with surprising completeness to the changed demands of contemporary social, economic and political life. The so-called provincial universities in England, being relatively young, have been quick to seize upon the opportunities of the present day for helpful and constructive service. The four noble universities of Scotland, apparently apart from the great waves of change and commotion, retain their distinction and their leadership from generation to generation. In the United States, the term *university* is so loosely used that the university problem does not present itself to public opinion with the clearness and definiteness which it should. Thirty-two universities are included in the membership of the Association of American Universities, but that is due to a very generous application of the term. Clear thinking and sound practice require that the words *college* and *university* be not confused, and that their very separate and different problems be understood and studied as they really are and not in a manner complicated by the misuse of words.

The metropolitan city of New York will in all likelihood become the effective and influential capital of the thought and conduct of the world for the next few hundred years. The conditions which will bring this about should be plain to the eye of any realistic observer. The old and ripe civilization of Western Europe has come to a point where it is obviously not easy to adapt itself to the wholly changed world conditions which now prevail. In the New World and from its great metropolitan capital where peoples of various national origins are gathered and mingled on a scale that is not found anywhere else on earth, and where both economic power and influence and intellectual leadership are found in highest degree, may well arise that new and much-needed source of intellectual strength that will guide mankind through the coming generations. Should such a condition come to pass, then surely the authority of Columbia University and its great company of productive scholars would be of highest importance in the history of the human race.

During my last visit to Professor Burgess at Newport, R. I., shortly before his death, he exacted from me a promise that if I were to write anything relative to the history of the organization and development of Columbia University, I should insert the following letter which he wrote to the Secretary, now the Provost, of the University on September 22, 1921. Except in execution of that promise to Professor Burgess the printing of his letter in this volume would not be becoming. It is written with all the friendly prejudice of a beloved teacher and an intimate companion for forty years.

I can conceive of nothing which would give me greater delight than to join you and the other colleagues in the greeting and ovation to our President on October 3rd next. The spirit is not only willing but eager, but, alas, the flesh is now weak, and, should I not be able to be with you in body, I shall certainly be present in thought and affection.

I doubt if there will be another among you who has had the opportunity and privilege of viewing and appreciating our noble chief from so many angles as I have.

First, I knew him as my favorite pupil. I can see at this very moment, that young face in the front row in my lecture room, always present, always prompt, intelligent, alert, deeply interested, taking in everything and giving it back with more precision and in better form than as received.

Then I remember the day when, to my great satisfaction, he took his seat in the Faculty as a colleague on the staff of our institution, and clearly recall the constancy and vigor with which he gave his support to all the genuine measures for the development of the University, at a time, too, when many of them were regarded with disfavor by the majority of our then associates.

After that, my memory of his most valuable services runs along to that famous evening in February of 1890, when we came together in mass meeting to discuss the plan for the organization of the University, which he, during the previous half decade, had done so much to evolve. As the youngest among us in age and in office, he was called upon to speak first, and his masterful presentation of the subject was so complete, so lucid, and so convincing, that those of us who came after him found little to change or to add.

Then followed those crucial years between 1891 and 1901, when he, as Dean of the newly created Faculty of Philosophy, worked hand in hand with me, as Dean of the older Faculty of Political Science, continuously, cordially, *and so commandingly,* in putting the plan of 1891 into operation, that, when in 1901 it became necessary to choose a new president of the University, there was no doubt nor hesitation in determining upon whose shoulders the heavy responsibility should be laid.

For twelve happy and prosperous years, I had the privilege of working with him as my chief, without hitch or friction, or even the slightest misunderstanding, during which period I saw him develop rapidly into the most capable educational organizer and executive in this country, yes, in the entire world, and I was witness, at close range, of still more than this. I saw him become one of the world's greatest publicists and practical statesmen, and I am bound to say that it is incomprehensible to me why, if there be a providential order in the universe of man, he is not today guiding the destinies of this country and, through it, of the world. His profound philosophical insight, his wide and varied attainments and his truly marvelous administrative ability fit him, as no other man in this Nation, to cope with the great problem of the restoration of this ruined and distracted world.

Nothing in my whole life ever gave me the disappointment which I felt when the choice of the Republican Party for the presidency of the United States in 1920 failed to fall upon him.

But I have, and we all have, one consolation in this, namely: he is preserved to the University to lead us on, as our Chief, to greater and ever greater things in our labors for the world's civilization. For this I am, and we all should be, deeply grateful; and long may he live in health, happiness and honor for the perfecting and realization of this transcendent purpose.

Kindly reserve me a modest place at the coming banquet, and, should I not be able to be there in person, please fill it with a representative, so that I may, at least by proxy, wave my greeting to our great leader and friend.

My considered judgment as to the commanding part played by President Low during his twelve years of service in the building of Columbia University is recorded in my first Annual Report as President of the University, submitted to the trustees for the year ending June 30, 1902.

So it was that when the twentieth century opened, Columbia University had come fully into existence with all the strength and all the ideals which were to make it an outstanding national and international powerhouse of scholarship and service. Surely, each and every scholar and administrator who took any part in this great accomplishment may truly say: *Si monumentum quæris, circumspice!*

VIII

FOUNDING TEACHERS COLLEGE

THE story of the origin and University relationship of Teachers College has been told at various times and is given in briefest form in my Annual Report as President of Columbia University for 1937. The fact that Teachers College came into existence in the winter of 1886–87 and received a provisional charter under the name of the New York College for the Training of Teachers from the Regents of the University of the State of New York on January 12, 1889, is due to a series of almost fortuitous circumstances.

The real origin of Teachers College and its inspiration are to be found in the Annual Reports of President Barnard, made to the Trustees of Columbia College, for the years 1881 and 1882.[1] The discussions by President Barnard in those reports of education as a science, of the need for the careful and scientific study of education as well as for thoroughly trained, well informed and well disciplined teachers have long since become classic. President Barnard was then blazing a wholly new path. It was his proposal that there be established in Columbia College

[1] *The Rise of a University*, Vol. I; edited by William F. Russell, Dean of Teachers College. New York: Columbia University Press, 1937. pp. 289–329.

a department of history, theory and practice of education. He outlined in detail the scope and the work of such a department. He sketched an ideal school of elementary training and brought the whole power of his scholarship and his years of reflective study to bear upon the presentation and interpretation of the subject that was so dear to his heart. Great as was the respect in which President Barnard was held, these recommendations seemed so novel and so revolutionary that they were received by the Trustees and Faculty of Columbia College not only without enthusiasm but with very marked skepticism. A department of education seemed as strange and as odd as a department of aviation would then have been!

In order to carry the matter forward, in the spring of 1886, with President Barnard's approval and connivance, I offered a course of four lectures on Saturday mornings to the teachers of New York City and vicinity on this new and horrendous subject. We were told that nobody would come to such lectures, that nobody was interested and that we were simply wasting our time. Consequently, President Barnard took no small pleasure in recording in his Annual Report for the year 1886 the fact that the largest hall available in Columbia College was packed with an audience to hear these lectures and that 1500 requests from teachers for admission had to be refused! It soon became clear, however, that no real progress could be made in developing this idea under conditions then existing in Columbia College. The evidence of this is furnished by these abstracts from the minutes of the Trustees of Columbia College:

February 7, 1887

The chairman presented a communication from Mr. Nicholas Murray Butler, Assistant in Philosophy, Ethics and Psychology, recommending a plan for the establishment of a Course in Pedagogy, which was referred to the Committee on the Course and Statutes.

.   .   .   .

May 2, 1887

The Committee have considered the communication from Mr. Nicholas Murray Butler, Assistant in Philosophy, Ethics, and Psychology, recommending a plan for the establishment of a course in Pedagogics. They find that it is Mr. Butler's wish that he should be permitted to give a course of instruction in that subject in the College, that it should be offered as an elective to undergraduates in the senior year, and that the lectures should be given at the rate of two or three each week. He further proposes that the course should be open to all persons whatsoever desirous of instruction in the subject, and that they should be permitted to join the Senior Class for that particular study. Mr. Butler, on being interrogated on that point, admitted, that the number of students likely to elect that subject would be exceedingly small; that he would not consider it worth while to do the work for them only; and that his chief object would be to bring to the College a large number of persons, not otherwise connected with it, for whose benefit in fact the scheme has been devised. Your Committee are not prepared to give their assent to the proposition; it appears to them that it is open to grave objection on many grounds. The number of students in the College likely to derive benefit from it would not exceed ten or twelve. The outsiders whom the establishment of such a course would immediately attract to the College would be according to Mr. Butler's estimate, as many as 150 to 200 in number, and of these, by the same estimate nine-tenths would be women, either already engaged in teaching or in training for that profession. It is obvious that the scheme would introduce entirely new elements into the work of the College, and that it could not be carried into effect without a departure from the fixed policy of the Board as to the inexpediency of admitting women to the classes in the undergraduate department. If persons from outside were to be admitted, on Mr. Butler's plan, they would be required to matriculate as other students, and the result would be to graft an outside co-educational department on the senior year. Your Committee are not able to discern any advantage likely to ensue to the College, which could be taken as an offset to the confusion which would result from the introduction of a scheme having reference to the outside public rather than to the youth under our own care; and they have therefore drafted a resolution to the effect that it is not expedient to adopt Mr. Butler's proposal.

. . . .

Resolved, that it is not expedient to adopt the plan presented by Mr. Nicholas Murray Butler, for the establishment of a Course in Pedagogics.

At the very moment when the path to progress in Columbia College itself seemed hopelessly blocked, a new and entirely unsuspected door was opened. There existed in New York at that time a group of men and women organized first as part of the parish work of St. Mark's Church in the Bouwerie under the leadership of a very remarkable woman, Miss Emily Huntington. This group was known as the Kitchen Garden Association. Its purpose was the training of young girls of school age in domestic duties—what we now call domestic science and domestic art, although those names were not yet in existence—and in the elements of gardening and caring for flowers and vegetables. Miss Huntington had classes in East Eleventh Street, late in the afternoons and on Saturday mornings. In the spring and autumn, when the weather was fine, she took groups of these young girls out into Westchester and up to Riverdale to the country places of those who were assisting this movement, and gave them there some notion of outdoor life, of plants, of flowers, of birds. Then during the week-day afternoons there was some specific instruction in the care of the household, with all its many ramifications.

Miss Huntington had gathered about her a group of eager women, at the head of whom were Miss Grace H.

Dodge, Miss S. Edwina Brown and Mrs. William T. Blodgett. They were giving her encouragement and financial support. During 1885–86, in the third year of the existence of the Kitchen Garden Association, it broadened its scope. It chose the President of the City College, General Alexander S. Webb, as its President, became the Industrial Education Association and set itself the task of developing the public interest in industrial education, in the training of the hand for industry and for the arts. In the spring of 1886 that Association held at Cosmopolitan Hall, Broadway and Forty-first Street, a very remarkable exhibit. That exhibit showed what could be done in these fields with proper guidance and with very small resources. The press supported the exhibition and the movement very vigorously. The question then arose, "What are we going to do next?"

The women who were interested in this movement were true philanthropists, eager for a practical and highly useful type of public service. They now wished to promote special training in any of the industries which affected the house and the home and which would enable those receiving such training to become self-supporting. They planned to prepare and to publish literature on this subject as well as to study methods by which domestic and industrial training might be introduced into existing schools. Their work advanced by leaps and bounds. A house at 54 East Eleventh Street was rented as its headquarters and with a view to rousing public opinion generally, public meetings were held and exhibitions of pupils' work were given. President Gilman of Johns Hopkins University was greatly interested in the work of the Association and aided it with his wise counsel. A number of men of high standing and great usefulness in the community were added to the Association's membership and board of control in the winter of 1886–87. General Webb then retired from the presidency and at the suggestion of John B. Pine, a devoted trustee of Columbia University, I was invited to succeed him in the presidency of the Industrial Education Association. This was a purely honorary office and in no sense a professional career. Almost immediately, however, the directors of the Industrial Education Association requested me to make the presidency an office of administration and to devote as much time to it as possible. I saw at once the opportunity to combine this useful movement with that which President Barnard desired pushed forward at Columbia College. I then explained to the directors of the Industrial Education Association that I could only accept such a position as they had in mind if the work of the Association was fundamentally changed and so broadened as to make it really an effective representative of President Barnard's ideals. This meant that the whole movement must be converted from a philanthropic enterprise into one for educational advancement and reform. My suggestion was accepted, but with much reluctance on the part of the women on the board of directors who feared that the philanthropy for which they cared so much would be overshadowed by academic interest and academic ideals. Nevertheless, a college for the training of teachers was organized and its work was begun. An excellent building, Number Nine University Place, which had just been vacated by the Union Theological Seminary to go to its new home on Park Avenue and Seventieth Street, was rented to be the seat of the new college. This building quickly became known affectionately for more than a decade by teachers and students alike as Number Nine. In the program of study of the college, manual and industrial training were emphasized, a model school named for Horace Mann was opened and special classes for teachers were planned, some of which were held at late afternoon and evening hours and during the summer vacation. So it was that by the grafting, so to speak, of President Barnard's educational ideals upon a philanthropic enterprise of outstanding importance, the New York College for the Training of Teachers came into existence, secured the funds necessary for its support and growth and was able to procure the provisional charter of 1889. This was followed by the permanent charter of 1892 when the name Teachers College was given to the institution. The story of the work and extraordinary growth of Teachers College is set out in its annual circulars of information and in the annual reports of its chief executive officers during the past half-century.

There was discussion from the very beginning as to what, if any, relation should exist between Teachers College and Columbia University. As early as January 27, 1892, the Chairman of the Trustees of Teachers College addressed to the Trustees of Columbia College a proposal that it be consolidated with the work of Columbia College at the end of a five-year period, so that its work might stand in the same relation to the developing University as would that of the Law School or of the College of Physicians and Surgeons. When this proposal reached the trustees, they invited the University Council to express its opinion and in due time the University Council rendered a report, of which the following is the substance, dealing with the whole subject.

The College for the Training of Teachers is an institution chartered by the Regents of the University of the State of New York for the purpose of giving a professional training of high grade to intending teachers. It has done and is now doing most excellent work of a character that is in part, if not as a whole, germane to the work of a university. This College is one of a large class of institutions situated in and near the city of New York, whose peculiar field touches that of Columbia at one or more points. It is a type, not an isolated case, and should be treated as such.

The proposition referred to this Committee contemplates the consolidation of the two institutions on lines similar to those laid down in the case of the College of Physicians and Surgeons. Two reasons influence your Committee to report against this plan. The first reason is that a necessary part of the organization of the College for the Training of Teachers is a school of observation and practice, in which every grade from the kindergarten to the high school must be represented. The maintenance and administration of such a school as part of Columbia College would involve many difficulties, and would very distinctly divert our administrative energy from its proper channel.

The second reason is that such a consolidation as is proposed would introduce co-education into Columbia in a most pronounced form. A large majority of the students in the College for the Training of Teachers are women, and this will always be the case. In this country more than sixty per cent of the entire teaching force are women, and the proportion is increasing. We believe that at this point in our development, when Columbia is becoming a university, and is laying the foundations of its reputation as such, it would be a mistake to commit the university to a policy of co-education, as such a consolidation would commit it. Either of the reasons given should be sufficient in our view to prevent consolidation, and both together seem to form an insuperable obstacle.

At the same time it is not to be denied that an alliance between Columbia and the College for the Training of Teachers might be formed that would be of advantage to both. Columbia might hope to gain a valuable ally, and opportunity for instruction in pedagogy both valuable and unique. To the latter institution might be assured a high standard of scholarship, much university instruction, and the benefits of a university atmosphere and a university library. For such an alliance we believe that Columbia's arrangement with Barnard College, with certain necessary modifications of detail, furnishes the correct type. It appears to your Committee to be vital that under any such arrangement Columbia should control so much of the work of the College for the Training of Teachers as is properly university work, and that the College for the Training of Teachers should itself give no degrees, while retaining the right to reward by certificates such of its students as are not qualified for the Columbia degree. It would be an essential feature also, of any arrangement, that the fees to be charged in the College for the Training of Teachers should be the same as those charged in Columbia both for candidates for the degrees and for special students in university work. Subject to these assumptions we believe that an alliance in this instance could be made with mutual advantage upon the following lines:

1. The New York College for the Training of Teachers should retain its charter, its separate board of trustees, and its independent financial status.

2. To such of the students of the College for the Training of Teachers as have had the requisite preliminary training, Columbia should give degrees upon such conditions as might be laid down by the University Council.

3. The educational control of the College for the Training of Teachers should be confided to a Board of Managers, or a Faculty, made up of representatives both of the technical and the university sides of its work. It is suggested that from the College for the Training of Teachers there should be in this body as many professors of pedagogy as may be necessary to give instruction in the methods of teaching the English language and literature, the classical languages, mathematics, natural science, the elementary school subjects, and the like. From Columbia there should be the members of the University Council representing the Faculty of Philosophy, ex-officio, and the professors having charge of the following subjects of university instruction, whether they are now in service or may hereafter be appointed:

History and Institutes of Education,	Ethics,
Philosophy,	Sociology,
Psychology,	History.

4. Appointments of the professors of pedagogy in the College for the Training of Teachers should be subject to confirmation by the President of Columbia. One of such professors of pedagogy should be designated by the Trustees of the College for the Train-

ing of Teachers as President of the College, and he should perform, subject to the determinations of the Board of Managers or Faculty, constituted as above proposed, all of the ordinary executive duties of the College for the Training of Teachers.

5. Each Columbia professor, who is a member of the Faculty as above, should give at least one course of instruction each year in the College for the Training of Teachers.

6. Candidates in Columbia College for the M.A. and Ph.D. degrees should be allowed to take one or both of their minor courses in the College for the Training of Teachers.

7. Students of the College for the Training of Teachers not qualified under the rules of Columbia to enter as students of Columbia should not be admitted to university privileges.

8. Students of the College for the Training of Teachers should have the privileges of the university library at the discretion of the President of Columbia in such numbers as may prove practicable.

Shortly thereafter the trustees took the following action based upon this report from a committee of which President Low was Chairman and of which the Reverend Doctor Morgan Dix, F. Augustus Schermerhorn, John B. Pine and the Reverend Doctor Marvin R. Vincent were members:

The Committee received from the University Council, as requested by the Trustees, a carefully prepared report upon the educational questions involved in the proposition. The University Council advise unanimously against the acceptance of the proposition submitted by the College for the Training of Teachers in its present form. They are opposed to the consolidation of the two institutions.

1st. On the ground that the schools for observation and practice maintained by the College for the Training of Teachers would be a distinct anomaly in the work of the University, and,

2d. On the ground that such a consolidation would introduce co-education into Columbia in a most pronounced form.

The University Council have, however, expressed it as their opinion that an alliance with the College for the Training of

Teachers might be formed which would be mutually advantageous. The Council point out, as it seems to your Committee justly, that this institution is one of many whose work touches ours at one or more points while involving in its further reach many matters that are foreign to our proper field. The Council, therefore, in their report have indicated the principles which in their judgment ought to apply to alliances of this kind and have endeavored to suggest the outlines of a scheme by which an alliance might advantageously be made in the present instance. Your Committee are disposed to consider the opinion expressed by the Council in regard to the desirability of an alliance with the College for the Training of Teachers, provided that the terms of such alliance may be made mutually satisfactory. Your Committee, however, have felt under restraint which they assume is likely to be shared by the Trustees in view of the fact that the proposition from the College for the Training of Teachers suggests consolidation only and does not, upon its face, offer any alternative. Your Committee, therefore, are constrained to report against the acceptance of the specific proposition submitted. At the same time they offer a resolution asking to be continued, in order to ascertain whether by conference with the College for the Training of Teachers a mutually satisfactory basis may be found for some alliance between the two institutions. Your Committee gladly bear testimony to the efficiency and high character of the work done by the College for the Training of Teachers in its own sphere, and they are inclined to believe that important benefits might accrue to both institutions as a result of the policy indicated. They greatly regret to be obliged to report unfavorably on the specific proposition submitted, but there appear to be elements involved in this proposition which are inseparable from the work of the College for the Training of Teachers that make it clearly impracticable from the point of view of Columbia College.

. . . .

Resolved, That the proposition of the College for the Training of Teachers for consolidation with Columbia College be respectfully declined.

Resolved, That the Select Committee be continued with leave to consider and report as to the possibility of effecting a satisfactory alliance between Columbia College and the College for the Training of Teachers, and in case it be found practicable and desirable in their view to submit a detailed plan therefor.

As a matter of fact, this whole movement reflected the discussions which had been going on for a decade over some of President Barnard's proposals and marked much more progress than a superficial reading of these reports would indicate. In his Annual Report for 1900 President Low called attention to the fact that new agreements had been made with Barnard College and with Teachers College during that year by which both of these corporations, while retaining their separate existence, had become in fact as completely a part of the educational system of the University as though the work that they were doing was being carried on under the University charter. This meant that another and long step had been taken in building Columbia University's educational system on a federal basis of co-operating corporations which, while having separate and independent financial responsibilities, were under one and the same University academic administration by reason of the jurisdiction of the President of the University and that of the University Council on which every School and Faculty has representation. Meanwhile, during this first half-century of its existence Teachers College has achieved and holds a position of outstanding leadership in its field of intellectual life and work, and exerts an influence in every part of the land in respect to all that concerns the administration and work of school organization and school instruction. President Barnard's dream has been fully realized.

IX

SOME FORTUNATE MEMORIES

I T IS a pleasure to tell some of the experiences of long ago in the work of the teaching profession and its organization in this country at a time when it was at a peak of distinction which has always seemed to me very remarkable, and which, so far as I can judge, it has never since reached. This was the period from about 1885 to about 1905. I fancy that the standard of excellence then attained may have been due to the effect of the Civil War on American life. That war and its after-happenings brought into American public service and into the intellectual life of the nation an exceptional number of outstanding personalities. It would be difficult to find any period, either earlier or later in our history, when there were so many striking personalities engaged in the work of public school education in this country as was the case from about 1875 to about 1900, or possibly a little later. The profession then attracted not only men of great ability, but men of exceptional character and personality. It may perhaps be that the business instinct and the power of the gain-seeking motive had not then become so strong as they did later, for we certainly had in the work of education at that time, in the superintendencies of our school system, in our elementary school and high school principalships and in many of our college professorships, a very extraordinary body of men.

Teachers College, as has been told, did not take corporate form until 1889, but as an idea and an ideal it began its life in the month of December, 1886. It took some little time for that idea and ideal to obtain the support necessary to enable it to take on concrete and organized form. In connection with the founding of Teachers College, there was a movement afoot, particularly strong in New York and vicinity, for the introduction of manual training and industrial and art education in the schools. Some of us identified ourselves heartily with this movement, which was just beginning to attract public attention and to arouse a certain measure of public interest and support. At that time there lived in Chicago a gentleman named Charles H. Ham, who was deeply interested in such a movement. He conceived the notion that the United States Commissioner of Education should be a person concerned with and interested in it. Without my knowledge, and of course without my consent, he undertook to have me appointed United States Commissioner of Education by President Harrison. The proposal was really quite ridiculous. I was but just out of college and was only getting started in the interesting things of life, with increasingly clear and definite plans with respect to my life-work in connection with the coming Teachers College and with Columbia University. Under no circumstances would I have deserted what I was then proposing to do in order to be United States Commissioner of Education. Nevertheless, on the urgent insistence of Mr. Ham and that of the scores of other persons whose support he enlisted, President Harrison sent for me shortly after his inauguration on March 4, 1889, and invited me to be United States Commissioner of Education. For a number

of years that post had been held by General John Eaton
of Ohio, who, upon the election of President Cleveland in
1884, was succeeded by Nathaniel H. R. Dawson of
Georgia. President Harrison proposed to make a change
in the office. Of course, I thanked him most warmly for
the compliment of his invitation, but pointed out that I
had no experience which qualified me to hold this position, that I had no personal fitness for it and, moreover,
that I had chosen a course of work in life from which I
had no wish to be tempted. "And, furthermore," I said
to the President, "there is available for this post the most
distinguished educational thinker in America, and he is
the man whom I should urge you to appoint." The President asked me whom I had in mind and I replied, "William T. Harris," then of Concord, Massachusetts, but
formerly of St. Louis, Missouri, where he had been Superintendent of Schools for nearly twelve years. The President
said he had never heard of Doctor Harris, to which I
replied, "Your Secretary of the Interior can tell you all
about him, for he was a member of the Board of Education in St. Louis while Doctor Harris was Superintendent."
Within thirty days President Harrison appointed Doctor
Harris to be United States Commissioner of Education.
He filled that office with commanding distinction until
the condition of his health required him to retire from it
in 1906. In recognition of his great personal service, Doctor Harris was chosen by the Trustees of the Carnegie
Foundation for the Advancement of Teaching to be the
first person named on their list of those to receive their
maximum retiring allowance, when that Foundation was
organized in the very year of Doctor Harris's retirement.

It would be quite impossible to overstate the ability,
the learning or the commanding intellectual influence of
Doctor Harris. To my thinking, his was the one great

philosophical mind which has appeared on this side of the Atlantic. In addition to his philosophical learning and power, he had a most extraordinary gift of very simple exposition and it was this which gave him his power over the teaching profession. Doctor Harris could stand up before an audience of any kind of teachers or principals and expound in the simplest language profound philosophical ideals and ideas, and so shape, in accordance with those ideals and ideas, the conduct of the thinking and action of those who heard him. In him there was a most remarkable combination of intellectual traits.

He has not been appreciated by the subsequent generation, and the reason is very simple. It is one which I may say I foresaw and tried to guard against. I used to say to him, time and time again during the later years of his life, that he owed it to himself and his future reputation to bring together his philosophical doctrines in a single volume, which could be studied and referred to by thoughtful men and women for generations to come. He never lived to do this, but continued to scatter his really marvelous writings through book reviews, comments, introductions to books and casual articles in a way which perhaps multiplied his immediate contemporary influence, but certainly prevented the erection of that literary monument which could be pointed to for all time. Some day an authoritative life of Doctor Harris will be written. If competently done, it will be an invaluable book. Doctor Harris was the ruling figure at all educational meetings in the United States during these very active years of his life. Every national meeting was dominated by his personality and his thought. When invited to a state meeting or to a group meeting, he was the one person to whom every one wished to speak and about whom every one wished to talk.

Doctor Harris was a New Englander, born on a farm near the village of North Killingly, Connecticut, in 1835. He entered Yale in 1854, but left in the middle of his Junior year, because he was "dissatisfied with both the school and its curriculum," to go to Missouri where he entered the public school service. He came in contact there with an extraordinary German of the 1848 movement, named Brockmeyer, who had marked philosophical capacity and subsequently became Lieutenant Governor of Missouri. Harris and Brockmeyer were the founders of the so-called St. Louis School of Philosophy, which was not a school in the ordinary sense but a group of serious students of philosophy. It was there that Doctor Harris's influence began, and from there that it grew until it became literally stupendous. He founded the *Journal of Speculative Philosophy,* and its volumes remain today an indispensable repository of philosophical learning and interpretation. He edited the *International Education Series* which, likewise, is of permanent value. His introductions to the volumes of this series are, many of them, unique and of lasting importance. In his own volume, *The Psychologic Foundations of Education,* the man is revealed at his best. In the large type of this book is printed what Doctor Harris has to say to the average teacher, but in the small type of the footnotes is to be found the profound philosophy of the author. One who reads the book without the footnotes gets a general notion of Doctor Harris's philosophical teaching, but one who reads the footnotes as well gains insight into the philosophy which lies behind the advice and interpretation which has been given on the printed pages above the footnotes.

He had a most engaging manner upon the platform and was very quick in retort when debate was in progress. When the Department of Superintendence of the National

WILLIAM T. HARRIS
[1835–1909]

United States Commissioner of Education, 1889–1906

Education Association met at Richmond, Virginia, in 1894, Doctor Harris read a paper which was criticized from the floor by Doctor William H. Maxwell, then Superintendent of Schools in Brooklyn and afterwards the first Superintendent of Schools in New York, himself one of the outstanding men in the profession. Doctor Harris retorted with some amusing and caustic references which made Doctor Maxwell's objections to what he had said seem rather trifling and caused the great audience to laugh heartily. Then some one called for Doctor Andrew S. Draper, who was at that time State Superintendent of Public Instruction in New York and afterwards President of the University of Illinois. Doctor Draper rose and said, "No, excuse me; I shall not debate with Doctor Harris. I have a wife and child at home." He did not wish to call down upon himself the gale of laughter which Doctor Harris had brought upon Doctor Maxwell.

In those days there were some exceedingly interesting happenings which have become landmarks in the progress of educational theory and practice in the United States. In 1894 when the National Education Association met at Asbury Park, the Council of Education assembled two or three days before the general meeting. At that time there was read what proved to be a most remarkable and significant paper by Doctor B. A. Hinsdale, Professor of Education at the University of Michigan. Doctor Hinsdale was the holder of the only important professorship of education which existed until Teachers College itself was established. This paper was a very searching examination of the dogma of formal discipline. Any one who will read the record of that meeting will see in Doctor Hinsdale's paper the beginning of a very great change in our educational theory and practice, to be attributed in high degree to his influence.

The following year, 1895, when the Department of Superintendence held its meeting at Cleveland, Ohio, there was still another mark of the beginnings of a development in American education. There was then presented the really great report of the Committee of Fifteen, of which Doctor William H. Maxwell was Chairman, appointed two years earlier to consider and examine some of the fundamental problems of elementary education. Among the members of this committee were Doctor William T. Harris, then United States Commissioner of Education, Superintendents Balliet of Springfield, Mass., Dougherty of Peoria, Ill., Powell of Washington, D. C., Tarbell of Providence, R. I., Jones of Indianapolis, Greenwood of Kansas City, Mo., Brooks of Philadelphia, Poland of New Jersey, Seaver of Boston, Lane of Chicago, Gilbert of St. Paul, Cooper of Galveston, and Andrew S. Draper, President of the University of Illinois. The report of the Subcommittee on the Correlation of Studies, presented by Doctor Harris at the Cleveland meeting, is an outstanding contribution to American educational philosophy. It led to a sharp discussion participated in by Charles De Garmo, then at Swarthmore College, and the two McMurrys, who were just at the beginning of their years of influence and leadership. These three men had recently returned from Jena where they had absorbed the Herbartian philosophy under the influence of Professor Rein. From that viewpoint they attacked Doctor Harris's exposition, and the battle was on. Other participants included Doctor Walter L. Hervey, then head of Teachers College, Doctor Emerson E. White of Columbus, Ohio, and Superintendent Dutton of Brookline, Mass., in addition to Doctor Harris himself. It may be that there have been other discussions of like or equal significance, but I venture to doubt it. The record of this discussion marks

the beginning of the influence of the Herbartian philosophy upon our theory and practice. These happenings were
not only quite out of the ordinary, but they marked definitely a movement of opinion in regard to educational
doctrine and practice which was of large significance.

At that time the National Education Association was
a great force in the intellectual life of the profession. It
was relatively small, compared to its membership at the
present time, but much more powerful because of the
quality of the membership. It had been organized as long
ago as 1857, but led a precarious existence until it was
strengthened by a transfusion of blood, so to speak, in
1884. This transfusion took place at the meeting held at
Madison, Wis., and the person who did the transfusing
was Thomas W. Bicknell of Rhode Island, a most energetic and active organizer and leader of men. From 1884
the Association steadily grew in authority and in influence
and in power until it changed its form and character about
thirty-five years ago.

In the time of which I speak, the meetings of the Association were attended statedly by the leaders of the
profession in every group. Not only the superintendents of
schools, principals of high schools and of normal schools,
but the heads of a great many institutions of higher learning in the liberal arts and sciences made a practice of
regularly attending these annual meetings and of participating in the discussion of the problems there considered.
For example, the meeting at Toronto in 1891 marked the
beginning of one of the most interesting and constructive
movements which has ever come into the field of organized education in the United States. Nothing of it is recorded on the program, but during the week that session
lasted there were constant consultations and discussions
going forward as to the new and severe problems pre-

sented to the high schools of the country by the regulations governing college admission. When preparation for college admission was largely a task for private secondary schools only, the problem was fairly simple, but when with the growth of public high schools this problem had wholly changed its form and scope, matters were very different. The problem, as it presented itself to the average high school principal at that time, was how he could treat his students who looked forward to entering different colleges at which examinations for admission were held at different times, with different requirements and sharply differing definitions of one and the same nominal requirement. If Latin is required for college admission, what is meant by Latin? One college insisted upon its definition and another college upon a different one. Mathematics is required for college admission. What is mathematics? The colleges paid no attention to the needs of the high schools and the high schools had no way of impressing their needs upon the colleges. All these matters were much discussed at Toronto in 1891, and during the following winter several informal conferences were convened in New York and elsewhere.

Finally, at Saratoga in 1892, the time seemed ripe to accomplish something. It was my fortune to introduce into the National Council of Education the motion which authorized a Committee of Ten to study and to consider the relations between the high schools and colleges. After some discussion the motion was carried. I then introduced a motion naming the committee. That, too, was carried and the famous Committee of Ten began its work. It was a very remarkable and a very representative committee. Its chairman was President Eliot of Harvard and with him were Doctor Harris, President Angell of the University of Michigan, Mr. John Tetlow, head of the famous

Girls' Grammar School in Boston, President Taylor of Vassar College, Principal Robinson of the Albany, N. Y., Academy, President Baker of the University of Colorado, President Jesse of the University of Missouri, Principal Mackenzie of the Lawrenceville, N. J., School, and Professor King of Oberlin College. This Committee of Ten and its work marked the beginning of the complete reorganization of the relationship between secondary schools and colleges in this country. We went to the Board of Directors of the National Education Association and, by a vote of twenty-one to nine, got an appropriation of $2100 to meet the expenses of the committee in conducting its inquiry. This was the first time that the directors had ever voted a dollar for educational work of any kind.

The first meeting of the Committee of Ten was held in my own apartment on Stuyvesant Square in New York, and their subsequent formal meetings were held in the Faculty Room of old Columbia College. When they submitted their report two years later there was started thereby the movement which resulted, after five years, in the establishment of the College Entrance Examination Board and the final solution of the administrative side of the problem of college admission. It took a long time, however, to get the colleges to agree to co-operate. Doctor Eliot was the outstanding exception among the heads of colleges. He was willing and ready to lead, but it was some years before he could get the Harvard College faculty to agree with him or to support him. President Taylor of Vassar College could not command the support of his faculty nor could President Jesse of the University of Missouri, but they went ahead just the same, and the faculties came along in due season. The situation had become such that any other course was quite impossible.

Colleges like Harvard and Yale and Princeton and Williams and Swarthmore and Dartmouth and Brown and the rest held admission examinations at different times —in May, in June, or even in July. They had widely varying requirements for admission and they defined one and the same term in contrary fashions. Cicero meant one thing to one college and something quite different to another. The same was true of algebra, of Homer, or of American history. The consequence was that the work of the secondary schools was completely wrecked during the last year of their teaching, so far as those students were concerned who were looking forward to college entrance. Some of them, in desperation, had to make a Harvard group, a Yale group, a Williams group and so on, to prepare the candidates for admission on the subject matter as those colleges defined it.

This whole problem came to a climax in 1899 when I had arranged to present a motion at the meeting of the Association of the Colleges and Preparatory Schools in the Middle States and Maryland, to be held at Trenton, N. J., endorsing the project for a College Entrance Examination Board and pledging the secondary schools of that area to support it. I had already secured a vote from the faculty of Columbia College endorsing this action.

President Eliot did a very characteristic thing at that meeting. Our Association was to meet at Trenton on the Friday after Thanksgiving Day. Doctor Eliot, who had no relation to that Association, came all the way from Boston by night-train in order to appear upon the platform and support my motion. Indeed, the College Entrance Examination Board owes everything to President Eliot.

After I had introduced my motion and made a speech in its support, President Patton of Princeton, one of the ablest of men, got up and made a very vigorous attack on the whole proposal and did it with a great deal of power. Then President Warfield of Lafayette arose. He was a very agreeable gentleman, devoted to the interests of the institution over which he presided. He declared that he could never agree to this proposal at all, since Lafayette College intended always to admit its own students in its own way. They would not be told by any board whom to admit and whom not to admit. Warfield went on to say that they might want to admit the son of a benefactor or the son of a trustee or the son of a member of the faculty, and if they thought such action to be to the interest of the college, they would not be prevented from so doing by any board. Then Eliot rose to close the debate. Those who never saw him can never appreciate his platform manner. He always stood perfectly erect, with heels tight together, and began to speak with his hands lowered, with fingers and thumbs closely touching. His habit was to start slowly, coldly, with no sign of emotion of any kind, but with the greatest precision and definiteness. On this occasion, after he had said some general things in favor of the project, he turned to President Warfield who was sitting near him on the platform and said, with just a suspicion of a smile on his face:

The President of Lafayette College has misunderstood Mr. Butler's proposal. This College Entrance Examination Board, if constituted, is not to admit students to any college but so to define the subjects of admission that they will be uniform, to conduct examinations in these subjects at uniform times throughout the world, and to issue to those who take the examinations certificates of performance—good, bad, or indifferent. And, President Warfield, it will be perfectly practicable, under this plan, for Lafayette College to say, if it so chooses, that it will only admit such students as cannot pass these examinations. No one proposes to deprive Lafayette College of that privilege.

The debate ended in a roar of laughter. When the vote was taken, the Association, with several hundred members present, voted unanimously for the establishment of the College Entrance Examination Board. This might never have happened if President Eliot had not come down from Cambridge to support the proposal and make that kind of a speech.

Shortly thereafter the College Entrance Examination Board came into existence and the whole problem which had given rise to its organization disappeared. Uniform examinations have since been held all over the world at one and the same time. Certificates of performance are issued, with which any college may do what it pleases. All this has now become part and parcel of our higher educational system, and the secondary schools and colleges have been given a medium of co-operation and understanding which could not have been constituted in any other way.

It is difficult to convey my sense of the real distinction of the men who in so great numbers adorned our educational system at that time. They were certainly a most extraordinary group. They were not all philosophers by any means, but they were almost without exception scholars. They were admirable administrators and, what is more important, they were powerful personalities. I recall, for instance, men like Seaver of Boston, Marble of Worcester, Mass., and Stanley Hall of Clark University, Tarbell of Providence, Rounds of New Hampshire, Balliet of Springfield, Cole and Downing of Albany, Emerson of Buffalo, Maxwell of Brooklyn, MacAlister, first of Milwaukee and then of Philadelphia, Lyte of Millersville, Pa., Schaeffer of Pennsylvania, White of Cincinnati, Jones and Rickoff of Cleveland, Corson of Ohio, Colonel Francis W. Parker, Albert G. Lane, and Orville T. Bright of

Chicago, Dougherty of Peoria, Ill., Brown of Blooming-
ton, Ill., Cook, first of Normal and then of DeKalb, Ill.,
Bryan of Indiana, Gilbert of St. Paul, Shepard of Winona,
Minn., Kiehle of Minnesota, Seerley and Sabin of Iowa,
Boone of Ypsilanti, Mich., Taylor of Emporia, Kan.,
Greenwood of Kansas City, Soldan of St. Louis, Canfield
of Nebraska, Fitzpatrick of Omaha, Gove and Smiley of
Denver, Preston of Mississippi, Payne of Nashville, Tenn.,
J. H. Phillips of Birmingham, Ala., Edwin A. Alderman,
then of Chapel Hill, N. C., Charles D. McIver of the
State Normal School at Greensboro, N. C., Cooper of
Texas, and Elmer E. Brown of Berkeley, Calif. All these
men were always ready to sit about a table and to consider open-mindedly and with great seriousness any problem or proposal which might be brought forward for
discussion. They were the real leaders of a profession and
they represented that profession not only before their several constituencies but before the nation. These men differed widely, sometimes sharply, in fundamental principle
and in respect to some contemporary policy, but that did
not interfere with their personal relationships. They were
on terms of great intimacy and friendship, and through
their co-operation accomplished a vast task for the improvement of education in the United States.

Outstanding among these men were Maxwell of Brooklyn, MacAlister of Philadelphia, Soldan of St. Louis, and
Greenwood of Kansas City. Those four men differed
greatly in temperament and in outlook, but each of them
held the school system of his city in the hollow of his
hand. He not merely administered it—he really directed
it, guided it and inspired it. These men were thinkers,
and they had both the time and the willingness to think.
My relation to them and to the movement which they
marked came through the work of Teachers College which

was then in the cradle. Without exception they were most encouraging, sympathetic and helpful. In those days it was not easy to secure public support or even widespread approval of such an undertaking. Teachers College then bore its earlier name, the New York College for the Training of Teachers, and in order to show their appreciation of our work, the Department of Superintendence came in 1890 to hold its annual meeting at Number 9, University Place, which was our home. They did this in order that the word might go around the country that the organized superintendents of schools were watching this undertaking, had an interest in it and wished to give it their support.

Moreover, at that time, our best literature of education was in the making. Perhaps the most striking contributions were those contained in the *International Education Series,* edited by Doctor Harris. For news service there was a weekly *Journal of Education* published at Boston and a weekly *School Journal* published at New York. Then there was a racy *School Bulletin* published at Syracuse by C. W. Bardeen, a very delightful man, who wielded a caustic as well as a humorous pen; but we lacked any organ for the expression of our serious educational thought. Therefore, it was that in 1890 I brought into existence the *Educational Review,* which had a life of thirty years. The first issue which appeared in January, 1891, contained articles by President Gilman of Johns Hopkins, by Doctor Harris, by Professor Josiah Royce of Harvard, the great philosopher, by Andrew S. Draper and by Charles De Garmo. That fact of itself established the publication on the high plane which it continued to occupy so long as it existed. It served as the organ for the expression of scholarly opinion by the leading students of education all over the world. It examined and interpreted the best contributions to the literature of education and it occupied a place which, unfortunately, is occupied no longer. The time arrived when the labor of conducting it was too severe because of my University duties. I myself should have let it die, but did not do so out of sheer laziness. If I had stopped it, I should have had to draw about twenty-four hundred checks and return to the subscribers the fractional amounts of their unfulfilled subscriptions. These would have run from 25 cents to $2.75. Rather than sign all these checks, I turned the *Educational Review* over to a publisher and in a short time it died. A fact of which I am very proud is that the publication of its sixty volumes never cost anybody anything. At the time I started the *Educational Review* I sent about a thousand letters to teachers, superintendents, and others interested in education throughout the country, announcing what was to be done and stating that the subscription price would be $3.00 a year. I received 800 subscriptions before the first issue was printed. That $2400 plus the advertising and renewals of subscriptions paid for the *Educational Review* for thirty years, and enabled us to pay for articles and book reviews without costing any one a cent.

Shortly afterward I started the *Great Educators Series,* published by the Scribners, for the purpose of presenting the history of education in biographic form. I invited ten scholars in this country and abroad each to contribute a biographical volume. They did strikingly excellent work, which has not been surpassed since by any one. Indeed, the volume on Loyola in this Series is far and away the best in the English language and the only easily available source of accurate information regarding that great man's educational work and influence. None of the other volumes in that Series have been superseded, and Compayré's *Abelard,* West's *Alcuin,* Monroe's *Comenius,* and Sir Joshua Fitch's interpretation of Thomas and Matthew Arnold and their influence, still stand without any rivals. It is interesting to note that, although the publication of this Series began in 1891, its volumes are still selling in no inconsiderable number after well-nigh half a century.

Three or four years later I began the *Teachers Professional Library,* published by the Macmillans. Professor David Eugene Smith presented in truly classic form the subject of mathematics, as did Professor Henry Johnson that of history. Josiah Royce's *Outlines of Psychology* is still unequalled of its kind. These volumes likewise, first published in 1895, are still being sold in considerable quantity.

Shortly thereafter, the whole situation began to change. The reasons for this change cannot be gone into here, and in any event they would be very difficult to give. The change became plain to every one after 1905. Doubtless, for one reason, it was due to the passing, one after another, of the great commanding personalities of whom I have spoken. Doctor Harris had retired as Commissioner of Education in 1906. Eliot retired from his work at Harvard three years later and no longer participated actively in our educational gatherings. Gilman of Johns Hopkins, who had become President of the Carnegie Institution at Washington, withdrew still earlier. So these great souls of whom I speak with so much affection passed one after another into the other world, and the epoch closed.

Of these great souls Eliot was outstanding and always a dominant force. He is one of the very great Americans who was never understood because, like another of our greatest Americans, Elihu Root, he concealed a heart of fire under an exterior of formal coldness, which led people to think that he did not have any feeling. As a matter of fact, his heart was his dominating characteristic, but he never let people know it. Therefore, that great man was never fully understood or appreciated—either in Cambridge or in Boston or anywhere else; but I have reason to understand him because of the charming and affectionate things which he did for me. My judgment of his importance as representative of intellectual life in the United States is recorded in this extract from a letter which I addressed, under date of December 20, 1898, to Karl J. Trübner, the well-known publisher of Strassburg:

It gives me great pleasure that you have decided to use next year for the frontispiece of *Minerva*, the portrait of an American scholar. I am very much complimented at your asking my judgment in the matter, and shall give you what I believe to be the best advice possible.

Since the death of Whitney of Yale University, the distinguished philologist, we have in this country no *Forscher* who so distinctly outranks all of his fellows as to mark him out for the prominence involved in using his portrait in *Minerva*. For this reason and for other reasons that I will give, I hope that you will decide to use the portrait of Charles W. Eliot, President of Harvard University. There are many reasons for this:

1. Mr. Eliot is the President of our oldest, largest and most influential University. During the thirty years of his presidency he has made a mark not only on the education, but on the culture and ideals, of the American people. Distinguished as an orator, as a man of letters, as an educator and as an administrator, he stands out easily as one of the very few great men that America has thus far contributed to the history of the nineteenth century. In his office and in his person, as well as in his achievements, he is typical of all that is best and highest in American education.

2. The office of President of an American University is *sui generis*. It has no counterpart in Europe. It is a peculiarity of our organization and academic life; it is an office of great power and influence. It seems, therefore, peculiarly fitting that the most distinguished incumbent at the present time of this high office

should be chosen to represent American university life and men in the new volume of *Minerva.*

I am so confident that Mr. Eliot is the proper person to represent us, that I do not even offer any suggestions as to a second or as to a third choice. Should you desire to ask any specific questions concerning him, it will give me great pleasure to answer them in detail.

Mr. Trübner used the photograph of President Eliot in the volume of *Minerva,* No. 9, for the year 1899–1900.

Whatever brought that great epoch into existence I do not know, unless it was the causes which I have suggested. What ended it I do not know, unless it was the passing of the individuals who, as a group, were so remarkable, so influential and in so close touch and communion with one another. It was really a great period, and to have lived in it and through it, to have been at work in education during that time, getting the inspiration of the companionship and counsel and thought of these many-sided men, was an experience which meant everything to me. They all had something to teach; they all had some inspiration to give; they all had some criticism to make, but it was kindly, generous and thoughtful criticism. They were all aflame with zeal for the higher and better things in our educational system. It was a great period; it ought to have a name—but what name? What name, unless it was the period when Harris ruled the educational philosophy of the United States and when Eliot was leading men on to strengthen and elevate the thought of the American people and to build sound and progressive policies not only for the schools but for the country.

X

FOURTEEN REPUBLICAN NATIONAL
CONVENTIONS

THAT happening in our American political life which most clearly and most fully reveals the nation's political habits and the forces which are either permanently or temporarily at work in shaping our public policies is the quadrennial national convention of each of the two great political parties, Democrat and Republican. Many thousand persons have attended at least one such convention. Probably several hundred persons have been members of two such conventions or more. A few score persons have been members of three or four such conventions. My experience is probably unique in that it covers attendance upon fourteen national conventions of the Republican Party, including membership in most of them, as well as upon two conventions of the Democrat Party. When the Fifteenth Republican National Convention met in Chicago on June 18, 1912, on comparing notes it was found that but four of the members of that convention, which was composed of 1078 delegates, had also been members of the Convention of 1888, held in Chicago nearly a quarter-century earlier. These were former Senator Powell Clayton of Arkansas, former Governor Henry C. Warmoth of Louisiana, Henry W. Bishop of Florida and myself.

It is at these gatherings that political enthusiasm as well as political antagonism and political bitterness reach the boiling point. Only a small portion of what really takes place appears in the newspapers or on the printed page of the published official reports of the proceedings of these conventions. The work of the convention is really directed, and the results arrived at are really planned and achieved, by a substantially unbroken series, or several series, of private conferences which go on, now here now there. It is at such times that men whose names are little heard by the public, but who hold important posts in the party organization in various states, come into their own. Time and again such men influence and have influenced the outcome of a convention far more than any holder of high public office. With no inconsiderable public reputation to support them, these high public officers are used as figureheads by the really controlling participants in the drama which is being enacted. The purpose of it all is the nomination for President of the United States of the preferred choice of the ruling group, this to be accomplished if possible without alienating or incurring the resentment of those elements in the party organization that are otherwise minded. To nominate a candidate in a Republican Convention requires only a clear majority of the total membership of the convention, whereas in a Democrat National Convention it is prescribed that a two-thirds vote is needed. It was the application of this rule which prevented the nomination of Champ Clark at Baltimore in 1912 instead of Woodrow Wilson.

1880

By far the most impressive and most exciting convention at which I have been present was the very first in order, that of 1880, which met at Chicago on June 2 and

which, after the most desperate of battles between those
on the one hand who were insistent on the nomination
of General Grant for a third term and those on the other
who were the eager and impassioned supporters of James
G. Blaine, resulted in the nomination of General Garfield. Not only was this convention of outstanding importance from the point of view of our American political
habits and happenings, but its constitution was most exceptional. There sat among its members no fewer than
three men destined to become President of the United
States: James A. Garfield of Ohio, Chester A. Arthur of
New York, and Benjamin Harrison of Indiana. Senator
Logan of Illinois was there, not knowing that he would
be nominated for the Vice-Presidency four years later.
By his side sat Emery A. Storrs, a leader of the Illinois
bar. J. S. Clarkson of Iowa had with him a future Speaker
of the House, David B. Henderson of Dubuque. Senator
Plumb of Kansas was there, as were William O. Bradley
of Kentucky, Senators Eugene Hale and William P. Frye
of Maine, Senator George F. Hoar and George F. Bout-
well of Massachusetts, Senator Omar D. Conger of Mich-
igan, Senator Dwight M. Sabin of Minnesota, Senator
Blanche K. Bruce of Mississippi, Chauncey I. Filley of
St. Louis, Senator William M. Chandler of New Hampshire, Senator William J. Sewell, George A. Halsey and
William Walter Phelps of New Jersey, Senator Roscoe
Conkling, Benjamin F. Tracy, Levi P. Morton, Thomas
C. Platt, Alonzo B. Cornell, and Stewart L. Woodford of
New York, Charles Foster and Benjamin Butterworth of
Ohio, Senator John H. Mitchell of Oregon, Senator Mat-
thew Stanley Quay of Pennsylvania, Governor Billings
of Vermont, and Senator Philetus C. Sawyer and Senator
Isaac Stevenson of Wisconsin, and many more of large
political influence and importance. It may well be doubted

whether so distinguished a company of men had been assembled in the United States at any time since the Constitutional Convention of 1787 met at Philadelphia.

From the instant that the convention was called to order the atmosphere was charged with political electricity. Every one knew that something exciting must soon happen and all were intent not to miss the happening when it came. They did not have long to wait. After Senator Hoar of Massachusetts, distinguished, dignified and impartial, had been unanimously chosen to serve as temporary chairman of the convention, the roll of states and territories was called. By accident the territory of Utah was omitted. It so happened that the National Committee had voted to place upon the roll of the convention two delegates from Utah whose seats were contested by supporters of General Grant. So soon as the omission was noticed, Senator Frye of Maine, whose voice rang throughout the great convention hall like a trumpet and who was at the moment seated upon the platform, jumped to his feet, stated that the territory of Utah had been omitted by accident and asked that it be now called. Senator Hoar repeated to the convention the request of Senator Frye and asked if there was any objection to its being granted. It was pretty generally assumed, both by members of the convention and by the vast audience, that since the facts were undoubtedly correctly stated by Senator Frye, unanimous consent would be given; but from his place on the main aisle of the convention hall there arose slowly and with great dignity and impressiveness the stately form of Senator Roscoe Conkling of New York. All eyes were upon him as he straightened his body to its extreme height, and then in silence lifted his right hand and slowly bringing it down to the level of his eye, pointed it straight at the chair, said: "Mr. Chairman, there *is* objection." This was the signal for the first outburst. The battle had begun and its first gun had been fired. From that instant until the work of the convention was over the nerves of the convention, its members and its audience were never relaxed for an instant.

It has usually been said that General Garfield was nominated primarily as the result of the very eloquent and noble paragraph with which he opened his speech placing the name of John Sherman of Ohio in nomination. When that speech was made the convention had been in storm and tempest throughout four days and nights. Nothing equal to the long-continued cheering, shouting and marching about by the followers of Grant and of Blaine had ever before been seen. It was this fact which gave profound impressiveness to these words with which General Garfield opened his nominating speech:

I have witnessed the extraordinary scenes of this convention with deep solicitude. Nothing touches my heart more quickly than a tribute of honor to a great and noble character; but as I sat in my seat and witnessed this demonstration, this assemblage seemed to me a human ocean in tempest. I have seen the sea lashed into fury and tossed into spray, and its grandeur moves the soul of the dullest man; but I remember that it is not the billows, but the calm level of the sea from which all heights and depths are measured.

When the storm has passed and the hour of calm settles on the ocean, when the sun-light bathes its peaceful surface, then the astronomer and surveyor take the level from which they measure all terrestrial heights and depths.

Gentlemen of the Convention, your present temper may not mark the healthful pulse of our people. When your enthusiasm has passed, when the emotions of this hour have subsided, we shall find below the storm and passion that calm level of public opinion from which the thoughts of a mighty people are to be measured, and by which their final action will be determined.

Not here, in this brilliant circle where 15,000 men and women are gathered, is the destiny of the Republic to be decreed for the next four years. Not here, where I see the enthusiastic faces of 756 delegates, waiting to cast their lots into the urn and determine the choice of the Republic; but by four millions of Republican firesides, where the thoughtful voters, with wives and children about them, with the calm thoughts inspired by love of home and country, with the history of the past, the hopes of the future, and reverence for the great men who have adorned and blessed our nation in days gone by, burning in their hearts—*there* God prepares the verdict which will determine the wisdom of our work tonight. Not in Chicago, in the heat of June, but at the ballot-boxes of the Republic, in the quiet of November, after the silence of deliberate judgment, will this question be settled.

Splendid as these words were and great as was the effect which they had upon the convention, General Garfield had earlier in its proceedings made the impression which finally turned the convention's eyes and thought to him as its candidate.

Without any particular congruity, Senator Conkling arose in his place on Friday morning, June 4, and offered the following very innocent-looking resolution:

Resolved, As the sense of this Convention, that every member of it is bound in honor to support its nominee, whoever that nominee may be; and that no man should hold a seat here who is not ready so to agree.

Delegates wondered what the reason for this was, but thinking it wholly innocent, proceeded to answer to the roll call which was demanded. Wyoming had not then been admitted to the Union, so that West Virginia was the last state to be called. Every state voted unanimously "Aye" until the name of West Virginia was read by the Secretary. Then the high-tempered chairman of the delegation, Archie Campbell, the well-known editor of the *Wheeling Intelligencer,* replied with emphasis, "West Virginia casts seven votes 'Aye' and three votes 'No.' "

At once there was commotion, which was renewed when the Secretary announced the vote on this resolution to be "Ayes" 753, "Noes" 3. Without an instant's delay Senator Conkling was on his feet and offered this resolution:

Resolved, That the delegates who have voted that they will not abide the action of the Convention, do not deserve, and have forfeited, their votes in this Convention.

He met his match in Archie Campbell, who proceeded in most vigorous and emphatic fashion to say that he and two of his associates on the delegation did not approve of the resolution and would not vote for it. He went on to say that they proposed to support the nominee of the convention, but would not fail to register their dissent from Senator Conkling's motion. As Conkling pressed his point, Campbell returned to the attack upon him with great vigor. He recalled that both he and Conkling had been delegates to the Republican National Convention held at Cincinnati in 1876, that neither his candidate nor the candidate of Senator Conkling had been nominated, but that he, Campbell, had gone upon the stump for many weeks urging the election of the candidate chosen by that convention, while Conkling had had important business abroad which prevented his taking part in the campaign. It was then that Garfield intervened. Speaking with the utmost impressiveness and in quiet fashion, he asked Conkling to withdraw his resolution. Garfield went on to say that the three dissenting delegates from West Virginia had not stated that they would not support the candidate of the convention, quite the contrary, but simply that they did not like this resolution. "If, therefore," said Garfield, "these three delegates are to be expelled from the convention, must we not after every roll call pause to expel the minority until finally the convention is reduced to two delegates who must settle matters between themselves by physical force?" The humor and good sense of this appeal and the quiet way in which it was made, profoundly impressed the convention, and from that instant Garfield became one of its heroes. Conkling withdrew his resolution.

Still another incident of 1880 was that attendant upon the speech by Conkling placing General Grant in nomination. The result of the work of the convention up to that time had been a great disappointment to the supporters of General Grant. They had begun to feel that he could not possibly be nominated. It was whispered about the convention and in the hotel corridors that Conkling was planning some coup and would bring about the nomination of a friend and supporter of General Grant in any event. Therefore, when he arose to make his nominating speech, while there was some applause, quiet soon reigned, for the listening thousands were on the *qui vive* to hear just what Conkling would say and whether or not he was to present some other name than that of Grant. Conkling himself then did a very unbecoming and ill-mannered act. Just in front of the platform of the convention, from which every other person who had addressed the delegates had spoken, was a long broad table where the newspaper men were assembled. There were scores of them, each with his writing materials and his records. Instead of going up on the convention platform Conkling climbed up on this press table, which was on a level perhaps two feet lower than the platform itself, and walking over all the papers which the table contained, he pushed everything right and left with one foot to make an open space on which to stand, and then looking defiantly into the faces of the delegates, he relieved them of all further suspense by these famous opening words:

> And when asked what State he hails from,
> Our sole reply shall be,
> He hails from Appomattox,
> And its famous apple tree.

All uncertainty was then removed. General Grant was in nomination and the fight on his behalf was to be carried through to the bitter end, and so it was.

The balloting, which began on the morning of Monday, June 7, continued until after midday on Tuesday, June 8, when General Garfield was nominated on the thirty-sixth ballot. The vote for General Grant, which was 304 on the first ballot, rose to 308 on the tenth, and to its maximum of 313 on the thirty-fifth, but 379 votes were needed to nominate. The stalwart 306 were recorded on the list in favor of General Grant's nomination on the last ballot. The vote for Mr. Blaine, which began at 284, rose to 285 on the thirteenth and fourteenth ballots, fell to 257 on the thirty-fifth ballot, and was but 42 on the final ballot, most of the Blaine votes having been transferred to General Garfield.

This struggle was most extraordinary by reason of its intensity and its bitterness. It left very deep marks on the Republican party organization, but it did not prevent General Garfield's election in November. It finally settled the principle that each congressional district was entitled to its own representation, and that no state-wide convention could deprive it of that privilege.

At this convention my father was a delegate from the old Fifth District of New Jersey, comprising the counties of Bergen, Passaic and Morris. As an undergraduate at Columbia, much below the voting age, and doing work occasionally for the old *New York Tribune* in order to help pay my college expenses, I went with him to the convention and was attached to the *Tribune* staff there.

As I recall, this staff consisted of seven persons and was under the direction of Count Seckendorff, then the very able and accomplished representative of the *Tribune* at Washington. The job assigned me was to watch for personal incidents on the floor of the convention and in the hotel lobby, and to note anything which seemed either dramatic or important. There was plenty to do. In addition to serving the *New York Tribune*, I was also commissioned by Mr. George Wurts, an intimate friend of my father, who was editor of the *Paterson* (N. J.) *Daily Press*, the evening Republican paper in my home town, to send a dispatch each day at noon, giving all details which would be of special interest to the people of New Jersey because of happenings in the delegation from that state. These two assignments kept me relatively busy, but the convention itself had an interest so unbroken and so absorbing that every detail of it has remained carved in memory from that day to this.

1884

Contrasted with the Convention of 1880 or even with that of 1888 which followed it, the gathering which met at Chicago in 1884 was quiet indeed. The nomination of Mr. Blaine was pretty much taken for granted, although the opposition to him was vigorous to the point of extreme bitterness. It is not often that the man chosen by the Republican National Committee to become temporary chairman of a convention is displaced for another, but just this happened in 1884. The well-known Powell Clayton of Arkansas, when nominated by the Republican National Committee, was opposed by Henry Cabot Lodge, George William Curtis and Theodore Roosevelt, who made his first appearance as a delegate to one of these national gatherings. He had just gotten started as a vigorous member of the New York State Assembly. These men proposed the name of John R. Lynch of Mississippi, a colored delegate, and after some display of oratory elected him by a small majority over Clayton. Otherwise, the work of the convention went forward without very much excitement, the Chairman of the Committee on Resolutions being William McKinley of Ohio, this being, likewise, his first appearance as a delegate.

In 1884, as four years earlier, I was once more on the staff of the *New York Tribune* and also sent dispatches relative to the New Jersey delegation and its happenings to the *Paterson* (N. J.) *Daily Press.*

1888

The Convention of 1888 was the only one within my recollection which met in a relatively small hall. It assembled June 19 at Chicago in the Auditorium, then newly completed and adjoining the hotel of the same name. The total number who could be seated in that theatre could hardly have exceeded 4000, so that any such tempestuous demonstrations as had marked the Convention of 1880 and were to mark the Convention of 1912 were quite impossible.

This was the first National Convention of which I was a member. My election was as alternate delegate from the Fifth District of New Jersey, but my principal having been taken ill on the very same day that the convention met, I succeeded to his place and served throughout all the sessions of the convention.

Of all the conventions that I have known, this is the only one which was really deliberative so far as its choice of a nominee for the Presidency was concerned. General Harrison, whom every one greatly respected but few liked, received 85 votes on the first ballot, this number being exceeded by those cast for John Sherman, 229, Chauncey M. Depew, 99. General Russell A. Alger received 84, Senator Allison of Iowa 72, while 35 were still stubbornly cast for Mr. Blaine, despite his frequently repeated statement that he did not wish to be voted for. To nominate 417 votes were needed. The more the leaders of the convention considered the situation which confronted them, the more strongly were they led to the conclusion that of all the candidates before them Benjamin Harrison would make the most competent and the ablest President of the United States.

The so-called Granger States, led by Iowa, were in violent opposition to Chauncey Depew, because he was president of a railroad. After he had withdrawn his name, he visited the headquarters of the Iowa delegation and aroused their unbounded enthusiasm by a speech which he addressed to them as his "Fellow Grangers," and in which he gave them information in detail and very specifically as to what the Chicago and Northwestern Railway and its operation meant to the people and the farmers of the State of Iowa. It was an amusing incident and one which illustrates admirably the contradictions and superficialities of so-called practical politics.

When Saturday came, the convention decided to adjourn over Sunday in order that serious and intimate consideration might be given to the selection of a candidate. A Committee of Five went over to Indianapolis by night train, met General Harrison on Sunday afternoon, discussed the whole situation with him, returned to Chicago and as a result he was nominated on the third ballot Monday morning. General Harrison's defects as a politician were so obvious and his manner was frequently so ungracious, that his outstanding intellectual ability was often overlooked. Surely there had been no occupant of the

White House since John Quincy Adams who was superior to Benjamin Harrison in sheer intellectual power.

This convention was marked by great bitterness aroused over the struggle between the two factions in Virginia, the one led by General William Mahone and the other by John S. Wise. Their abuse of each other was unbounded and their fiery eloquence both interested the convention and called out demonstrations of great enthusiasm. It was here that we first heard the story of General Mahone, which was told many times afterward on the stump in the State of Virginia, particularly, I believe, by Senator Daniels. General Mahone, so the story goes, having passed from earth, presented himself at the gates of the Heavenly City and knocked for admittance. The Apostle Peter, who was in charge, opened the door on a crack and asked the General what might be his name. "General William Mahone," was the answer, "from Virginia." "General Mahone, are you on foot or mounted?" "On foot," replied the General. "You cannot enter," was the answer of Peter. General Mahone turned away and shortly espied in the distance a colored man also making for the gates of the Heavenly City. The General explained to the colored man that there would be no hope of his entering unless he were mounted, but that if he would get down on his hands and knees and let the General sit astride of him, when they reached the heavenly gates, the General being mounted would be allowed to enter and the colored man being his horse, so to speak, would enter with him and all would be well. But, the story continued, when General Mahone, thus mounted, presented himself at the gates of the Heavenly City for a second time, he was asked his name and whether he was on foot or mounted. When he confidently replied, "Mounted," the answer came, "Tie your horse outside, General Mahone, and come in."

This, it was pointed out, was characteristic of General Mahone's attitude toward the colored man. He would use him for his personal purposes, but beyond that nothing would happen. The story, well told, created great hilarity among the delegates.

There is one intensely interesting incident of this convention which has no place in the printed record of its proceedings. It has to do with Colonel Robert G. Ingersoll, then at the very apex of his fame and influence as an orator. Although not a delegate to the convention, Colonel Ingersoll was seated on the platform and several times when there was a lull in the proceedings there were loud calls for him to speak. On one occasion he did so. This was on the afternoon of Friday, June 22, when the convention adjourned until evening after a very brief session, leaving the delegates disappointed and unhappy because there was nothing to keep them interested or entertained. So just as soon as the motion for a recess had been carried, there were loud shouts for Ingersoll, who then arose to address the assembled multitude, both delegates and audience remaining in their seats to hear him. To the great surprise of every one, instead of speaking in general terms on some political topic, he plunged into an enthusiastic eulogy of Judge Walter Q. Gresham of Indiana, who was one of the candidates before the convention. This was so unfair and in so indescribably bad taste, Colonel Ingersoll not himself being a member of the convention, that immediately there was an outburst of objections and interruptions. This demonstration was so substantially unanimous that after speaking two or three minutes, Colonel Ingersoll was driven from the platform and the crowd dispersed. It was quite certain that never before in his life had he had such an experience, but he deserved it.

1892

In 1892 the convention met at Minneapolis under conditions which may properly be described as rather nervous. There seemed to be no escape from the nomination of General Harrison for a second term, and yet it was felt that his re-election was, to say the least, doubtful in high degree. The strong Blaine sentiment still remained in the party organization and nothing that Blaine himself could say, do or write would prevent the continual mention of his name and the urging of him as a candidate for the Presidency.

William McKinley, who had appeared at two previous conventions and had each time served as chairman of the Committee on Resolutions, had a very strong hold on the Republican Party of that day, and when introduced to the convention as its permanent chairman he was received with almost boundless enthusiasm. Indeed, as many as 182 delegates, chiefly from Kansas, Massachusetts, Michigan, New York, Ohio and Pennsylvania, insisted on voting for him on the one ballot which was required to renominate General Harrison. After the convention had adjourned, a group of some ten or a dozen of us assembled in Major McKinley's rooms at the Hotel West where he was lying on the bed, fanning himself vigorously and resting after his labors as chairman of the convention. While we were talking matters over, the door opened and in came Mark Hanna, dripping with perspiration and looking very much fatigued. He walked up to the bed on which McKinley was lying and said, "Well, William, that is what I call a damn tight squeak!" He had been greatly alarmed lest McKinley should be the nominee of the convention, since he foresaw defeat in November and had made plans to nominate McKinley later on when the outlook would be more favorable.

1896

That time came at St. Louis four years later, where the crucial contest was not so much over the presidential nomination as over the so-called gold plank in the platform. The pressure upon Hanna from either side of those who carried on this bitter controversy was as strong as can well be imagined. The advocates of bimetallism and of free coinage of silver were numerous and influential. Their opponents were still more numerous and still more influential, and the fight waxed hot as the time for the delegates to assemble approached.

Probably two dozen persons have told the world that they, individually, were responsible for the gold plank in the platform of 1896. The exact facts may now be told with propriety. The convention was to meet on Tuesday, June 16, and Charles W. Fairbanks of Indiana, soon to be Senator, had been agreed upon as the temporary chairman. On the Saturday preceding there were present in Mark Hanna's rooms, when he finally agreed to accept the gold plank, just five persons and no more. These were Mr. Hanna himself, former Governor W. R. Merriam of Minnesota, Henry C. Payne of Wisconsin, H. H. Kohlsaat of Chicago, and myself. If any one man deserves credit for the gold plank in the platform of 1896 it is Payne of Wisconsin, whose way of stating the question at issue and whose insistence upon its political importance were very convincing. Governor Merriam and Mr. Kohlsaat were equally emphatic, and finally, after Mark Hanna had had his famous long-distance talk with McKinley at Canton—which is often said to have been the first long-distance telephone call of the kind—and McKinley had agreed to accept whatever plank Hanna thought best, he announced at the end of three or four hours of discussion that he would accept a gold plank. He added that not a word must be said about it until the following Tuesday, since he was afraid of the effect of his decision on the support of McKinley from the states west of the Missouri River. He added that only one delegate from that section, and he a German from Nebraska, was in favor of a gold plank and that great care must be taken lest the McKinley forces be disrupted. Whatever may have been the personal views of Henry Cabot Lodge, of Thomas C. Platt or a score of others, no one of them had anything whatever to do with the plank itself, as it was presented to Hanna and accepted by him before any of these gentlemen had reached St. Louis.

The nominee of this convention for the Vice-Presidency was my father's friend and mine, Garret A. Hobart of Paterson, N. J., then the very effective head of the Republican party organization in that state. During the short time that he served as Vice-President he proved to be the best presiding officer that the United States Senate has ever had in my lifetime and probably the best in the whole history of that highly self-conscious body.

Senator Henry M. Teller of Colorado, who marched out of this convention at the head of his supporting group, was a very pathetic spectacle and aroused the deepest sympathy among the delegates. He had been a lifelong and devoted member of the Republican Party and it cut him to the quick to find that an issue of principle had arisen on which he felt so strongly that he must withdraw from the convention. He carried with him the sympathy and in large part the affection of most of the delegates, who profoundly regretted that any question of principle or policy could cut so deep into the party organization.

Such was the case, however, and had not Hanna conducted the campaign in the way in which he did, particularly in the states of Ohio, Michigan, Indiana, Illinois and
Iowa, Bryan would have been elected in the following
November on his free-silver platform. Had the vote been
taken early in September, Bryan would almost certainly
have been elected.

1900

The Convention of 1900 was one of the few which
met elsewhere than at Chicago. It was called to meet in
Philadelphia, and on the surface there appeared to be no
reason why it should not be a very humdrum affair.
President McKinley was at the height of his popularity,
and his renomination, to be followed by his re-election,
was looked upon as quite certain. The one matter awaiting
settlement was the nominee for Vice-President, since Mr.
Hobart of New Jersey had died in the middle of his term.
Political conditions in the State of New York were such
that the reigning magnates of the Republican party organization there were exceedingly anxious to dispense
with the further services of Theodore Roosevelt as Governor. They had placed him in nomination in 1898 only
because they feared that, unless they did so, both the
governorship and control of the Legislature would pass
to the Democrats, which would be quite too awful to be
calmly contemplated. As a matter of fact they won in
1898 in New York by the narrowest of margins, for
Colonel Roosevelt's plurality over his Democrat opponent
was only about 18,000. His independent conduct in executive office and his willingness to be perfectly agreeable,
combined with his unwillingness to be controlled, had
made these party leaders sad indeed, and they had made
up their minds to get rid of him. It would not do to fail

to renominate him for governor, but the fortunate fact that a new candidate for Vice-President must be found to run with McKinley seemed to them to open the door of opportunity. They proceeded to act accordingly, although very quietly, and secured allies in the party organization of several other states. Roosevelt was quickly aware of this and immediately started a counter movement to prevent his own nomination for the Vice-Presidency. He issued public statements to say that he declined to be a candidate, and he wrote letters to friends in all parts of the country on some phase or aspect of this matter.

As a result, one of the liveliest and most interesting incidents in connection with the political career of Theodore Roosevelt or which has ever taken place in any national party convention followed.

The fact is that T. R. had set his heart on being renominated for governor of New York, and did not hesitate to say so, both to his political friends and to his political enemies. President McKinley was exceedingly popular and apparently in the best of health. He had the united support of his party for renomination in 1900 and while T. R. was well enough liked by the President and those who surrounded him, he was not of their intimate circle and they did not have confidence in his judgment or wisdom. As governor, T. R. had done one or two excellent things and in doing them had run counter to the wishes and personal commitments of Senator Thomas C. Platt, then leader of the Republican party organization in the State of New York. Senator Platt, in consultation with Senator Quay of Pennsylvania, had made up his mind as early as January, 1900, to secure the nomination of T. R. for the Vice-Presidency if possible, not because he loved T. R., but because he wished to get him out of the way by putting him in an innocuous office, and particu-

larly because he wished to get him out of the governorship
at all costs. Naturally news of this drifted to T. R. and he
resented being thus cavalierly disposed of against his will.
Early in March, 1900, he discussed the whole situation
with me and asked me to go to Washington and find out
what was up as to the Vice-Presidency. He especially
charged me to tell President McKinley and Senator
Hanna that he was not a candidate for the Vice-Presidency, did not wish to be nominated and would not accept
if nominated. Despite his later denials of this statement,
this is precisely what he instructed me to say and it is
precisely what I said. President McKinley took the matter
in good part and, after laughing with me a little about
some of T. R.'s characteristics, told me to talk the matter
over with Senator Hanna. The Senator was explosive
and abundant in expletives. He banged on the table and
said that he proposed to control the Philadelphia convention absolutely and that under no circumstances would
or could T. R. be nominated for the Vice-Presidency. He,
Senator Hanna, would not have it. I reminded Senator
Hanna of this conversation a few weeks later at Philadelphia.

When I took this news back to Albany, T. R. was in
part pleased and in part chagrined. He was pleased to
think that Platt and Quay would not be able to dispose
of him politically and he was chagrined to find in how
little political esteem he was held by the President and
Senator Hanna.

As time went on and the date of the convention approached, the newspapers in various parts of the country
and many party leaders urged the nomination of T. R.
for the Vice-Presidency in order to represent the younger
element in the party. Vice-President Hobart having died
in office, there was no complication on his account and

there were no very conspicuous candidates brought forward. There was some talk of John D. Long of Massachusetts and of two or three others, but it was not very
serious since none of them had any considerable measure
of public support. Before the convention met, Roosevelt
asked me, together with Frederick W. Holls and Albert
Shaw, to represent his interests at Philadelphia, to be
always at his personal headquarters and to resist every
effort to nominate him for the Vice-Presidency. Holls and
I went to Philadelphia several days before the date fixed
for the convention and took a quiet apartment on Walnut
Street where we could sleep in peace and away from the
turmoil and uproar of the Hotel Walton. Until Saturday
afternoon, June 15, there was absolutely no interest in the
work of the convention. McKinley was to be renominated
by acclamation. There was no controversy over anything
and all was as dull as dull could be. During the afternoon
of that day, the New York delegation arrived, T. R. being
with them. He walked into the main corridor of the Hotel
Walton with his quick nervous stride and his invariable
soft black felt hat, and at once the crowd waked up.
T. R.'s name was on every lip and the question as to
whether or not he should be forced to take the Vice-Presidency pushed every other question into the background.
Holls, Shaw and myself took charge of his personal headquarters, met the delegations which visited him and explained to them T. R.'s position and the ground for his
unwillingness to surrender the governorship in order to
take the Vice-Presidency. All Saturday evening the delegations kept coming and it was perfectly evident to me
on Sunday morning that only the most drastic steps would
prevent T. R.'s nomination. Two incidents occurred which
confirmed me in this belief.

Among these groups was the Kansas delegation, headed

by J. R. Burton, who afterward went to the United States Senate for a term and then to the penitentiary for a like period. He and his fellow-delegates had in their button-holes huge artificial sunflowers, and when the lapel of the coat was turned over there was this legend on the back in large letters:

I'M FROM KANSAS!
NOW, DAMN YOU, LAUGH!

Burton announced that the Kansas delegation did not care what Colonel Roosevelt's desires or preferences might be. They proposed to support his nomination for the Vice-Presidency and to do everything in their power to bring it about. Burton went on with undisguised impudence to say that he cared nothing about Colonel Roosevelt personally, but that with Roosevelt's name on the ticket he, Burton, would be sure of election to the Senate from Kansas.

On the following morning a still more significant incident occurred. A committee of the Pennsylvania delegation called to say that the entire body of delegates from Pennsylvania intended to vote for Roosevelt's nomination. Their spokesman was that very shrewd and experienced politician, Congressman Bingham of Philadelphia, and nothing that he said could be taken lightly.

Following this interview and one or two other similar happenings, Holls and I went down to Senator Hanna's room for a further talk with him. We told him of our experiences at the Roosevelt headquarters, and strongly expressed the opinion that "You cannot beat somebody with nobody," and that the only way to keep Roosevelt from being nominated was to produce a candidate for the Vice-Presidency whose personality and fitness were of so compelling a character that the convention would rally quickly to his support. Hanna greeted these statements with another outburst of profanity, and again affirmed with all vehemence that Roosevelt would not be nominated because he, Hanna, would not permit it. In response to our continued urging he finally stated that he proposed to have the convention nominate John D. Long of Massachusetts for Vice-President. Our reply was that while we had the greatest respect for Governor Long, there was no possible chance of inducing the convention to prefer him to Roosevelt. Hanna brusquely informed us that we did not know what we were talking about, and we withdrew.

During the afternoon and evening of Sunday matters got steadily worse hour by hour, and when Monday morning came we were quite unable to see how Roosevelt's nomination could be prevented by anybody, no matter how politically powerful he might think himself.

The end was reached on Monday. Colonel Roosevelt, General Francis V. Greene of New York—who was not without hopes that the vice-presidential lightning would strike him—and I went together for luncheon with Mrs. Roosevelt to the house of a friend near by with whom Mrs. Roosevelt was stopping. Senator Lodge was there also, wearing a huge blue silk badge on which appeared in bold gilt letters: "FOR VICE PRESIDENT, JOHN D. LONG."

George H. Lyman, then Collector of the Port of Boston, was also present. During luncheon I pressed T. R. for a definite refusal to accept the nomination and was joined by General Greene and George Lyman. Lodge said little or nothing, for as a matter of fact he was really red hot to have T. R. nominated although wearing a Long badge conspicuously on his coat. Mrs. Roosevelt agreed with us entirely. Immediately after luncheon had been served,

Lodge left us, saying with brusque cynicism, "I must go back and be loyal to Long." We then had a heart-to-heart talk with Roosevelt over the situation which had developed, and told him flatly that unless he was prepared, then and there, to write a statement which might be given to the press at four o'clock, when the newspaper men were coming to his headquarters, making it perfectly definite and final that he would not accept the nomination if tendered, he was certain to be nominated on Thursday. He walked up and down for some little time, muttering and protesting, and then said with much impatience: "What is it you want me to say? I am willing to say it." Thereupon I sat down at the writing-table in the room and wrote a brief statement to the effect that, while he was most grateful for the friendly support which had been offered him from all parts of the country, yet he felt that his duty at the moment was to the State of New York; that he was not a candidate for the vice-presidential nomination and that he could not accept even if nominated. I handed this to Mrs. Roosevelt who approved it, and then said to T. R.: "If you will sign that paper and give it out this afternoon, you will not be nominated." T. R. screwed up his face as he had a way of doing when in perplexity, and said he was in favor of that statement but thought he could improve its phrasing. So he sat down at the desk and wrote a statement of his own. Having finished, he handed it to us and said: "There, that is what you want." I read it carefully and then, after reading it a second time, said: "Theodore, if that is all you will say, you will certainly be nominated. You have taken out of the statement all of the finality and definiteness that was in mine." We had a vigorous debate over this point for perhaps half an hour, but T. R. refused to budge from his position. I then began to suspect for the first time that he was really willing to be nominated in order to score upon his opponents in the State of New York.

On going back to the hotel, we found that the newspaper men were already assembling and by four o'clock the Roosevelt headquarters were packed full to overflowing with them. Indeed, so numerous were they that some of us were compelled to stand upon the bed while Roosevelt slowly read the statement. At the foot of the bed were Senator Platt's son, Frank H. Platt, and his henchman, Lemuel Ely Quigg, both of whom had their eyes fixed upon Roosevelt with closest attention. When they heard the words of the statement, their faces were wreathed in smiles and they darted for the door to report to Senator Platt that all was well and that he had won his fight. And so he had.

Beyond the incidents concerned with Roosevelt's nomination, this convention went its way in orderly and unexciting fashion. The only important happening was the very eloquent speech of Senator E. O. Wolcott of Colorado as temporary chairman.

1904

The Convention of 1904 was peace and quiet itself. Its outstanding event was the brilliant and eloquent speech of Elihu Root as temporary chairman of the convention. This truly admirable and most persuasive argument was felt to be so important and so convincing that it was the document most used by the National Committee in carrying on the campaign which followed. Of course, there was no opposition whatever to the nomination of Theodore Roosevelt and nothing arose to disturb the harmony and good order of the convention save the usual quarrels over contested seats, which represented personal and factional struggles and differences in various states and districts

This is the original draft, in Mr. Roosevelt's own writing, of his statement as to the vice-presidency, read by him to the newspaper reporters in Room 524, Hotel Walton, Philadelphia, at 4 p.m. on Monday, June 18, 1900.

It was written by him at the house of Mrs. Brack, 1417 Spruce St, & the only persons to whom it was read before it was made public were Mrs. Roosevelt, Francis V. Greene, George K. Lyman of Boston, Mass, & N. M. B.

Nicholas Murray Butler

In the view of the revival
of the talk of myself as
a Vice Presidential candidate,
I have this to say. It is
~~can not~~ impossible too deeply to express
how touched I am by
~~my~~ ~~appreciation~~ of the
attitude of those delegates,
~~especially from the ~~,
who have ~~asked~~ wished me to take
the ~~this~~ nomination; the ~~I can not~~
~~say how~~ deeply ~~I am touched~~
~~by their of attitude toward~~
~~me.~~ Moreover, it is not necessary to
~~I need not~~ say
how thoroughly I understand the
high honor and dignity of
the office ~~of which they~~ desire
~~to make me a candidate~~; an
office so high and so honorable

that it is well worthy the ambition
of any man in the United
States. But while I appreciate
all this to the full, I nevertheless
remain feel most deeply that
the field of my best usefulness to
the public and to the party
is in New York State; and
that, if in its wisdom the party
should see fit to renominate
me for Governor, I can in that
position help the National
ticket as in no other way.

I very earnestly hope and
ask that every friend of
mine in the convention
will respect my wish
and my judgement in
this matter.

Theodore Roosevelt

Philadelphia, June 18th 1900

throughout the country. The most interesting and probably the most important of these contests was over the four delegates at large from Wisconsin, where those headed by Governor LaFollette were unseated and their places given to those headed by Senator Spooner.

After Speaker Cannon had been chosen permanent chairman and had delivered a characteristic speech, Senator Lodge presented a report of the Committee on Resolutions which was pretty long and pretty boastful. The speech by Governor Black of New York placing Theodore Roosevelt in nomination was one of the very best of its kind, and was received with unbounded enthusiasm. The seconding speeches by Senator Beveridge of Indiana and George A. Knight of California were of the same general character and the cheers were loud and prolonged.

After the roll-call had proceeded so far as the State of New Jersey, Governor Franklin Murphy of that state rose and asked that the further calling of the roll be dispensed with and that Theodore Roosevelt be chosen by acclamation. This proposal was greeted with loud cries of "No! No!" so the roll-call went on to its end and recorded 994 votes, all of them for the nomination of Theodore Roosevelt. It did not take long to choose Senator Fairbanks of Indiana as candidate for Vice-President, and the work of this harmonious body was over.

It was during the sessions of this convention that my friend and fellow-delegate, William N. Cohen, afterwards Justice of the Supreme Court of the State of New York, told me of the confidential conferences of the leaders of the party organization in New York at which it was decided that I was to be the party nominee for governor when the State Convention met in September. It shortly developed that what Governor Odell, William Barnes of Albany, Francis Hendricks of Onondaga, George W. Aldridge of Monroe, J. Sloat Fassett of Chemung, Speaker Nixon of Chautauqua, Louis F. Payn of Columbia, Elon R. Brown of Jefferson, William L. Ward of Westchester —all of whom were delegates to this convention—and the others of their group had in mind was that if I were elected governor—a fact which they took for granted— and if all went well, I was to be renominated and re-elected to that office in 1906 and then brought forward in 1908 by the party organization, with the full support of President Theodore Roosevelt—who, it soon appeared, was a party to the scheme—as candidate for the presidential nomination. This amazing plan, conceived in the most friendly and indeed flattering spirit, would mean, if I assented to it, the complete abandonment of my self-chosen and clearly conceived life work upon which my mind and heart were set. It took three months of time and an exhibition of persistent stubbornness, which some thought was ingratitude and others evidence of a lack of common sense, to prevent this plan from being under-taken. What was said, written and done to bring that plan to an end occupied all the weeks from June until September; but that is a story by itself and has no proper place here.[1]

The way in which I came to attend the Democrat National Convention of 1904 held at St. Louis is rather interesting. I went there at the personal request of President Roosevelt, who suffered from the same complex in 1904 that took possession of President Lincoln in 1864. Just as Lincoln felt that he was certain to be defeated by McClellan, so forty years later did Roosevelt think that he would fail of re-election. He was most anxious that I should attend the Democrat Convention, observe what was said and done and report to him in detail as soon as

[1]See Chapter XII, On Keeping out of Public Office.

practicable. All these things I did. I heard the temporary chairman, Senator John Sharp Williams of Mississippi, make a stupendously long speech—it covers thirty-five printed pages of the official report—which while amusing in parts distinctly fatigued the assembled delegates. Champ Clark of Missouri, who followed him as permament chairman, made a good speech, but it also was far too long.

The work of the convention centered about the declaration as to silver, since the conventions of 1896 and 1900 and the results of the elections which followed were uppermost in the minds of all the delegates. What the Committee on Resolutions really did was to sidestep the issue, and by a vote of 35 to 15 to exclude from the platform the so-called gold plank, which had been offered by the sound-money element of the party.

The story of the nomination of Parker and his famous dispatch declining the nomination unless it was understood that he was to support the gold standard, and the subsequent happenings, are all on record and are perfectly familiar.

What is not widely known is the brilliant and impressive opening of the speech made by William Jennings Bryan, just as dawn was breaking on Friday, July 8, when he rose to second the nomination of Senator Cockrell of Missouri. The convention had been in session for many hours and was very tired. The heat was intense and the early dawn was fighting with the electric lights, giving a weird effect to the convention hall. Bryan himself was white, his face was drawn and he was visibly greatly fatigued. After saying that he had had no sleep for two nights and that his voice was almost gone, he spoke these impressive words to a most attentive audience of many thousands:

"Eight years ago a Democratic National Convention placed in my hands the standard of the party and commissioned me as its candidate. Four years later that commission was renewed. I come tonight to this Democratic National Convention to return the commission. You may dispute whether I have fought a good fight, you may dispute whether I have finished my course, but you cannot deny that I have kept the faith."

In an instant the whole vast audience was on its feet, deeply moved by this very sincere and pathetic appeal to their feelings. It was some time before the crowd could settle down to listen to Bryan's speech, for he had exhibited oratorical power of a very high and impressive type.

1908

In 1908 the convention was distinctly dull. This was largely because despite murmurs and mutterings and despite the prediction often confidentially made that the nomination of Theodore Roosevelt for a third term would be insisted upon, it was pretty clear that Secretary Taft would be the nominee. The oratory at this convention was less interesting than usual and its proceedings were marked by a certain dullness which was novel to me. Senator Lodge of Massachusetts was made permanent chairman and on the first ballot, 980 votes being cast, Taft received 702, including at least one from every state except Indiana, which cast its 30 votes solidly for Senator Fairbanks. Three votes from Pennsylvania were cast for Roosevelt, while 65 of the 78 New York votes were cast for Governor Hughes. A small number of votes were cast for Speaker Cannon, for Senator Fairbanks, and for Senator Joseph B. Foraker of Ohio. In order to keep peace in the political family and at the urgent request of Speaker Cannon, Congressman James S. Sherman of New York was nominated for Vice-President and the work of the campaign began.

1912

The happenings of 1912 were remindful of those of 1880, for once again bitterness and passion amounting to fury were in evidence on every side. The schism in the Republican party organization which had been growing more or less rapidly for some years and which was made evident by the result of the Congressional elections in 1910, came to its climax when the National Convention met at Chicago. So evenly did the two factions appear to be balanced, that it was not unlikely that the control of the convention would be found to depend upon the temporary roll as made up by the National Committee, after hearing the numerous contests which were presented to them for action. The committee had been in session for several days and had decided most of the contests in favor of the Taft delegates and against the Roosevelt delegates. No sooner had the Acting Chairman of the Republican National Committee called the convention to order, than Governor Herbert S. Hadley of Missouri, who was to be the floor leader of the Roosevelt forces, rose and demanded information as to whether a temporary roll of the delegates had been prepared and was in the hands of the Secretary. Before an answer could be given, James E. Watson of Indiana, who was to be the floor leader of the Taft forces, made the point of order that this question was out of order until after the convention itself had been properly organized. Despite this objection, Governor Hadley promptly moved that the list of delegates prepared by the National Committee, known as the temporary roll, be amended by striking out the names of certain delegates which he handed to the Chair and by substituting certain other delegates therefor. Watson renewed his point of order, that this motion was out of order until the convention had been organized. After some discussion of the point of order the Chairman upheld it and when Governor Hadley appealed from the decision of the Chair and Watson moved to lay the appeal on the table, both motions were declared to be out of order for the reason that the only business before the convention was that which the Chairman of the National Committee would submit, at the direction of that committee: the name of a delegate for temporary chairman. The Chairman thereupon submitted the name of Elihu Root, a delegate from the State of New York. Wisconsin dissented and nominated Governor McGovern of that state. A long and angry debate followed and it was some hours before the roll was called. The result of the ballot was Root, 558; McGovern, 501; with some 20 delegates returned as voting for other candidates. Of the New York votes all were cast for Root except three from Brooklyn, three from Manhattan, three from Westchester, two from Monroe, and two from other upstate counties. As Mr. Root took the Chair, the accomplished, cultivated and polite William Flinn of Pennsylvania yelled at the top of his lungs: "Receiver of stolen goods!" and Richard R. Quay of Pennsylvania added: "You are a protector of stolen goods!" Root's speech was, of course, on the highest possible plane and was admirably received despite the factional bitterness manifest in the convention. Governor Hadley immediately resumed the fight to unseat seventy-four delegates from various states, whose names he insisted had been improperly put upon the list.

There were some amusing incidents despite all the tragic performances of this convention. Senator Boies Penrose of Pennsylvania, who had been defeated as a candidate for delegate-at-large by the Roosevelt forces, was seated on the platform in a comfortable chair fanning himself and looking down at the disturbance going forward on the floor of the convention. At one time when this was at its height and some of the delegates from Pennsylvania were behaving like madmen, dancing and shouting and screaming at the top of their lungs, I asked Senator Penrose how in the name of common sense men of that sort got themselves elected as delegates to a Republican National Convention, for I had never seen anything of the kind outside of a street riot. Penrose, fanning himself placidly, remarked with his inimitable twang: "Oh, those are the corks, bottles and banana peels washed up by the Roosevelt tide!" To any one who had ever seen a ferry-slip on the Hudson River at high tide with a west wind blowing, this was a perfect description. At one time during the uproar there was a delegate from Pennsylvania who made himself particularly obnoxious by the noise he was making. Root, having been brought to the very edge of the limits of patience, came forward to the edge of the platform and holding his gavel by its head and pointing the handle at the noise-making delegate, could be heard above the uproar saying: "If the delegate from Pennsylvania who is so disturbing this convention does not take his seat, the Chair will order the Sergeant-at-Arms to eject him from the hall." This very definite threat produced for a few moments a measure of silence and the characteristic voice of Senator Penrose could be heard saying: "Hear how rough he talks to the Mayor of McKeesport!"

Hours were spent in the prolonged and really tempestuous discussion of the roll of the convention, since it had become clear that if the roll remained as made up by the National Committee, after its hearing of the various contests, there would be a majority of the delegates against the nomination of Theodore Roosevelt and in favor of the

renomination of President Taft. Once these questions were
settled, the work of the convention proceeded rapidly to
its end, a number of the Roosevelt delegates withdraw-
ing from further participation in its work. After President
Taft's name had been presented in an impressive speech
by Warren Harding of Ohio and seconded in an unim-
pressive speech by John Wanamaker of Pennsylvania, the
voting proceeded and on the first ballot Taft was nominated, receiving 561 votes. For Theodore Roosevelt 107
votes were cast, for Governor LaFollette of Wisconsin 41,
for Senator Cummins of Iowa 17, and 349 were recorded
as present and not voting. After the Chairman had announced the renomination of President Taft and while the
cheering was still going on, Senator Reed Smoot of Utah,
whose delegation had seats in the hall somewhat farther
back than those assigned to the delegates from the State
of New York, came down the aisle and said to me with
a smile: "Well, she's did! What next?" The "what next"
was the result in the following November, and the complete disruption of the old Republican Party, which disruption has continued in fact, although not in form, from
that day to this.

So complete was the Republican defeat in 1912 that we
all kept pretty quiet for some time thereafter. My own
first political speech after the defeat was made at a dinner
given by the Middlesex Club of Boston, Mass., in celebration of Grant's birthday on April 27, 1913, former
Governor John D. Long presiding. On the journey by
train from New York to Boston, I found that my neighbor
in the parlor car was former Governor Hadley, who had
been the floor leader of the Roosevelt forces at the convention. It turned out that we were both going to speak
at the same dinner in Boston, and that we had been invited because we represented the two wings, or elements,
into which the year 1912 had broken the Republican

Party. During the course of the journey I said to the Governor: "It is all past now, but I should be very much interested to know how you arrived at the decision to make contests of 74 seats at the convention last June? Why 74 instead of 174 or 274?" Governor Hadley smiled and said: "I will tell you. After the National Committee had heard the various contests and reached their conclusions, Borah, Frank Kellogg and I decided that in twenty-four cases we had been literally defrauded of our representation. We recognized that we had a very strong case in respect to other contests, but that there were debatable questions, every one of which, however, had been decided against us. There remained twenty-four contests in which we felt that we had been outraged and that injustice had plainly been done. So we three went to Colonel Roosevelt and told him this fact. We said we were going to contest these twenty-four seats on the floor of the convention. On hearing this statement, Colonel Roosevelt cried with great vehemence: 'Twenty-four seats! Twenty-four! What is the use of contesting twenty-four? You must contest seventy-four if you expect to get anywhere.' So we raised the number to seventy-four."

This was Hadley's own statement to me. It entirely confirmed what Senator Murray Crane had previously told me, namely, that all doubtful cases had been decided in favor of the Taft contestants, but that there were a few cases in which much was to be said for the other side.

This was the first convention of which Lafayette B. Gleason of New York was secretary, he having become chief assistant secretary in 1908. At every convention since 1912 Mr. Gleason has held the secretaryship, discharging its duties admirably and to the satisfaction of all elements in the party organization.

It amused me not a little that after the Convention of

1912, I was generally referred to as a reactionary. From my earliest participation in politics as an undergraduate I had been looked upon as a rather disturbing progressive, being usually in revolt against the party organization, particularly the Platt organization in New York. That I was a close and intimate friend and political adviser of Theodore Roosevelt is evidenced by the fact that in my copy of the volume entitled *Public Papers of Theodore Roosevelt, Governor, 1899,*[1] there appears in Roosevelt's handwriting this inscription:

To

Nicholas Murray Butler, who has walked these papers in advance on the installment plan, and has helped prepare not a few of them,

from

Theodore Roosevelt

June 10th, 1900

[1]Albany, N. Y.: Brandow Printing Company, 1899.

In 1912, for reasons that I deemed good and sufficient, and without in any way lessening my regard for Theodore Roosevelt, I preferred to follow Taft in the fracas of that year. Although my principles and policies had not changed in the least, I found myself thereby transferred by the newspapers from progressive to reactionary. This, no doubt, was in large part due to the fact that with a view to defining the attitude of the New York delegation I wrote the following resolution which that delegation adopted on June 15, 1912:

The Delegates from the State of New York, in conformance with the expressed wish of the Republican State Convention of Rochester, wish to impress upon their fellow delegates the supreme importance of the issue of principle that now confronts the party.

That issue we believe to be whether or not the Republican Party shall enter upon a campaign pledged to reform abuses, to remove evils, and to effect needed reforms, without at the same time destroying the essentials of a stable and permanent popular government, namely:

1. Government by the people through representative institutions.
2. The Constitutional guarantee of the civil liberty of the individual.
3. The integrity and independence of the Courts of justice, as the sole protection of the weak against the strong.

This issue of principle we believe to be paramount. We ask the support of our fellow delegates in contending for the preservation of these essentials of our American form of government.

1916

The Convention of 1916 was of exceptional importance and was planned for long in advance. The leaders of the party, and indeed the great mass of the enrolled voters, had one dominating idea, which was that Theodore Roosevelt, who had left the party in 1912 and who had attacked it most viciously and caused its defeat, should not be nominated in 1916.

During the autumn of 1915 many conferences were held in New York and elsewhere for the purpose of ascertaining the general trend of party opinion and of party preference. Previous to this time Theodore E. Burton of Ohio, Senator Albert B. Cummins of Iowa and Senator John W. Weeks of Massachusetts had more or less formally announced their candidacy. Indiana was understood to be getting ready to name Mr. Fairbanks and Illinois held a similar attitude towards Senator Sherman. While these gentlemen might, and did, differ in competence and in availability, the political distinctions between them were not sufficient to give to any one of them a commanding lead over his fellows. Burton prosecuted the most active personal canvass, although Senator Weeks did nearly as well and in addition had better organization and more support, financial and otherwise, than did Mr. Burton. Representatives of Senator Weeks were active in the border states and in the South, particularly in Maryland, in North Carolina, and in Alabama, while the friends of Mr. Fairbanks laid special siege to the neighboring State of Kentucky. Sentiment favorable to Senator Cummins existed in Minnesota, in South Dakota, in Nebraska, and in Montana.

The situation in Pennsylvania was very mixed, so much so that Senator Penrose had great difficulty in deciding upon, and in following, a course of action. While he himself had been re-elected to the Senate by a large majority in 1914, the heavy Progressive vote cast in 1912 still exerted much influence and was a factor to be reckoned with. The vanity of Governor Brumbaugh led him to fall an easy prey to those who whispered that, having been elected governor of Pennsylvania, the path to the White

House now lay open before him. Mr. Knox was anxious to return to the Senate but some of his friends, including Mr. Frick, were anxious, in the early stages of the campaign, that he should be brought forward as a candidate for the Presidency. If left to himself, Senator Penrose would undoubtedly have supported Mr. Fairbanks, but he could not well do so in face of the fact that Governor Brumbaugh was a receptive candidate, and in face of the further fact that Roosevelt still had a very large and very influential following in Pennsylvania. During the past few years Senator Penrose had fallen out with the Vares, contractors in Philadelphia, one of whom was a member of Congress. These gentlemen were very influential in South Philadelphia and their chief concern was not so much with the Presidency of the United States as with contracts for public work in Philadelphia and elsewhere in Pennsylvania. With a view to embarrassing Senator Penrose the Vares espoused the cause of Governor Brumbaugh, and Penrose found himself driven to negotiate with the friends of Roosevelt in order to maintain himself. During the winter of 1916 Mr. Knox was sent for to come north from Palm Beach and attend a conference at which his Presidential candidacy was carefully discussed. Despite the urgings of some of his Philadelphia and Pittsburgh friends, Knox, on looking the situation over, declined to permit the use of his name and returned to Palm Beach, having announced that he would remain a candidate for the United States Senate. The date of the Pennsylvania primaries was unusually late—May 16—and therefore Senator Penrose was kept on tenter-hooks until the very last moment. One reason for the persistence of the notion that Roosevelt might yet be nominated at Chicago was to be found in the fact that Senator Penrose was under such pressure at home, and

was in such close negotiation with Mr. Perkins, Mr. Wilkinson, and other of Roosevelt's friends and advisers, that these felt justified in believing that sooner or later he would be driven to declare for Roosevelt in self-defense. Had he done so, of course Roosevelt's strength in the Chicago Convention would have been notably increased, but under no circumstances could he have been nominated.

A most amusing episode developed because of Senator Murray Crane's anxiety over what he believed was Senator Penrose's very important political conferences with Colonel Roosevelt and his supporters. So one day Senator Crane asked me to see Penrose and find out just what the facts were. I called upon Penrose at the old Waldorf-Astoria and found him sitting placidly there in a comfortable chair as if there was nothing in the world either to disturb or to interest him. After a few preliminary sentences, I told him that Senator Crane was concerned about the Oyster Bay visit and the character of the conferences with Colonel Roosevelt, and had asked me to ascertain the facts and to learn what was to be his, Penrose's, attitude at Chicago. Penrose made a perfectly characteristic reply. He said, "My dear boy, you people must remember that the Progressives carried Pennsylvania in 1912, and that they are very strong there now. I am going to have a hard fight in the primaries next Tuesday, so I have entered into partnership with the Roosevelt men, which partnership will be dissolved on Tuesday afternoon at six o'clock. I shall have all the assets and they will get all the liabilities." Senator Crane was greatly cheered by this news.

The situation in Massachusetts was also extremely complicated. This was due in part to the candidacy of Senator Weeks, in part to the action and the egotism of Senator Lodge and in part to the ambitions of Governor McCall.

Senator Weeks was put forward, in part at least, by men prominently associated with the United Shoe Machinery Company and other large financial and commercial organizations in Boston. This of itself was no ground for criticism, but it was made such by the press of the state and by those who were unfriendly, for various reasons, to Senator Weeks. As early as December, 1915, Senator Lodge had made a public declaration in support of Senator Weeks, but, as the event proved, he had not the slightest idea of seriously aiding to bring about his nomination. Indeed he was at this very moment, in the Senate cloakrooms, commending Justice Hughes as a possible candidate, and at the same time he was in constant and confidential communication with Roosevelt in a way that might well have justified the latter in believing that Senator Lodge was really friendly to him. The Roosevelt sentiment had been very strong in Massachusetts in 1912 and, as a result of the primary fight for Governor in 1915 between Governor McCall and Grafton D. Cushing, the lines of demarcation between the two elements in the party had been emphasized anew. Finally, at the instigation of Congressman Gardner, four men, of whom Grafton D. Cushing was one, announced that they had decided to offer themselves as candidates for election as delegates-at-large to the National Convention pledged to the support of Roosevelt. Their action precipitated a direct fight on the question of Roosevelt's candidacy. Ex-Senator Crane undertook the difficult and delicate task of uniting all the other elements in Massachusetts in support of a ticket that, while opposed to the nomination of Roosevelt, would be unpledged so far as any other candidate was concerned. By the exercise of his most unusual skill and tact, he succeeded in inducing Governor McCall, Senator Lodge and Senator Weeks to join with him in becoming candidates for delegate-at-large in opposition to the ticket headed by Congressman Gardner. This so-called un-pledged ticket, while containing in itself elements of sharp dissension, won at the primaries, and with its victory the final death knell of Roosevelt's hopes was sounded so that everybody could hear it. Yet this delegation was not really for Mr. Weeks, nor was it ready to support Governor McCall. It was, with the exception of Senator Lodge, strongly opposed to the nomination of Roosevelt, but, as it afterwards showed, it could not be united in support of any candidate when the balloting began.

In the State of New York the situation was as pathetic as usual when a national convention is to be held. The extremely small men (with the notable exception of Chairman Hilles) who had managed to get into conspicuous public and party positions were concerned first and chiefly with such relatively unimportant questions as who should be chairman of the delegation, who should be chairman of the State Committee, and who should be member of the National Committee. They were much less concerned with the question as to who should be nominated for President of the United States. In December and in January there were many signs that the opinion of the party in New York State was turning towards Root. William Barnes, whose skill and foresight included the making of what he called "pictures" to impress and to instruct public opinion, was insistent that Mr. Root should be chosen to be temporary chairman of the State Convention called to meet in Carnegie Hall, New York City, on February 15, 1916. His object was to have Elihu Root make a speech of such commanding ability and of such statesmanlike power that it would, first, serve to focus the mind of the party on the real issues of the coming campaign, and, second, bring forward Root himself as a desirable and available candidate for the Presidential nomination. Root made the expected speech and it had a profound effect. It desperately offended the pro-German element and it failed to influence the votes of many Republican congressmen on the McLemore Resolution, warning Americans against travelling on English or French vessels, which came before the House of Representatives not long afterward. The *New York Times* and other papers friendly to President Wilson did not hesitate to point out that, whatever might be said for the strength of Root's position, it was not the position of a majority of the Republican Party as was evidenced by the votes in Congress. Meanwhile, Root himself had vetoed the proposal that he should be either endorsed for the Presidency or presented to the country as a candidate by the Republican State Convention. A resolution to do either of these things would have been carried, but it would have been vigorously fought, behind the scenes if necessary, by Governor Whitman, Speaker Sweet, Herbert Parsons and others.

The result was that a large part of the political activity of the State of New York during the winter and spring of 1916 was spent upon purely local and personal squabbles, leaving the Presidential candidate a matter of minor importance. When the delegates were elected it was found that about thirty-five of them were ready to declare themselves instantly and uncompromisingly in favor of Root, and that two of them believed that Roosevelt should be nominated. The remainder were either allied with the group opposed to Root or were uncertain. It was not until the roll had actually been called in the convention that it was known where one or two of the delegates stood. That roll call showed forty-three for Root, forty-two for Hughes, and two for Roosevelt; so that once more, as in 1880, 1884, 1892, 1896, and 1908, the State of New York

was so thoroughly divided in sentiment as to destroy what
should have been and should always be its really controlling position in the National Convention. As a result of the
Convention of 1912 the intellectual leadership of the State
of New York in the Republican Party had been made
secure. As late as the Christmas holidays of 1915, the un-
precedented sight could be seen of prominent Western
party leaders coming to New York to ask what New York
wanted and what attitude New York was going to take.
A month or two afterward the situation had so changed
that no Western leader cared what New York wanted or
what attitude New York was going to take.

The delegation was on the whole one of high tone and
good representative capacity. There were some members
of it who sincerely believed that, while Root was incom-
parably the best-fitted candidate for the presidency, he
was not so likely to be elected as Charles Evans Hughes
or some one else. To this group belonged Herbert Parsons,
Ogden L. Mills and two or three more. Then there were
those who were simply playing state politics and who had
no interest whatever in either Root or Hughes, although in
private conversation they were frank to admit the commanding ability of Root and their personal dislike of
Hughes. Among those were William L. Ward of Westchester and George W. Aldridge of Monroe.

The Southern States, as usual, had their local fights
but the usual amount of money was not spent upon them
and the results were correspondingly happy.

As early as January, 1916, there were conferences as to
the organization of the convention and I was asked whether
I would take either the temporary or the permanent chairmanship, and which I would prefer. I pointed out that
I could not under any circumstances take the temporary
chairmanship since, in our anxiety to put our convention

a week ahead of the Democrat convention, the date of its opening session had been fixed for the same day as the annual Commencement of Columbia University, from which I could not be absent. The question as to the permanent chairmanship I took under advisement. While I was in Seattle about March 20, a dispatch was published in the newspapers saying that the Committee on Arrangements for the National Convention was in session in Chicago, and that my name among others was being considered for the temporary chairmanship. I at once wired to Chairman Charles D. Hilles reminding him of the conflict of dates and again pointing out that I could not be present at Chicago on the opening day of the convention and that therefore my name must not under any circumstances be considered for the temporary chairmanship. Chairman Hilles told me afterward that he understood this perfectly, but that some other members of the Committee on Arrangements had felt that I ought to be willing to sacrifice the University Commencement and accept the temporary chairmanship as asked. As the record shows, the matter was held over until a later meeting and then Senator Harding of Ohio was chosen and proved a most capable and acceptable officer. During the month of April the matter of the permanent chairmanship was again brought forward and I agreed to accept it if chosen. Shortly afterwards, however, William Barnes and Congressman John W. Dwight, together with James R. Sheffield and Cornelius N. Bliss, made the point that the speech nominating Root was much more important than the permanent chairmanship and that they wished me to make that speech. We discussed this matter for two or three days and it was finally decided that I should make the Root nominating speech and that Senator Harding should be continued as permanent chairman, unless, acting upon a suggestion of mine, we could find some delegate from the Pacific Coast who was competent to discharge the duties of permanent chairman. It seemed to me that, in view of the fact that California, Oregon and Washington had all been heavily Progressive in 1912 and were now safely back in the party ranks, it would be a graceful thing to select a permanent chairman from there if any one was available for the position. The names of Scott Bone of Washington and Judge Walter Bordwell of California were discussed but both were set aside as not having the voice adequate to the performance of the chairman's task. It was then settled that Senator Harding should be temporary and permanent chairman.

Meanwhile Charles B. Warren of Detroit was working on the rules, a subject of which he had made a specialty, and Chairman Hilles was beginning to give thought to the platform. About May 1 he wrote to twelve or fifteen prominent Republicans in various parts of the country asking them for suggestions, first as to the importance and order of treatment of topics for the platform and second as to specific paragraphs dealing with particular subjects. As fast as he received replies he sent them to me to be digested and classified. Then he invited a group of representative men, almost all of whom were delegates to the convention, to meet in New York on May 15 and 16 to discuss the platform in confidential conference. Those invited included Charles F. Scott of Kansas, John T. Adams of Iowa, James P. Goodrich of Indiana, H. C. Ogden of West Virginia, General Felix Agnus of Maryland, Charles Hopkins Clark of Connecticut, ex-Senator W. Murray Crane of Massachusetts and William Barnes, Elon R. Brown, Herbert Parsons, Henry L. Stimson, James R. Sheffield and myself of New York. We worked for two days practically from ten in the morning until six o'clock at night and came to substantially unanimous conclusions as to the tone, temper and contents of the platform. I was then requested to draft, within the next few days, a platform expressing the conclusions arrived at. I did this and sent a confidential copy to each participant in the conference and three copies to Chairman Hilles, who by that time had gone to Chicago. Reference to a draft of this proposed platform will show that it is far more progressive, more definite and more constructive than the platform actually adopted by the convention, which was the work of Senator Lodge. After the New York conference, I was asked to serve as Chairman of the Committee on Resolutions and to present for consideration the platform there agreed upon. I could not do this for the same reason that I could not accept the temporary chairmanship. On Wednesday, June 7, when I must be in New York, the Committee on Resolutions would be appointed and would immediately go into session. Then Charles Hopkins Clark of Connecticut was asked to take the chairmanship, but he felt that he was not in sufficiently robust health to stand the strain of an all-night session and of the close and active discussions that were certain to accompany the work of the committee. So it was that the position went by default to Senator Lodge, who had been anxiously asking for it for some weeks. When Mr. Clark presented the New York draft of the platform, Senator Lodge refused to have anything to do with it and insisted on using a draft of his own, which was, with a few committee amendments, reported to the convention and adopted as the platform of 1916. By common consent it is a sorry document and far below the Democrat platform, both in literary style, in progressiveness and in definiteness. The Republican Party owes this to Senator Lodge and not at all to its own lack of convictions at that time or of ability to express them.

The convention opened at eleven o'clock on the morning of June 7, and at 2:45 P.M. on that day we left New York for Chicago, getting the speech of the temporary chairman at Albany in the *Evening Journal*. On reaching Chicago the next morning there was lively interest manifested in the possible relations between the two conventions, the Republican and the Progressive. It was not known what might result from the establishment of friendly relations between these two conventions. If no relations were established it was felt that the Republicans would nominate either Root or Hughes or some person whose name had as yet hardly been mentioned. Shortly after reaching the convention hall, I was told by Chairman Hilles that the Progressive convention had asked for a conference and that each convention would probably appoint a committee of five conferees, who might be found to hold the fate of the party in their hands. At the same time he told me that if the convention adopted the resolution accepting the invitation of the Progressives to a conference, I would be named as one of the Republican conferees. He warned me to get ready for this and so to arrange my other convention work and obligations as to give the conference precedence over everything else. Shortly afterwards the resolution providing for a conference was introduced and passed unanimously without debate. There was a noticeable stir both in the convention and in the galleries as it was felt that this move might possibly produce some dramatic or unexpected result. Some even thought that it insured the nomination of Roosevelt by both conventions.

The chairman at once appointed the Republican conferees as follows: Reed Smoot of Utah, W. Murray Crane of Massachusetts, William E. Borah of Idaho, Nicholas Murray Butler of New York and A. R. Johnson of Ohio. As soon as the convention adjourned Senator Crane suggested that the Republican conferees should dine together at the Chicago Club at 7:30 and that the Progressive conferees should be invited to join us at 9 o'clock. This program was carried out. During dinner we discussed our own attitude and were unanimous in feeling that, since the Progressives had asked for the conference, they must take the initiative in the discussions and that we would be guided by events. Shortly after 9 o'clock the Progressive conferees arrived. They were: George W. Perkins of New York, Charles J. Bonaparte of Maryland, Hiram Johnson of California, John M. Parker of Louisiana and Horace S. Wilkinson of New York. Several of the conferees, most of whom knew each other personally, exchanged most cordial and hearty greetings and after a little informal chat we proceeded to the serious business of the conference. George Perkins opened the discussion by stating that, since the Progressives had asked for the conference they would probably be expected to speak first. He thereupon called upon Mr. Bonaparte to present the Progressive point of view. Bonaparte, speaking with his characteristic and curious drawl, proceeded for thirty minutes to state the Progressive position, first as to the issues of the campaign and second as to the candidate. Everything which he said as to the issues of the campaign was cordially assented to by the Republican conferees and within ten minutes it was plain to every one in the room that, so far as the platform was concerned, both conventions were in entire accord. So soon as this became evident, Mr. Bonaparte turned his attention entirely to the question of a candidate. He stated that the Progressives had canvassed the entire field of possible candidates, had weighed the claims and the advantages of many different men, but always came back to the conclusion that Roosevelt was not only the best-fitted man for the Presidency, but also the one man so associated with the dominant issues of the campaign as to be indicated the logical and almost the necessary candidate. All this took some time and was done with great good temper and excellent feeling. Mr. Bonaparte was followed by Mr. Parker of Louisiana, who harped upon the old and tuneless string of carrying the solid South for Republican principles. His argument was that this could be done if the Republican principles were nicknamed Progressive, and if the Republican candidate were Roosevelt. He was certain that Roosevelt could carry Louisiana, North Carolina, and probably other Southern States, and that if the Republican Party were given a Progressive veneer so as to overcome the long-time antipathy of the Southerner to the very name "Republican," all that he hoped for would be speedily accomplished. Governor Johnson of California followed and showed his very best side. He wholly lacked the violence, the temper and the bad manners which marked his appearance in the Convention of 1912. He referred to the very great importance of this conference, saying that he felt as if he were acting in the discharge of a really sacred duty. He, too, joined in saying that Roosevelt was really the only possible candidate. Then Mr. Wilkinson spoke and at some length. He discussed financial and commercial questions, and the relation of Roosevelt's candidacy and probable election to the business interests of the country and to prosperity generally. Mr. Perkins spoke last and rather briefly. He vigorously but quietly sustained the thesis that Roosevelt was by far the best candidate to unite upon, and he gave the reasons which he had often given publicly. All this took, perhaps, two and a half hours, so that it was midnight when Senator Smoot turned to me and asked me to make a statement for the Republicans.

My remarks were very, very brief and consisted, first, in expressing my great satisfaction at the conference and at the tone and temper with which it was being conducted; second, my appreciation of the personality, the ability and past services of Roosevelt; and, third, my conviction that under no circumstances whatever would the Republican convention consent to his nomination. I stated that it seemed to me only just and fair to the Progressive conferees that they should not be left in doubt upon this perfectly clear and certain point and that they should not be misled by concealing it from them. Perkins interrupted to say that he thought this was a full and free conference, and if we were not prepared to discuss the nomination of Roosevelt he did not see what use there was in coming together. My reply was that we were having a full and free conference; that the Progressive conferees had stated a fact, namely, that Roosevelt seemed to them the best candidate and that they all favored his nomination and had no second choice; that in reply I was stating a second fact, namely, that whatever Roosevelt's merits he could not be nominated by the Republican convention. It seemed to me, therefore, that with these two facts before us we ought to be ready to go forward to the consideration of the third fact, which was upon what candidate other than Roosevelt can we agree. To this all the Progressive conferees replied that they had no second choice and that they were not prepared to discuss anybody but Roosevelt. Senator Borah then spoke saying that so far as he was concerned he would be glad to vote to nominate Roosevelt at any time, and that no one could excel him in appreciation of Roosevelt's abilities and character, but that he too was of opinion that under no circumstances would the Republican convention nominate Roosevelt and that we might just as well accept that fact

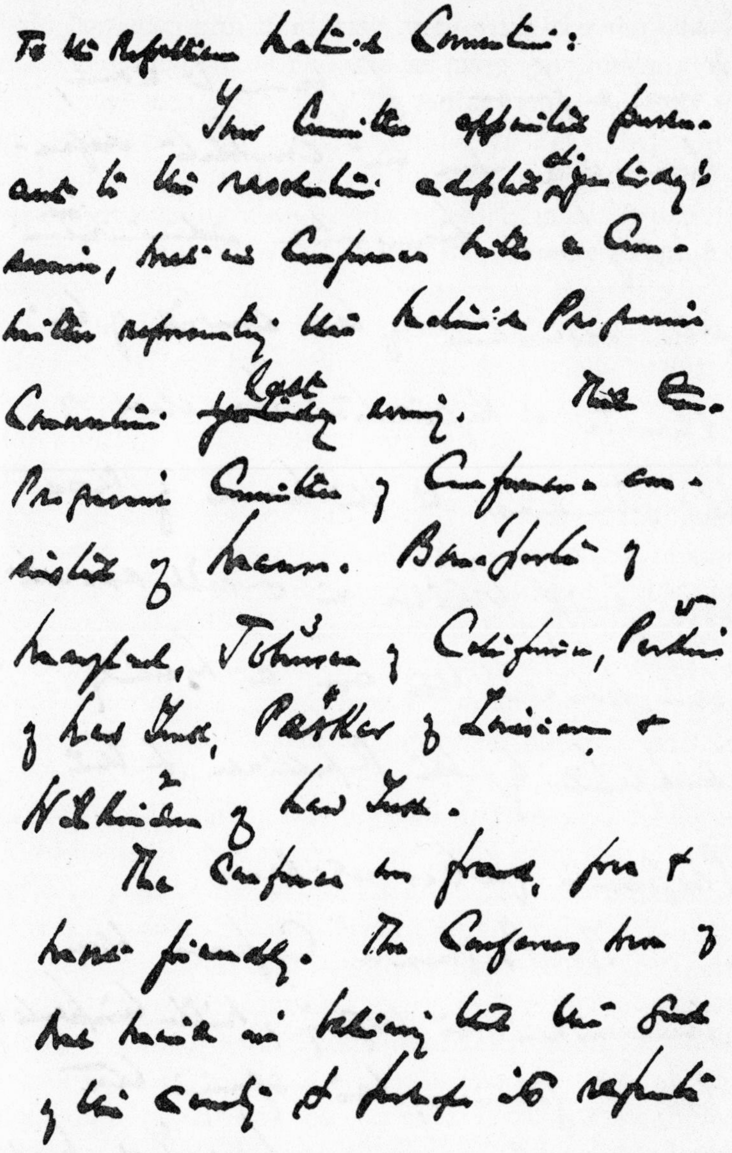
To the Republican National Convention:

Your Committee appointed pursuant to the resolution adopted yesterday morning, that we confer with a Committee representing the National Progressive Convention last evening. The Progressive Committee of Conference consisted of Messrs. Bonaparte of Maryland, Johnson of California, Perkins of New York, Parker of Louisiana & Wilkinson of New York.

The Conference was frank, free & most friendly. The Conferees were of one mind in believing that the good of the country & perhaps its salvation

[1]Report in the author's handwriting, with the original signatures, presented to the Repulican National Convention on behalf of the Republican conferees, June 9, 1916.

...and influence for years to come, depended upon the complete defeat of the present Democratic administration & the restriction of the control of the executive & legislative branches of the Government to the hands of those who firmly believe in & will execute the policies that are as heartily supported by the Republican & the Progressive parties alike.

The Progressive Congress then consisted in urging & holding conferences & families, the committee that Theodore Roosevelt of New York had

31

so large a personal following &
such a close personal relation to
the issues of this coming campaign
as to make him the most desirable
candidate upon which to unite.

He has agreed that your Conferees would report these facts to
their Convention.

June 9, 1916

Respectfully submitted,

Reed Smoot
W Murray Crane
W E Borah
Nicholas Murray Butler
R J Johnson

at once. This led to more general and informal discussion, during which Perkins asked whether the Republican conferees were ready to propose any name to the Progressive conferees. The Republican conferees replied that they were not ready to do any such thing. They pointed out that the Republican convention had not yet balloted, and that at least ten names were to come before it, some of which had been endorsed at primary elections in various states, and some of which had been endorsed by state conventions. In advance of some indication of preference of the convention itself the conferees did not feel that they had the right to select one candidate from this group or to eliminate others.

All this took until about three o'clock in the morning and then it was decided that the Republican conferees should prepare a short statement by way of report to the convention and that this report should be simply a statement of fact without any recommendation or expression of opinion. Thereupon Senator Smoot and I went downstairs to the writing-room and I wrote the following report to the convention. Perkins asked whether he might see this report, and a copy of it was made by Senator Smoot for the Progressive conferees. However, they did not show us in advance the report which they presented to their convention the following morning and which gave the impression that the Republican conferees had stood in the way of a united report in favor of some one candidate. When we separated at about 3 : 30 A.M. on Friday, June 9, it was with the understanding that we should reassemble at the Chicago Club thirty minutes after the adjournment of the Republican convention. It was then thought that this adjournment would take place about six o'clock in the afternoon. As a matter of fact, the nominating speeches were so numerous and so long, and the interruptions by applause and by demonstrations were so great, that it was after nine o'clock when the convention adjourned.

Throughout the conference the Progressive conferees kept emphasizing the fact that it was with the greatest difficulty that the Progressive convention had been kept from nominating Roosevelt on Thursday, and that they could not assure us that despite the continuance of the conference he would not be nominated during the sessions of Friday. We replied that we understood this situation perfectly and that we too were proposing to ballot on Friday afternoon, and that while we did not expect that the convention would nominate on the first or second ballot, of course it might do so, and that we could not be responsible for the result if it did. The Progressive conferees stated that they appreciated this situation and took it into full account.

The report of the Republican conferees was read to the convention by Senator Smoot on Friday morning. He read it with fine elocutionary effect and it produced a distinctly good impression. Indeed, so good was the impression that some persons who did not follow its language closely thought at first that the report recommended the nomination of Roosevelt. After the nominating speeches had been concluded two ballots were taken, in accordance with a previously arranged program. The first ballot was expected to clear the air as far as instructions and merely formal preferences were concerned; the second ballot was expected to show the drift of the convention's mind. Hughes received 328½ votes, Root 98½, Weeks 79, Burton of Ohio 76½, while as many as twelve other candidates were voted for. Adjournment until Saturday morning was proposed. Some of the more stupid of the advocates of Hughes resisted the motion to adjourn, on the theory that if a third or a fourth ballot could be had immediately Hughes would be nominated. They were quite wrong about that, for on Friday night Hughes had polled his full strength in that convention as matters then stood. He might have received ten or twenty more votes on a third or fourth ballot, but no more than that until the situation with the Progressives had been cleared up or until it was quite certain that Theodore Roosevelt would under no circumstances make a statement in advocacy of Elihu Root. The first choice of the convention's head and heart was, by an overwhelming majority, Mr. Root. There was no dissent from the statement as to his peculiar fitness for the Presidency, but there was a feeling that it might not be possible to elect him unless Roosevelt would either advocate his election or at least state that he would not oppose him. A great many delegates in the convention were waiting for a final demonstration of Roosevelt's attitude in this respect. Not before they were convinced that it would be unsafe to nominate Root were they ready to go to Hughes.

As soon as the convention adjourned the conferees took the shortest possible time to refresh themselves and to change, and hastened to the Chicago Club for a late dinner and a resumption of the conference. The conferees all assembled at about 10:30 P.M. and resumed the discussion where they had broken it off in the early morning. The Progressive conferees again stated that their convention had with great difficulty been persuaded to refrain from nominating Roosevelt during the day, and that they were more convinced than ever before that he was the only candidate upon whom both parties ought to unite, or indeed could unite. The Republican conferees reiterated their statement of opinion that under no circumstances would the Republican convention nominate

Roosevelt, and pointed to his sixty-five votes on the first ballot and his eighty-one votes on the second ballot as evidences of his very small support in the convention. The Progressive conferees were then asked whether there was any name on the list of Republican candidates which they would consider as a possible second choice. Their answer was that they had no second choice and that there was no name on that list which they would so consider. Mr. Perkins in turn asked the Republicans whether they were ready to bring forward any name as a possible candidate for both parties. The Republicans replied that they could not do this, since although the convention had balloted twice they were substantially in the same position as the night before. While it was plain that Hughes had more support than any single candidate for the nomination, eight candidates had received fifty votes or more each, and the history of past conventions proved that a candidate in that position might well be nominated later on. At this point the Progressive conferees manifested some impatience at the attitude of the Republicans in neither accepting Roosevelt nor proposing a substitute. The discussion was continued amicably but fruitlessly for a long time and finally at 3 A.M. on Saturday the conference adjourned to meet again at 9 o'clock in the morning. The Republican convention had adjourned until 11 o'clock, and the Progressive convention until 10:30, therefore the time was growing very short within which to arrive at a conclusion.

As soon as the conference adjourned I called at the Congress Hotel and found that a number of the leaders were then in the rooms of the Indiana delegation and that they wished me to join them at once. I went there, and found, in addition to John W. Dwight, Will H. Hays, Chairman of the Indiana State Committee, ex-Senator

Hemenway, Senator McKinley of Illinois, National Committeeman King of Connecticut, and Senator Penrose. I outlined to them the proceedings of the conference. I also said that just before leaving the Chicago Club, Perkins had asked me whether, in view of the critical situation in which we all were, I would be willing to talk with Roosevelt on the telephone, using his (Perkins') private wire. I told Perkins that I would let him know in an hour's time. Meanwhile I had asked Senator Smoot what he thought of the suggestion and he had advised me to do it by all means. The group of gentlemen assembled at the Indiana headquarters gave me the same advice. We then discussed what I should say to Roosevelt.

They told me that at a conference held earlier in the evening they had been unable to concentrate on any one candidate in opposition to Mr. Hughes, that the hoped-for concentration on Root had failed because of Senator Penrose's refusal to co-operate, and that concentration upon Mr. Fairbanks had failed because a number of delegates not specially favorable to Hughes preferred him to Mr. Fairbanks. This group of gentlemen then suggested that in talking to Roosevelt I should suggest to him the names of Mr. Root, Mr. Knox and Mr. Fairbanks, and in that order, and ask whether he would be willing to advise his Progressive friends to support any one of them. What I learned in this conversation made it doubly clear that Hughes was certain to be nominated when the convention reassembled in the morning, unless Roosevelt would support some other name. As I was leaving the room Penrose called after me: "Tell Roosevelt that we will nominate you if he will agree to support you." My answer was: "Au revoir!" accompanied by a sarcastic wave of the hand.

By this time it was 4 A.M. and I went over to the Blackstone to Perkins' rooms, where he was awaiting me. I told him that I was ready to talk with Roosevelt on the telephone if Roosevelt desired it, and in a very few minutes Mr. Perkins told me that Roosevelt was at the Oyster Bay end of the wire. As soon as we had exchanged "Hellos," I said, "Good morning, Mr. President," and he replied with great precision of utterance, "Good morning, Mr. President of Columbia." He then went on to say that he wished to thank me personally for the form of report submitted to the Republican convention on Friday morning by the conferees and for the very nice mention of his name. He added that he understood from Perkins that the Republican conferees were unanimous in the opinion that he himself could not be nominated, and asked whether I held this opinion. I said that this was undoubtedly the fact, that under no circumstances could he be nominated, and that unless he was willing to indicate his support of some other name, Justice Hughes would certainly be nominated on the first or second ballot when the convention reassembled. Roosevelt said that he thought this was true; what names had I to suggest? In reply I said that I had just come from an important conference of leaders and that I had three names to suggest to him and in a definite order; and then I named Mr. Root, Mr. Knox and Mr. Fairbanks. After an instant's hesitation, Roosevelt said that he was not in a position to discuss Mr. Root, something which I, of course, deeply regretted, and which he did not further explain. Of Mr. Knox, he said that of course he held him in high regard and thought him a very able man, but that he believed him to be quite as much responsible for the Mexican mess as was President Wilson, and that since we were going to fight this campaign in large part upon the issue of Mexico, we could not possibly do it with Knox as a candidate. Fairbanks he said he greatly liked. "He is a very able and a very nice man, but I am not sure what my Progressive friends would say. I shall have to talk it over with them."

Roosevelt then said: "Is there any chance whatever for a wholly new man?" I replied: "There is a chance for anybody who is fit for the office and upon whom we can agree. Any man upon whom you and I agree now over this telephone can be nominated tomorrow morning at 11 o'clock." "Well," he said, "what about Leonard Wood? Could he be nominated?" I said, "No. He could not. General Wood is a very able man; he is much more than a soldier, as his administration in the Philippine Islands and in Cuba amply demonstrated. But," I added, "at a time when we are asking the country to take a new attitude as to foreign affairs and as to military preparedness, we cannot possibly ask them, at the same time, to take a man from the active army to be President." I added that it was going to be hard enough to bring the Middle West to the support of our program, and that this section would revolt beyond any question if we asked them to take both our program and a soldier; that never was there a clearer case for the nomination of a civilian on every possible political and public ground. Roosevelt quickly added, "I thought it might be that way; there is a good deal in that." Then he said, "What about Lodge?" and proceeded for two or three minutes to outline Mr. Lodge's experience and knowledge very much as he described them at greater length in the message which he shortly afterwards addressed to the Progressive conferees. I replied: "Of course Mr. Lodge is a Republican in good standing, and a statesman of large experience. He is entitled to be considered in connection with the Presidency. What the Republican convention will say to his name, or what his vote-getting qualities may be, I do not know. As to those matters, I shall have to consult some of my colleagues, but I will do that and let Mr. Perkins know the result." After a few more sentences we closed a most agreeable conversation that had lasted over perhaps fifteen or twenty minutes and I turned the wire over to Perkins.

In five minutes Perkins rejoined me and said, "The Colonel has just been telling me of his conversation with you, but those suggestions of Leonard Wood and Lodge are ridiculous. We have discussed them time and time again. They are impossible." Then he added, "You heard what the Colonel said about Knox, which is perfectly true, but we cannot do anything with Fairbanks. Penrose has been trying to get us to do that for weeks and has offered us everything in return. We turned all that down long ago, and there is no use in going over it again." Curiously enough Perkins, like Roosevelt, could not or would not discuss Mr. Root, but there was something in the minds of both of them which they did not choose to communicate to me which stood in the way of their saying the word that would have nominated him and thereby have changed the whole history of our country and of the world for the past twenty years. For he would almost certainly have been elected President.

By this time it was 5 o'clock in the morning and I then went upstairs to Dwight's room where were assembled the group that I had left at the Congress Hotel two hours earlier, waiting to hear my report. I outlined my conversation with Roosevelt and we separated about 6 A.M., all with the conviction that Hughes would be nominated before many hours had passed, and that then the question would be, would or would not Roosevelt support him?

At 6:15 I went in for a short sleep, but was back at

the Chicago Club for breakfast at 8:30 and ready to
resume our conference at 9. This time neither Governor
Johnson nor Mr. Parker turned up, but the rest of us were
all there. We at once stated to Mr. Perkins that we were
now ready to advance beyond the position that we had
taken the night before inasmuch as conferences held during the night, which had supplemented the two ballots
taken on Friday evening, made it plain to us that Hughes
was or soon would be the choice of the Republican convention. We therefore presented his name to the Progressive conferees as a candidate upon whom both parties
should unite. Before Mr. Perkins came in Senator Smoot
and I had again gone to the writing-room and I had dictated the statement to the conferees of the National Progressive Party. As soon as Mr. Perkins heard the statement he said: "Are you unanimous as to this?" We said
we were. He said: "Well, I must consult Governor Johnson and others and I will telephone you our answer here
before 10:30 at which hour the Progressive convention is
to reconvene."

It was just 10:29 when Mr. Perkins called Senator
Smoot on the telephone and read him a short statement
to the effect that the Progressive conferees, following our
precedent of the day before, would report our recommendation to their convention without comment. This
they shortly did, and their convention laid our recommendation on the table. We had treated their recommendation of the day before a little better, for our convention
had actually voted on their candidate.

We then went back to the Convention Hall and going
on the platform asked Senator Harding to call the convention to order promptly so that our report might be
heard and the balloting proceeded with. Just as Senator
Harding was raising his gavel to call the convention to

order, Mr. McGrath, Roosevelt's secretary, arrived on the platform bearing a communication for Senator Smoot. As soon as Senator Smoot opened it, it was apparent from his expression that the paper was important. He immediately summoned us to the National Committee room in the rear, and asked Senator Harding to postpone calling the convention to order and to have the band play for a time until we could see what this communication was and what ought to be done with it. The communication proved to be a copy of Roosevelt's message to the Progressive conferees suggesting the name of Senator Lodge as a compromise candidate. He had dictated this message over the telephone between 5 and 6 o'clock in the morning, almost immediately after concluding his conversation with me. The fact that Lodge either had a copy of it, or knew about it, was evidenced by the fact that he was absent from the Saturday morning session of the convention, probably out of excessive modesty. As soon as we read the communication, we saw how unwelcome the suggestion of Lodge would be both to the Progressive and to the Republican conventions. Nevertheless, for tactical reasons we wanted to have the Progressive convention act first. Therefore we waited in the committee room while Senator Borah called up Mr. O. K. Davis, Secretary of the Progressive convention, and got word from him that Roosevelt's letter, as well as the suggestion of the name of Hughes, had been laid on the table. As soon as he turned from the telephone Senator Borah said to us: "It is very important to get that message confirmed, as on its correctness may turn one of the issues of this campaign." Our whole group of conferees, therefore, now enlarged by the presence of Senator Lippitt of Rhode Island and Mr. Charles B. Warren of Detroit, stood about the telephone while Mr. Hilles called up Mr. Perkins at the

Progressive convention. Each time he asked Mr. Perkins a question, Mr. Hilles repeated to us Mr. Perkins's answer so that our whole group of seven or eight got the entire conversation. Mr. Perkins told Mr. Hilles, as Mr. Davis had told Senator Borah, that the Progressive convention had laid Roosevelt's letter on the table.

This fact made our course perfectly clear. It was to go back to the convention, to report what we had proposed to the Progressive conferees, to read Roosevelt's letter and then to resume balloting. This we did. Roosevelt's suggestion of Senator Lodge, which was received in the Progressive convention with jeers and hoots, was received in the Republican convention quietly and with an amused smile. Senator Penrose was particularly sarcastic in commenting upon the suggestion.

While the prayer was being offered, a newspaper man who I understood represented the *Philadelphia Evening Telegraph,* told me that it was a mistake to say that the Progressive convention had laid Roosevelt's letter on the table. He said that he had been in that convention and that what was done was to lay it over for later consideration. I rushed back to the platform and tried to get this information to Senator Smoot, but before I reached there the prayer was concluded and Smoot had gone forward to make his report. The result every one knows. The concentration on Hughes began at once and there was competition between the two conventions as to which should nominate first. According to the newspaper reports the Republicans nominated Hughes two minutes before the Progressive convention nominated Roosevelt.

After the adjournment of the convention on Saturday afternoon, I was sitting with a group in the Chicago Club with Melville E. Stone of the Associated Press. Stone stated that he had received word that the Chairman of the Progressive convention, Raymond Robins, on hearing that Senator Smoot had reported to the Republican convention that the Progressive convention had laid Roosevelt's letter on the table, had publicly denounced that statement as a characteristic Republican trick and Republican lie. I then recited to these gentlemen what pains had been taken, at Senator Borah's instance, to confirm the accuracy of our information on that point. While we were talking, President Benjamin Ide Wheeler of the University of California joined the group and, on hearing what we were discussing, said that he could explain the whole matter. President Wheeler stated that he was in the Progressive convention when the action in question was taken and that the motion made by a delegate was that Roosevelt's letter be laid over for later consideration, but that in putting the motion, Chairman Robins had stated it as one to lay upon the table, and that in that form the motion prevailed. President Wheeler's opinion was that, while the Progressive convention intended to lay Roosevelt's letter over for later consideration, as a matter of fact, owing to an error on the part of its own chairman, it had actually laid Roosevelt's letter on the table. President Wheeler's statement, therefore, makes it perfectly clear that if there was any misunderstanding in regard to this matter, it was due to the action of the Chairman of the Progressive convention and that Senator Smoot was absolutely correct in his statement to the Republican convention.

In many ways the convention of 1916 was the critical point in the later history of the Republican Party. The fact that the bitter opposition of Senator Penrose and the fears of Senator Murray Crane, of Charles B. Warren of Michigan and others prevented the nomination of Elihu Root proved tragic in high degree. The party was quite prepared, under Root's effective and highly intellectual leadership, to go forward constructively to new and progressive policies, including those of leadership in that international co-operation which is absolutely necessary if war is to be abolished and world trade established and made secure. This would mean peace and prosperity not for our own land alone, but for every land, and a new era of modern history would open. Because this could not be accomplished, the Republican Party was sentenced to a hopelessly timorous and incompetent campaign and to a defeat which it deserved. It is customary to attribute this defeat to the unfortunate experiences of candidate Hughes in the State of California, and those experiences were, of course, a painfully contributing factor. More important, however, was the cowardly campaign conducted in the State of Ohio which, in consequence, was lost by a majority of some 40,000, together with the Governorship, the United States Senatorship and many Congressmen.[1]

1920

As the Convention of 1920 approached, the situation was one of great party disorganization and uncertainty. The Democrats had been in power for eight years, and that influential patronage which had ordinarily been in Republican hands for the better part of a half-century was now lost to the party organization. There was no noticeable drift toward any one candidate for the Presidential nomination, as had been the case in the days of Blaine and of McKinley. This led to the bringing forward of a number of candidacies, sometimes with and sometimes without the active support of those whose names were used. Probably the largest body of organized support

[1]See Chapter XI, Behind the Scenes in Politics, "Indiana in the National Election of 1916."

favored the nomination of General Leonard Wood, but there was vigorous, widespread and earnest support for former Governor Frank O. Lowden of Illinois, whose public service both at Washington and in the State of Illinois had been admirable. In addition, he possessed a very charming personality which endeared many persons to him. When placed in nomination by Congressman Rodenberg, his name was received with great enthusiasm. Senator Hiram Johnson of California also had a very considerable following, reminiscent of some of the groups and episodes of the conventions of 1912 and 1916. On the first ballot no fewer than fifteen candidates were voted for, the larger number of votes being cast for General Wood, 287½; Governor Lowden, 211½, and Senator Johnson, 133½. Senator Harding's nomination was brought about late on Saturday afternoon on the tenth ballot by a concentration of the friends of all the other candidates except those of General Wood and Senator Johnson, for both of whom a very substantial number of votes was still cast.

A group of personal and political friends, drawn from a dozen or more states, arranged to have my name presented to this convention for the Presidential nomination, with assurance of widespread and powerful support provided certain conditions could be met. This proved to be impossible and, therefore, these delegates voted almost to a man for the nomination of my warm friend, former Governor Frank O. Lowden of Illinois, who I had hoped would be the convention's choice.

Senator Harding's nomination is widely attributed to personalities and causes which had nothing to do with it whatever. Colonel George Harvey, who claimed the honor of having brought the nomination about, not only was not concerned in it in any important way, but was secretly supporting another person and planning a coup, which had it not been for the stubborn independence of the Connecticut delegation might have resulted in success. Another man who is often supposed to have played a controlling part in bringing about Harding's nomination, but who in reality had nothing whatever to do with it, was Senator Penrose of Pennsylvania. Penrose had conceived the idea of nominating Senator Philander C. Knox, his colleague, and he had approached William Barnes of New York on the subject three months before the convention met. Just as he completed all his personal arrangements for the convention, Penrose was taken gravely ill and passed wholly out of the picture. He died a few months later. The notion that John T. King of Connecticut was in constant communication by telephone with Senator Penrose at his home in Washington during this convention is a myth. Penrose was too ill to telephone.

There were certain elements of chance in the nomination of Harding which must not be overlooked. In the first place, there was the excellent impression which Harding's personality and power of speech made upon the Convention of 1916, when he was chosen Temporary Chairman. The stunning character of his appearance at that time and the effect of his voice and manner, both upon the members of the convention and upon the vast audience assembled in the hall, are not likely to be forgotten by those who witnessed them. His selection as Temporary Chairman was, in turn, the result of accident, as has already been described in connection with the Convention of 1916, but it was an accident destined to have large consequences. Of course, the carefully planned and assiduous work done on Harding's behalf by Harry M. Daugherty was of greatest importance, but even that would not have won the battle had not a group of Senators put their heads together to nominate a man who, as one of them cynically said, would, when elected, sign whatever bills the Senate sent him and not send bills to the Senate to pass.

On Friday morning, June 9, while the nominating speeches were making at the Convention Hall, I sat alone with Warren Harding in his rooms at the Auditorium Hotel. The weather was very hot and he had taken off his coat and waistcoat and was fanning himself vigorously. In the course of our conversation he said: "I cannot afford to keep these rooms any longer and I have sent word downstairs to say that I am giving them up this evening. This convention will never nominate me. I do not propose to go back to the Senate. I am going to quit politics and devote myself to my newspaper." These words were spoken between eleven and twelve o'clock on Friday morning. At about six-fifteen on the following afternoon Warren Harding had been nominated for President of the United States. At the moment when his nomination was made, Frank Lowden and I were sitting with Harding in one of the small rooms back of the platform of the Convention Hall. We three were alone. The roll was being called on the tenth ballot. Suddenly, there was a tremendous roar from the Convention Hall. In an instant, the door of the room in which we three were sitting burst open and Charles B. Warren of Michigan leapt into the room, shouting: "Pennsylvania has voted for you, Harding, and you are nominated!" Harding rose, and with one hand in Lowden's and one in mine, he said with choking voice: "If the great honor of the Presidency is to come to me, I shall need all the help that you two friends can give me." In another instant Harry Daugherty arrived, seized Harding and took him back to the Auditorium Hotel before a crowd could assemble.

1924

In 1924 the convention was called to meet at Cleveland
and the sentiment of the entire party was for the renomination of Calvin Coolidge. His quiet and well-balanced
personality and his hard common sense had made a very
distinct appeal to the people of the United States, and no
other name than his was to be considered. On Saturday
morning before the convention met, James R. Sheffield of
New York and I arrived in Cleveland and called upon
our friend, Secretary John W. Weeks of Massachusetts,
for a friendly chat. Quite casually, we happened to say to
Weeks, "What are you doing about the Vice-Presidency?"
He responded, "Nothing. What are you two doing?" We
replied, "Nothing." Thereupon we three decided to do
something, and during the next few hours we brought
together under the informal chairmanship of Weeks a
small group, the purpose of which was to select a candidate for the Vice-Presidency whom we might all support.
By Monday morning the group included Secretary Mellon of Pennsylvania, Secretary New of Indiana, Senator
Curtis of Kansas, Speaker Gillett of Massachusetts,
Charles D. Hilles of New York, Congressman Longworth
of Ohio, Senator Watson of Indiana and three or four
more. We discussed every sort and kind of name, hour by
hour, by night and by day. Some one had objections to
make to every name that was proposed. Finally, at about
four o'clock one morning, Harry New rose and said solemnly: "I am going off to bed. The kind of man you
are looking for as Vice-President was crucified nineteen
hundred years ago." Among others we discussed former
Governor Herbert S. Hadley of Missouri, who had played
so important a part in the Convention of 1912, and who
was now Chancellor of Washington University, St. Louis.

I telephoned him to ask whether we might consider his name, but he said, "No." Finally, we came to the conclusion that probably the best thing to do would be to offer the nomination to Senator Curtis of Kansas. When that conclusion was reached, it was proposed that we should then go down to the room of Mr. William M. Butler of Massachusetts, who was the Coolidge manager at the convention, and tell him what was proposed. Objection was made to this on the ground that if we did so, the several score of newspapermen who were waiting in the halls outside our rooms would say that we had gone to Butler to get our orders, and that, therefore, we must bring him up to see us instead of our going down to see him. This was done and between one and two o'clock in the morning Chairman Butler arrived, escorted by Charles D. Hilles. John Weeks told him of our discussions and deliberations and of our conclusions. Butler looked at Weeks with a perfectly impassive face and said: "I have just been talking by telephone to the White House. We must nominate Borah for Vice-President." This statement was received with a silence which could have been cut with a knife. Finally, Chairman Butler said to Weeks: "Mr. Secretary, what do you think of Borah?" Weeks, coming forward to the front of his chair, replied with a stream of adjectives and expletives which would not look well in print. There was more silence. Then Chairman Butler turned to Secretary Mellon and said to him: "Mr. Secretary, what do you think of Borah?" The Secretary, looking dreamily off in the distance, took his characteristic little cigar from his mouth and said placidly: "I never think of him unless somebody mentions his name." Chairman Butler then withdrew. Of course, we were all familiar with the conversations which had been going on in Washington, but the convention had not the slightest intention of being controlled by them. The delegates were off on a rampage so far as the nomination for Vice-President was concerned and were wholly uninterested in the preferences of President Coolidge or his convention manager. They regarded the nomination and re-election of Coolidge as certain and were going to have the quite unusual fun of picking the candidate for Vice-President themselves instead of having a candidate handed to them by anybody. As a matter of fact, they were so foolish as to nominate Governor Lowden for Vice-President, despite the fact that he had told all his friends that under no circumstances would he accept the nomination. This nomination took place on the second ballot when no fewer than sixteen names were voted for. Governor Lowden's declination was repeated with emphasis in various forms, and at an adjourned session in the evening Charles G. Dawes was named in his stead. The nomination of Dawes was brought about at the urgent insistence of the delegation from New Jersey under the leadership of Senator Edge and of that from Nebraska with which state Dawes had had long and close association.

The Convention of 1924 was the first of three on a rapidly descending scale of competence, intelligence and courage. The addresses at Cleveland by both the temporary and the permanent chairman of the convention, and the appallingly long platform which, as was humorously said, resembled a Memorial Day parade in that it took an hour to pass a given point, made an impression of intellectual sterility which time has done nothing to remove.

1928 AND 1932

Both in 1928 and 1932 matters grew steadily worse. The speeches of the chairman and the platforms presented

gave evidence of a combination of intellectual confusion
and moral cowardice which were reflected in the steadily
weakening hold of the party organization on the people
of the country, particularly those of the younger generation. The campaign of 1928 would have been lost had it
not made mean-spirited use of widespread religious bigotry and intolerance in its fight, partly open and partly
concealed, on the candidate of the Democrats.

The story of the resolution which I presented at this
convention relative to the repeal of the Eighteenth
Amendment is told elsewhere.[1]

The Convention of 1932 represented the lowest level
that had yet been reached. The literally appalling
speeches of the temporary and permanent chairmen
and the platform, which played on every string of dema-
gogy and cowardice, were listened to with stolid disap-
proval. The spectacle of three members of the Cabinet
and the legal adviser of the National Republican Committee running about the floor of the convention in order
to influence the delegates to vote against their real convictions in the matter of a declaration for the repeal of
the Eighteenth Amendment was the most offensive happening which any convention has seen. The natural and
necessary result, of course, was the cataclysm of November, 1932. Returning to New York after the adjournment of the Convention of 1932, my daughter, who had
been Vice-Chairman of the New York State Republican
Committee for a decade, and I were agreed that we had
taken part in our last Republican National Convention.
The record which had been made was so deplorable that
we felt that for us to continue in active work with the party
organization was impossible. So it was when, in 1936,
Republican Party leaders urged me once more to become

[1]See Vol. II, *Repeal of the Eighteenth Amendment,* 1920.

a delegate to the convention of that year, I declined with thanks and said that my service to the party organization as then constituted was at an end.

LOOKING BACKWARD 1880–1939

As one looks back across well-nigh sixty years and reads the record of these highly important political gatherings, he cannot fail to be impressed by the very unsatisfactory character of almost all of the declarations of principle and policy known as platforms, which were adopted by one convention after another. Almost without exception they are diffuse and long-winded, as well as lacking in that definiteness and precision of statement in regard to debatable questions which high intelligence and courage demand. Time and time again these platforms hedge and qualify and side-step as to matters of large public concern, in order to meet the views of those so-called practical politicians who have in mind the support of some local or sectional faction, usually a small fraction of the voting population. Unhappily, the best and most forward-facing declarations of policy were frequently those to be most completely disregarded by the party representatives in Washington after they had been elected.

Having taken part for a long term of years in preparing platforms for state and local political conventions, first in New Jersey and then in New York, it was natural that I should be associated with work on the several national platforms almost from the beginning of my convention experiences. The usual practice was for some one chosen by the Chairman of the National Committee to prepare a draft platform and to bring it to the convention for submission to the Committee on Resolutions when appointed. That committee would as a rule accept the draft platform in major part. Some additions would be made here and some excisions there. Some statements would be modified in form and some in fact, but as a rule the draft platform survived all these processes in most respects. What was stricken out was almost always that which was progressive and forward-facing.

For a number of years this preliminary work was done, and most effectively done, by Charles Emory Smith, editor of the *Philadelphia Press*. After his death in 1908 this job was turned over to me for the three following conventions. What happened to the platform prepared for consideration by the Convention of 1916 has already been recorded. In 1908 the preliminary draft was completed at a conference held at the Hotel Plaza in the city of New York in the rooms of Senator Aldrich of Rhode Island. There were present in addition to Senator Aldrich and myself, Senator Eugene Hale of Maine, Senator John C. Spooner of Wisconsin, and Senator Albert J. Hopkins of Illinois, who was to be chairman of the Committee on Resolutions. Several times during the day and evening over which this conference extended, Senator Aldrich called up Secretary Taft at Washington and got his comment or criticism or approval of some proposed declaration.

In 1912 the major part of the platform was adopted precisely as I drafted it with three exceptions. When I read it to Senator Fairbanks, who was to be chairman of the Committee on Resolutions, he expressed the opinion that it should contain some reference to Lincoln, and thereupon he wrote the second paragraph of the platform in which Lincoln's name is mentioned. The short paragraphs, after those relating to conservation and the parcel-post, were suggested by other members of the committee when they had the platform before them for consideration. One short declaration the committee struck out entirely on the ground that it was "too weird." It was a statement that in revising the tariff schedules with a view to their reduction and the promotion of international trade, all efforts should be made to put this policy into effect in ways that would raise the standard of living not only in our own country but in those other countries with which we did business. A quarter-century has elapsed and the principle underlying this proposed declaration of 1912 has come to have a far greater importance than any one could then have foreseen. I was never able to get into any platform a straightforward declaration in favor of economic and social security through a system of social insurance against unemployment, disability and dependent old age.

Literally thousands of different political workers and leaders passed under the eye of any one who sat and watched the proceedings of these fourteen Republican National Conventions. They included men of every kind and type, and were a true cross-section of American political life and American political thought. Of all the severely practical politicians I unhesitatingly put William Barnes of New York at the head. Grandson of Thurlow Weed and having had an excellent education, he became not only an expert practical politician, but a keen and well-read student of political theory. The literature of political science in France and in Germany as well as in England, was familiar to him. He was skillful in high degree in the management of men and, unlike most of his fellow practical politicians, held fast to a set of fundamental principles from which no influence or power could budge him. William Barnes might be defeated, but he would neither compromise nor surrender.

In the long procession of men who tramped across the

political stage during these years there are four personalities which are outstanding—Garfield, McKinley, Foraker and Elihu Root. Garfield attended but one convention, that of 1880, which ended by nominating him for
the Presidency. He was a most accomplished orator, with
far more scholarship and distinction of manner than were
the fortune of most of his political companions.

McKinley first came to the Convention of 1884, when
he was made a chairman of the Committee on Resolutions. He returned in 1888 to hold the same distinguished
post and again in 1892, when he was chosen permanent
chairman. It was then that he escaped by a hairbreadth
being nominated for the Presidency at a time when his
election was probably out of the question. McKinley was
an admirable speaker, but his power over men lay very
largely in the charm and gentleness and kindliness of his
manner. He lacked the scholarship of Garfield, but he
excelled him in personal attractiveness.

Foraker had a most exceptional personality, full of fire
and vigor, speaking always with great emphasis and
jumping to his feet from time to time with a lightning-
like quickness which never failed to command attention.
He appeared first at the Convention of 1884, returned
in 1888 to nominate John Sherman, served on the Committee on Resolutions in 1892, was chairman of that
committee in 1896 and also placed McKinley in nomination in 1900. He appeared for the last time at the
Convention of 1904.

Elihu Root attended but two conventions, those of 1904
and 1912. On the first occasion he was temporary chairman, and on the latter he occupied the chair throughout
the entire series of troubled sessions. The source of Root's
power was intellectual. No American in the last half
century has equalled him in the field of constructive states-

manship or in intellectual grasp and power of exposition. A present Justice of the United States Supreme Court has said in conversation that our American political history has produced no one, save Alexander Hamilton, who takes rank as high as, or higher than, Root. Had Boies Penrose given way and permitted the nomination of Root in 1916, the whole subsequent history of our country and of the world would almost certainly have been very different.

George William Curtis was a member of but one convention, that of 1884. Warren Harding was a delegate in both 1912 and 1916, and presided over the last-named convention as both temporary and permanent chairman. Benjamin Harrison was a delegate in 1880 and again in 1884. Theodore Roosevelt appeared twice, first in 1884 and again in 1900. Mark Hanna was a delegate in 1884, 1888 and 1896, and was present at the convention in 1900 as Chairman of the National Republican Committee and, in all respects but one, its controlling force.

The figure that made the least appeal throughout all these years was that of Henry Cabot Lodge. He was able, vain, intensely egotistical, narrow-minded, dogmatic and provincial. For him Pittsfield, Mass., represented the Farthest West except on the quadrennial occasions when he was willing to cross the state boundary to attend a Republican National Convention at Cleveland, at Chicago or at St. Louis. One would hardly have suspected his background of education and literary work. Lodge came first to the Convention of 1880 and was present again in 1884, but he was not a member of the Conventions of 1888 or 1892. He was a delegate in 1896, 1900, 1904, 1908, 1916, 1920 and 1924. His persistence in asking honors for himself made him permanent chairman of the Conventions of 1900 and 1908, and both temporary and permanent chairman of the Convention of 1920. He was chairman of the Committee on Resolutions in 1904 and 1916, but in 1924 he cut a sorry figure. So much out of touch was he with the controlling forces of that convention, that both he and Colonel George Harvey wandered together about the corridors of the Cleveland Hotel asking the newspaper men what the news might be. The crowning revelation of Lodge's political character was made by his conduct at the Convention of 1916. In an impassioned speech he placed the name of John W. Weeks of Massachusetts in nomination for President and cast his vote for him on the first ballot. On the second ballot he deserted his candidate and voted for Theodore Roosevelt. When the third ballot was taken he remained outside the Convention Hall because of excessive modesty, since he hoped that by reason of Theodore Roosevelt's intervention the nomination might come to himself. A few minutes afterwards, when Hughes was nominated, Lodge appeared upon the platform and made a speech in high praise of him. This rather swift boxing of the political compass was the subject of well-nigh universal comment and universal hilarity.

Largely owing to Lodge's control of the Republican majority in the Senate, and his dominance of the Committee on Foreign Relations, the party organization had been going steadily downhill since the summer of 1919 in respect to everything which related to vision, to high intelligence and to forward-facing, liberal policies in the field of international relations, as well as in leadership in all that pertains to social service and economic development. The power of the Republican name remained still very great and millions of earnest men and women throughout the land clung to it, hoping almost against hope, that somehow and from somewhere constructive leadership would be provided to give representation to their ideas and their ideals but this was not to be. Stolid self-contentment and the pride of political possession held the field, and would not yield a jot or tittle until the whole of the party's political structure was brought down in one great crash by the voters of the nation. There is where it is today, and there it will stay until ideas and ideals, as well as courage to expound and to defend genuine American principles in a spirit of true forward-facing liberalism with full recognition of the new international world that time and circumstance have created, come to take possession of it and to transfuse it with new and vivifying blood so that it may offer that new, liberal and constructive leadership to the youth of the land. This almost tragic collapse would not have happened had the representatives of the party in the Congress of the United States hearkened to these noble words, spoken by President McKinley on September 5, 1901, the very day before his assassination:

> The period of exclusiveness is past. The expansion of our trade and commerce is the pressing problem. Commercial wars are unprofitable. A policy of good will and friendly trade relations will prevent reprisals. Reciprocity treaties are in harmony with the spirit of the times, measures of retaliation are not.

Instead of responding to McKinley's eloquent appeal, there followed as the result of the power of highly organized, self-seeking groups, three tariff acts—the Payne-Aldrich Act of 1909, the Fordney-McCumber Act of 1922 and the Smoot-Hawley Act of 1930—which contradicted flatly and in every detail the sound doctrine which McKinley so finely stated. These three tariff acts which, in effect, put a large portion of American industry upon the dole in defiance of the public interest in trade and commerce, both nation-wide and international, paved the way for the economic collapse of 1929–30, the effects of which are still oppressing and depressing the American people.

The refusal of those same Republican representatives to write into public policy the definite pledges of the party national platforms of 1920, 1924 and 1928 as to international organization, a permanent court of international justice and the development of international trade was followed by complete lack of public confidence in the party's professions and promises. The contemptuous neglect of the declaration of Harding in his speech made at Marion, Ohio, on August 28, 1920, as Republican candidate for the Presidency, in favor of a society of free nations so organized and so participated in as to make the actual attainment of peace a reasonable possibility, dashed the hopes of the civilized world for quick progress toward the avoidance of international war and the up-building of a world-wide system of prosperity and peace.

In the face of this record what ground can there be for surprise that the people repudiated the Republican Party in most overwhelming fashion?

Surely, it is little less than grotesque to continue to describe as liberal those public men who are definitely and vigorously opposed to almost every constructive policy which is offered at the moment, simply because they gained for themselves that adjective under the conditions which prevailed a quarter-century ago. Certainly, the time is ripe for presenting to American public opinion a political program which will not be one of mere criticism and attack, but one of constructive and definite proposal for the solution of the many new and pressing economic, social and political problems that confront our people. Such few of these as are primarily national are inextricably mixed with the many that are international. Senatorial dealers in political antiques continue to repeat and to applaud sentences torn from Washington's Farewell Address and from Jefferson's First Inaugural, without any regard to their historical background, in the attempt to persuade the American people to uphold policies and ideals which affront everything for which Washington and Jefferson themselves so definitely labored. Those men were not building a self-centered or an isolated America. They were building an America to be to all the world an example of the true meaning of liberty and a national influence for public service and for peace and good will throughout the earth.

Prosperity is not, and can no longer be, the characteristic of one nation only or of a few nations. If it exists at all, it will be, generally speaking, world-wide. International peace can no longer be the concern only of two governments which may be on the verge of conflict, for events have made it the concern of every government which really cares for the happiness and security of its own people. Economic war may be quite as destructive of national prosperity as is armed warfare. If the Republican party organization of tomorrow is intelligent enough and sufficiently open-minded to see these facts and to act upon them, the Republican Party may well begin another long period of helpful service to the American people. Today there are millions of Republicans, but there is no Republican Party.

XI

BEHIND THE SCENES IN POLITICS

O N INAUGURATION DAY, March 4, 1889, the weather in Washington was abominable. There was cold wind and rain, sometimes turning into snow, and a dark, heavy sky that were depressing in the extreme. After witnessing the immensely impressive ceremonies in the Senate Chamber, and after hearing the first few sentences of President Harrison's inaugural address, I made my way to the Cosmos Club to get warm and dry. Two or three men whom I knew were there, and while the inaugural parade was passing in dismal procession up Pennsylvania Avenue, we were enjoying the glow of a bright fire and the delights of intimate conversation on men and things. In a few moments Congressman Thomas B. Reed of Maine came into the club and joined our group in front of the fire. After some characteristically cutting remarks in reference to inaugurations, inaugural parades and Inaugural Day weather generally, Reed began to talk about the session of Congress that had just closed. He denounced in unmeasured terms the rules of the House of Representatives which made it possible for a few men to break a quorum for the transaction of business and to carry on a prolonged filibuster in the face of

the obvious wish of a large majority of the House. He
went into some detail and gave us illustrations of his
meaning. He then added that he thought he might be
chosen Speaker of the House in the Fifty-first Congress
and that if so chosen, he proposed to bring to an end the
situation that had so long existed, by insisting upon the
power and the duty of the Speaker to declare the presence
of a quorum if a quorum was visibly present, no matter
whether all who were present answered the call of the roll
or not. To all of us this was a new idea and we asked a
good many questions concerning what was in Reed's
mind. In reply he gave us a most elaborate and convincing exposition of the fundamental processes of parliamentary law and procedure, pointing out that the object
of a parliamentary body was to transact business and that
any rule which indefinitely prevented the transaction of
business against the will of the majority was in principle
revolutionary and preposterous. He pointed out very
shrewdly that recognition by the Speaker, whether such
recognition was visual or aural, was the basis upon which
the determination of a quorum rested, since whether the
person answering to a given name on the roll call was in
fact that person or some one else was something which
in last resort the Speaker must himself determine. "Therefore," said Reed, "the principle is the same whether the
Speaker declares a quorum to be present because he himself counts enough members of the House physically present to constitute a quorum, or whether he determines
that a sufficient number have in fact answered to their
several names when those names were called." We stayed
before the fire until after four o'clock while Reed unfolded his plans and the theory upon which they rested.

This whole episode interested me enormously since I
was convinced that Reed was right both in law and in

common sense, and I wanted to be present when the matter was settled in the House.

The next winter I followed closely the proceedings of the House, of which Mr. Reed was chosen Speaker after a stiff contest in the Republican caucus, and fully intended to go to Washington to be present in the gallery when the struggle over the rules should come. At that time 166 members of the House were a quorum and the Republicans had exactly that number. Not long after the Congress met, however, one Republican member died, reducing the party's strength to 165 and making it obvious that it would be almost impossible to maintain for any length of time a quorum of Republicans alone—a quorum now being 165—for the transaction of business. Of course the Democrat minority saw this clearly and they set about the task of compelling all the Republicans to remain in their places or to prevent the transaction of any business to which they did not themselves consent. Such a situation was an ideal one for the development of sharp and bitter partisanship. The Democrats instituted the practice of remaining silent, although present in the House, whenever a quorum was needed for the transaction of business in which the Republican majority was greatly interested, and since the Republicans could not often muster a quorum of their own, a deadlock resulted.

Toward the end of January, 1890, matters came to a crisis and, on a hint from the Speaker, I took a midnight train for Washington and was in the Press Gallery directly over Speaker Reed's head during the session when he carried through his memorable ruling as to counting a quorum. The matter before the House was a resolution offered in a contested election case, and when a quorum was demanded by the minority leader only 163 members of the House responded—two less than a quorum—although every seat was occupied. During the roll call it was most interesting to watch the Speaker. The House was excited and inclined to be turbulent. On the minority side there were constant mutterings and murmurings. From my place in the Press Gallery I could see that the Speaker had in his hand a printed roll of the House, and that as every man's name was called he quickly noted on the paper before him the fact whether or not a given member was present and not voting. The roll call had not proceeded very far before it became apparent to every one what the Speaker was doing, and the Democrats gathered in little knots to determine upon their course of action to prevent the Speaker, if possible, from carrying out his declared purpose to count a quorum. After the usual formalities, the roll call was justified and the Clerk handed his tally sheet to the Speaker. Then the Speaker, in that slow, nasal drawl which was so characteristic of him, started to make announcement to a House that was suddenly hushed. "On this question," said the Speaker, "the yeas are 161, the nays 2." At which point Mr. Crisp of Georgia, subsequently himself a Speaker of the House, called out: "No quorum!" Speaker Reed went quietly on: "The Chair directs the Clerk to record the following names of members present and refusing to vote. . . ." At this point there was a roar like that of a great tempest and the Democrat side broke out in shouts, yells, catcalls and hisses, through which were heard the cries of "No quorum!" "No quorum!" Members on that side rushed down the aisles and, becoming white with rage, shook their fists at the Speaker and hurled all sorts of epithets at him. Without seeming in the least disturbed and apparently as placid as a May morning, the Speaker went on with his announcement which not many in the turbulent House could hear, but which from my favored position only a few feet above his head I could hear clearly. He proceeded to read a list of names which few people heard, for, as the member to whom a given name on this list belonged heard it called out, he protested with every exhibition of fury and noise of which he was capable. The matter became ridiculous, however, when a distinguished member from Kentucky, a former governor of that state and afterwards to be senator, Mr. McCreary, got recognition and proceeded to read from a legal authority that he could not be counted as present unless he personally answered to the roll call. The Speaker's reply was, "The Chair is making a statement of the fact that the gentleman from Kentucky is present. Does he deny it?" It was this *reductio ad absurdum,* rather than Mr. Reed's powerful arguments, which ended the struggle in his favor. The whole country and even the angry minority came to see that the contention of the Speaker was logical, rational and in the public interest. Violent as was the controversy over its first declaration, Speaker Reed's ruling was quickly accepted as parliamentary law and no one would any longer think of questioning it.

So strongly did Mr. Reed feel upon this subject and so insistent was he that the bad practice of the House of Representatives should be brought to an end, that he had fully determined to resign from Congress if his position was not sustained by the Republican majority. Elihu Root, whom he had consulted before making his ruling and who strongly supported his position, had tendered Reed an invitation to join him in the practice of the law if the Speaker should feel it his duty to resign his seat in Congress.

Speaker Reed easily belongs to the group of very great personalities that American public life has produced. He was doubtless too intellectual, too high-principled and too strong-willed to be as widely popular as are men of softer and gentler mold than he, but he commanded what is far better than popularity, and that is the respect and admiration of men whose respect and admiration are worth having. His place in the parliamentary history of the United States is secure.

SPEAKER REED ON THE AMERICAN IDEA OF WAR

During the month of April, 1897, there was held in Washington an International Postal Conference to which the British Government sent as delegates Sir Spencer Walpole and H. Buxton Forman. While they were in Washington, Henry Cabot Lodge, who was then serving his first term as Senator from Massachusetts, gave a dinner in honor of these two gentlemen. Among the guests were Speaker Thomas B. Reed, Theodore Roosevelt, who had just become Assistant Secretary of the Navy in President McKinley's Cabinet, and myself. After dinner the talk turned for some reason or other upon war, and both Lodge and Roosevelt were very emphatic in their eulogies of war as a necessary means of settling great national and international differences and problems. Doubtless they exaggerated a good deal, but even allowing for exaggeration, what they said was quite grotesque. The two Englishmen were plainly staggered by all this and their amazement was written on their faces.

Finally, Sir Spencer Walpole turned to Reed and said: "But Mr. Reed, the American idea of war must be very peculiar. It must be something very different from ours. We could not possibly talk of war in this lighthearted way. Tell me, what is the American idea of war?"

Reed, without changing his expression a particle and with that peculiar manner and voice which added im-

mensely to the humor of what he said, drawled out: "The
American idea of war is to take the farmer from his plow,
and to return him to his plow—with a pension!" Surely
subsequent history has fully justified Reed's definition of
forty years ago.

SPEAKER REED AND THE CUBAN BELLIGERENCY
RESOLUTION

On February 15, 1898, the battleship *Maine,* lying at
anchor in the harbor of Havana, was blown up. Public
opinion in the United States, already much excited over
conditions in Cuba, was quickly in a state of flame. The
less responsible newspapers were yelling at the top of
their voices for war, and they redoubled their cries when,
a few weeks later, the special board of inquiry reported
that the *Maine* had been blown up by an explosion from
outside. President McKinley kept his head and bore himself with consistent dignity and firmness. Speaker Reed
gave him staunch support and shared the President's view
that if only a little time could be had, a satisfactory solution of the Cuban question would be worked out without
war. General Woodford, American minister in Madrid,
firmly held this view and, indeed, he reasserted it until
the day of his death. The jingo newspapers kept up their
alarums, however, and as usual produced a good deal of
effect on both houses of Congress. During March, 1898,
the President summoned a group of his personal and political friends to Washington and asked them to remain
for some days in order to assist him in controlling the
war spirit that manifested itself, both in the Senate and
in the House of Representatives. I was among those sent
for and remained in Washington some ten days or two
weeks in all. During this time Speaker Reed was constantly at work and he was at his very best.

The President was particularly solicitous that no action should be taken by the Congress to recognize the Republic of Cuba as a belligerent power, since he felt that such action would gravely limit his freedom of action and endanger his success in securing a peaceful solution of the problem. Unfortunately a number of Republican senators were ready to vote with the opposition in favor of such a declaration and it was only a question of time when it would be passed by the Senate with a large majority. Speaker Reed declared that it should not be permitted to pass the House and that he would see that it did not. One evening at about this time a group of the Speaker's friends were seated with him in his apartment at the Shoreham Hotel discussing the outlook when, following a knock at the door, a servant entered and handed the Speaker a card. "Show him in," said the Speaker in his high-pitched, nasal voice. The door opened and in came Lemuel Ely Quigg, member of Congress from New York, immaculately dressed in evening clothes and visibly embarrassed at finding the Speaker not alone. After a more-or-less awkward greeting of the company, most of whom he knew, Mr. Quigg walked up to the Speaker and whispered something in his ear. "Tell it right out, Quigg," said the Speaker. "These are all my friends. There are no secrets here." Quigg demurred, first in whispers and afterwards aloud, but the Speaker insisted that whatever was to be said must be said in the hearing of all of us, and continued with unruffled countenance to rock placidly backward and forward in his comfortable armchair. Finally, seeing that protest was useless, Mr. Quigg cleared his throat, squared himself and said substantially this: "Mr. Speaker, I come from a conference of fifty-two Republican members of the House to say that we propose to vote tomorrow with the Democrats to call up and pass the Cuban Belligerency Resolution." All were aghast at this announcement except Speaker Reed whose countenance never changed and whose rocking-chair never stopped in its rhythmic motion. We all realized that if Quigg's threat was carried out, President McKinley would be rebuked by a Republican Congress and war with Spain would be inevitable without farther notice and without preparation. So we all kept breathless silence, waiting for the Speaker's reply, which did not come. Quigg, plainly nettled, said, "Mr. Speaker, perhaps you do not fully realize what I have said. It is a very serious matter," and then repeated his former statement. "Yes, Quigg, I heard you," said the Speaker, unruffled of countenance and unceasing in the motion of his rocking-chair. From the rest of us came only silence and a good deal of it. After another moment, Quigg backed himself out and left the room, plainly in great anger. The door closed behind him and still the Speaker said nothing, but silently rocked and looked straight ahead of him. Finally, after what seemed hours, but was probably only a half minute of time, the Speaker came forward on his rocking-chair, stopped its motion and his face broke into a good-humored smile as he looked around at us and said, "They won't do it, boys; I won't let 'em." And he did not—at that time.

On April 13, however, a resolution recognizing the independence of the Republic of Cuba and directing the President to employ immediately the land and naval forces of the United States in aiding the Republic of Cuba to maintain its independence, passed the House of Representatives by a vote of 325 to 19. The damage was done and another wholly unnecessary war was entered upon by the Government of the United States.

SPEAKER REED AND CONGRESSMAN YOUNG

Another illustration of Speaker Reed's power over his colleagues in the House was given at about the same time by Congressman James R. Young of Pennsylvania. Mr. Young had formerly been executive clerk of the Senate and then represented a Philadelphia district in Congress. He was well known in Washington and had a wide acquaintance. The President heard that Mr. Young was threatening to vote in favor of the Cuban Belligerency Resolution in the House and asked me to argue with him and try to prevent him from doing so. I found Mr. Young one afternoon at about five o'clock in Shoemaker's, in those days a famous resort on Pennsylvania Avenue where senators and congressmen often dropped in late in the afternoon. Mr. Young was declaiming to a crowd of admirers, that he was for war and proposed to vote for the Cuban Belligerency Resolution, no matter what the President said. I broke in and said, "Well, Mr. Young, why? You represent a big Quaker district in Philadelphia. Your people are not for war if this issue can be honorably settled otherwise. What are your reasons?" To this Mr. Young responded with another outbreak more forcible than elegant, but one which left no doubt of his position. William E. Annin, the famous Billie Annin, one of the best newspaper men of that day in Washington and a leading member of the Gridiron Club, was standing near by. He walked up to Young and, shaking his finger in his face, said, "Why, Congressman, you talk like a fool! You know perfectly well that you won't vote to call up the Cuban Belligerency Resolution and force war. No matter what you say now, when you get in the House tomorrow morning Speaker Reed will come to you and say, 'Young, sit down there and vote for peace to support the President,' and you will do it." "That is just the devil of it," said Young with a leer. The crowd laughed, for they knew that Annin was right.

SPEAKER REED AND THE LIBRARY OF CONGRESS

Speaker Reed was not always so well disposed toward President McKinley's policies and acts as in the case of the Spanish war. An amusing illustration of this occurred in connection with the Library of Congress, for which new and splendid provision had been made and for which a competent administrative head was being sought when President McKinley's administration began. I had taken a very great interest in the Library of Congress, in securing appropriations for the present building and in working out an administrative scheme that would permit it to become a center of enlightenment and scholarship worthy of the nation. To this end it seemed to me important that the annual appropriations for the support of the Library be much increased and that a first-rate librarian be appointed by the President. I saw Speaker Reed on both these questions some time before the session of Congress opened and he promised me to support my proposals for larger appropriations for the Library and expressed his interest in the appointment of a suitable person to be librarian. On the latter point I discussed names with President McKinley at some length and told him that in my judgment what was wanted was a first-rate administrator with a knowledge of men and of books rather than a mere bureaucrat or a mere bibliophile. He agreed to this and asked me to suggest names. After some consideration of other names, I proposed to him Doctor James H. Canfield, then President of the State University of Ohio, whom President McKinley knew since Doctor Canfield had been his official neighbor

while he was governor. I pointed out that Doctor Canfield had had large and valuable experience in human
contacts in Kansas and in Nebraska before going to Ohio,
and that he had gained a nation-wide reputation as an
educational administrator. He seemed to me just the man
for the place. President McKinley, while not definitely
promising to appoint him, said that he was very much
interested in the subject and asked me to sound Doctor
Canfield as to his willingness to accept the position if
named. I took the matter up with Canfield. He expressed
his interest in the subject and his willingness to consider
it most sympathetically if chosen. Armed with this information, I went back to the President and asked him to
appoint Doctor Canfield to be Librarian of Congress. In
his quiet way, he said, "Butler, I am sorry to say that
I can't do it. I have unexpectedly had to make another
arrangement since you were here. My old friend, John
Russell Young, had expected to go as minister to China,
but he now tells me that his wife's physician advises that
she could not stand the climate of Peking. He has therefore asked me for some appointment here at home, and
the only thing that I have to offer is the Library. I am
going to appoint Young. You explain the facts to Doctor
Canfield and tell him how sorry I am that I cannot appoint him." To this I protested as strongly as seemed
appropriate. I told the President that John Russell Young
was no longer young and he had had no experience whatever to justify appointing him to this important position.
The President persisted however and, as is known, the
appointment was made shortly after. A few months later
I met Speaker Reed and asked him to make good his
promise to support the movement to get increased appropriations for the Library. "No, Butler, I can't do it," he
drawled, "and what's more, I won't do it." I expressed

my complete surprise and reminded him of our earlier conversations on the subject. "Oh, yes," he answered, "I remember; that's all so, but when an incompetent man is chosen for the head of a great public institution for the reason that his wife can't stand the climate of Peking, China, I lose interest in that institution and don't care what becomes of it."

Mr. Young lived but a short time after his appointment, and as his successor we were fortunately able, by the efforts of Senator Hoar of Massachusetts, to secure Mr. Herbert Putnam, than whom no one could be better. Incidentally, I then suggested Doctor Canfield to President Low for appointment to be Librarian of Columbia University and in that position he remained until his death some ten years later.

ABRAM S. HEWITT'S ACCOUNT OF HOW HE LOST THE GOVERNORSHIP OF NEW YORK AND POSSIBLY THE PRESIDENCY

One of the most absorbingly interesting political stories to which I ever listened was told by the late Abram S. Hewitt on December 17, 1891, under the circumstances which I shall relate. How far Mr. Hewitt was accurate in his recollection and statement of facts, and how far he allowed his imagination to be guided by his feeling and his ambition, I do not know, but certainly the story is one of greatest interest.

On December 17, 1891, the newly established Drexel Institute in Philadelphia, of which my warm friend, Doctor James MacAlister, had been chosen president, was to be formally dedicated. Mr. J. Pierpont Morgan invited a company of friends to be his guests for this occasion and to make the trip to Philadelphia in his private car. Among the group were Abram S. Hewitt, Bishop Henry

C. Potter, Andrew Carnegie, Thomas L. James, Chauncey M. Depew, H. McK. Twombly and Morris K. Jesup. An open fire was burning brightly in the sitting room at the rear end of the car and about it we quickly gathered. How Mr. Hewitt got started, I do not know, but it was not long before he took the floor and held it all the way to Philadelphia while he recounted his story of how Grover Cleveland came to be in the White House instead of Mr. Hewitt himself.

Mr. Hewitt was intimately concerned with the conduct of Mr. Tilden's campaign for the Presidency in 1876. He occupied a position of great influence in the direction of the Democrat campaign. As Election Day approached and the fight waxed constantly hotter, daily conferences were held at Mr. Tilden's house in Gramercy Park, where invariably his friends and neighbors, Mr. Hewitt and Mr. David Dudley Field, came each morning. All during the month of October the Republicans were making headway against Mr. Tilden with the widely published charge that, if elected to the Presidency, he would be committed to having the so-called Rebel Debt paid by the Government of the United States. Mr. Hewitt urgently pressed Mr. Tilden to repudiate this charge and to put himself publicly on record to the contrary effect. Mr. Tilden, always vacillating and anxious to avoid positive decision, delayed acceding to Mr. Hewitt's request although he professed a willingness to do so at the proper time. Meanwhile the Republican attack grew in force and Mr. Hewitt's urgency steadily increased. Finally on the morning of October 24, 1876, with Election Day close at hand and the issue plainly doubtful, Mr. Hewitt went to Mr. Tilden's house for his usual morning visit, carrying in his hand a statement on the subject of the so-called Rebel Debt which he asked Mr. Tilden to sign for publication.

Mr. Tilden demurred, but Mr. Hewitt insisted and finally went so far as to say that if Mr. Tilden did not then and there sign what he, Mr. Hewitt, had written, and allow it to be published, he, Mr. Hewitt, would withdraw from all further connection with the campaign. Mr. Tilden, thus driven into a corner, took Mr. Hewitt's paper, looked it over, and, having altered the final paragraph, signed it. The paper as drawn by Mr. Hewitt ended with the sentence: "Let the dead past bury its dead." Mr. Tilden changed this into "Let by-gones be by-gones," and added a score or more words of his own. As soon as Mr. Tilden had signed the paper, Mr. Hewitt took it and quickly left the house for the party headquarters on Fifth Avenue, since he knew enough of Mr. Tilden's nature to feel that in a few moments Mr. Tilden would regret his signature and ask to have the paper brought back to him. Sure enough, before Mr. Hewitt reached the corner of Fourth Avenue, Mr. Tilden's negro servant came running after him to say that Mr. Tilden wanted him to come back with that paper. Mr. Hewitt emphatically answered: "No, the paper has been given to the newspapers." He made his way as fast as possible to the headquarters of the Democrat National Committee and gave to the newspapers the letter signed by Mr. Tilden, which was published throughout the country on the morning of October 25, 1876, and which put Mr. Tilden emphatically on record against the payment of the Rebel Debt by the Government of the United States.

Mr. Hewitt said that Mr. Tilden never forgave him for this act although it was plainly to Mr. Tilden's advantage, and the breach thus created grew during the next few weeks when Mr. Hewitt was working for the determination of the result of the disputed presidential election through the appointment of the Electoral Commission. By this means he hoped to avoid resort to force or lapse into anarchy. Mr. Hewitt insisted that Mr. Tilden would, at that time, have gone to any lengths to obtain the Presidency and that he, Mr. Hewitt, was one of the powerful restraining forces which kept Mr. Tilden from precipitating a conflict and perhaps bringing on a new Civil War. Mr. Hewitt stated this several times with much emphasis and was plainly entirely convinced of the correctness of his view.

As affects Mr. Tilden, the sequel is well known, but Mr. Hewitt's recital of the sequel as it affected him has, to the best of my knowledge and belief, never been made public.

The rest of the story is this, and was doubtless suggested by the fact that at the time Mr. Hewitt was speaking, President Harrison's term as President was approaching its completion and there was already discussion of the possibility of again nominating Grover Cleveland as the Democrat candidate for the Presidency at the election of 1892.

Mr. Hewitt began by saying that he and not Grover Cleveland should have been elected President in 1884 and that this would have happened were it not for the following circumstance, which is immediately related to what has already been told.

It appears that after the Republicans had nominated Secretary Charles J. Folger for governor of New York in 1882, the Democrats felt sure of their ability to defeat him at the polls and began to look about for a candidate in all respects satisfactory. Despite Mr. Folger's personal character and high qualities he was felt to represent one faction of the Republican Party, and those who in 1884 were to support Mr. Blaine against President Arthur, were very vigorous in their opposition to him. There was much talk in the press of General Henry W. Slocum of Brooklyn and of Roswell P. Flower of Watertown and New York, as probable Democrat candidates for governor. Mr. Hewitt went on to say that a confidential conference of leaders was held and that under the guidance of John Kelly, then the master of Tammany Hall, he, Mr. Hewitt, was agreed upon as the party nominee of the convention to be held at Syracuse on September 22, 1882. Mr. Hewitt stated that nearly all the leaders, or at least a large majority of them, agreed to this program and that many of them assured him that he would be chosen governor in 1882 and then nominated and elected President in 1884. Two or three days before the convention was to meet at Syracuse, some one suggested that it was hardly proper to go forward with this program without at least taking into their confidence the titular leader of the party, the Sage of Greystone, Mr. Tilden. This was agreed to and two or three important Democrats called upon Mr. Tilden to outline that program. Upon hearing what was proposed, Mr. Tilden flew into a rage and announced that he would never support Mr. Hewitt, that Mr. Hewitt had been untrue to him in 1876 and 1877 and that if Mr. Hewitt were nominated, he, Mr. Tilden, would write an open letter against his election. This quite unexpected development staggered John Kelly and the other leaders, and they went to Syracuse dismayed and wholly unable to agree upon a candidate. For various reasons they were not satisfied with either General Slocum or Mr. Flower. Conference after conference was held in the Syracuse hotels and finally a hearing was given to an eager body of young Democrats from Buffalo, who were urging the nomination of the mayor of that city, Grover Cleveland. John Kelly said he wanted to see Cleveland and look him over. He, Mr. Cleveland, was sent for to come to Syracuse and apparently passed inspection satisfactorily. He was made the nominee of the convention and, as all the world knows, was elected Governor by the then record majority of 192,000, and was at once in the eye of the public as the Democrat nominee for the Presidency in 1884. To that office he was nominated and elected. Mr. Hewitt's point was that Mr. Cleveland was a child of fortune and grasped the place which he, Mr. Hewitt, had earned and deserved, and which he would have gained had it not been for the implacable enmity of Mr. Tilden incurred through doing what he, Mr. Hewitt, believed to be service in the interest of his country.

Mr. Hewitt told the story with great animation and complete conviction of the accuracy of its every detail.

THEODORE ROOSEVELT'S PART IN DEFEATING THE RATIFICATION OF THE HAY-PAUNCEFOTE TREATY

The circumstances in connection with the issuing of a statement on February 12, 1900, in criticism of the pending Hay-Pauncefote Treaty by Theodore Roosevelt, are these. Frederick W. Holls, who made his charming house in the outskirts of Yonkers the center of many delightful political gatherings and conferences, had invited for the week-end preceding Lincoln's Birthday, 1900: Theodore Roosevelt, then governor of New York; Andrew D. White, but recently returned from The Hague Peace Conference where he had been first American delegate; David Jayne Hill, who was then first Assistant Secretary of State; Doctor Albert Shaw, editor of the *Review of Reviews,* and myself. The conversation turned on the pending Hay-Pauncefote Treaty and the possibilities of a future Panama Canal with all that that implied in politics and economics. Mr. Holls took from his shelves a volume containing the declarations on this subject by James G. Blaine, and these were discussed and generally assented to by the entire company. Finally some one, probably Mr. Holls himself, urged that Theodore Roosevelt should issue a public statement along the lines of Mr. Blaine's doctrine, which of course antagonized the policy Secretary Hay was then urging upon the Senate. This matter was discussed for several hours and finally Theodore Roosevelt took a pen and wrote a brief statement which appeared in the newspapers of the following morning, and which is believed to have been the real cause for the failure of the Senate to ratify the Treaty. John Hay was very much provoked at the whole matter and was particularly incensed when he learned that Doctor Hill, his associate in the State Department, was present at Mr. Holls's house when the statement was prepared. Poor Doctor Hill was, however, perfectly innocent in the matter, for in accepting Holls's invitation he could never have dreamed of what was going to take place. The statement was given to me, and I made a trip to New York Sunday evening in order to give it to the newspapers. I have in my possession the original manuscript of the statement with T. R.'s interlineations and erasures.

THEODORE ROOSEVELT'S SUCCESSION TO THE PRESIDENCY

When President McKinley was shot at Buffalo, I was spending the summer at Rye Beach, N. H. Because of my cordial political and personal relations with the President and my intimate friendship with Theodore Roosevelt, then Vice-President, I was even more agitated and concerned than most others. I immediately communicated with friends in Buffalo, and found that it was not desirable for any more of the President's friends to assemble there. So I remained at Rye Beach and awaited the outcome of the President's injury. I was, however, in occasional telegraphic communication with T. R., whose headquarters were in the Adirondacks. Finally, when President McKinley died, T. R. telegraphed me to follow him to Buffalo. But that seemed to me injudicious, and I telegraphed a reply putting myself entirely at his service but suggesting that I go to Washington after the funeral rather than to Buffalo. This was arranged, so I proceeded to Washington and arrived at the house of the President's sister, Mrs. W. S. Cowles, where he was stopping before he took possession of the White House itself.

It was in late September, and daylight began to fade about six o'clock. A little before that hour, as I recall, T. R. marched in, clad in the presidential frock coat and silk hat, and after greeting me said that he wanted to go for a walk before dinner. We started off together in the dusk and walked at great speed straight out Sixteenth Street. We must have walked nearly or quite two miles before we turned and walked back to the house of Mrs. Cowles. T. R. talked vehemently and volubly all the time, and was in a great state of emotional excitement. Our intimacy was such that he could let himself go, and so relieve his pent-up feelings. He said a hundred interesting things, many of them important, but I am now able to recall but a few of them.

I was particularly shocked by his criticisms, favorable and unfavorable, of various public men, and he already showed the maleficent influence of Henry Cabot Lodge, who, true to his instinct as a professional politician, had hastened to warn T. R. against bringing with him to Washington any of his close friends in New York. Lodge had chiefly in mind Frederick W. Holls and Albert Shaw,

and possibly myself as well. He need not have bothered himself about me, because there was no office in the gift of the President that I would accept, a fact which the President very quickly ascertained. I doubt whether Albert Shaw would have accepted public office. But Holls would have been glad to do so, and would have been a distinguished ornament to the administration, as well as a great practical help to it. He had unusual political knowledge, particularly in regard to foreign affairs, and unflagging industry, together with a very wide and influential acquaintance in Europe.

During this hour or more of rapid-fire conversation, T. R. expressed with great vigor his lack of confidence in himself as President and his feeling that his administration would not be successful. He repeated this thought over and over again in varying forms and from different points of view. Finally, as we were approaching the end of our walk, I said to him: "Theodore, you are entirely mistaken. You will be an enormous success as President. You are here for seven and one-half years beyond peradventure. Your youth, your vitality, your many-sided interests, will all captivate the American people, so soon as they come to know you better. I have no fear whatever of the success of your administration. Your real problem, as I see it, is something quite different. You have come to the Presidency at an amazingly early age, and you will go out of the presidential office at fifty. The real problem that confronts you is whether you can be a sage at fifty. If you can, your permanent reputation seems to me certain. If you cannot, then the outlook is different."

I think that, as matters turned out, the question as to whether T. R. could be a sage at fifty was the most important that he ever had to answer. It surely was a trying test of temperament and character.

PRESIDENT THEODORE ROOSEVELT AND THE ORGANIZATION
OF THE CARNEGIE INSTITUTION

An amusing incident occurred in connection with the organization of the Carnegie Institution at Washington, which was the occasion of my writing a message to the Congress of the United States which was never sent, and of which I still have the original manuscript. The circumstances were these:

Mr. Carnegie had consulted me relative to his plan for the organization of an endowed national university at Washington and I had pointed out to him the folly and wastefulness of any such project, urging in its stead the establishment of a fund for the promotion of scientific research of every kind under the most generous and catholic provisions. My plan for the organization of the Carnegie Institution differed from that finally adopted, which was largely the result of the influence of Doctor John Shaw Billings and Doctor Daniel C. Gilman, whom Mr. Carnegie also consulted. When the plans for the undertaking were well under way, Mr. Carnegie conceived the notion of having it organized as the Smithsonian Institution is organized, thus making it, in a certain sense, an official government undertaking, or at least giving it official government recognition. Mr. Carnegie persuaded President Roosevelt that this would be a good thing to do and he urged the President to ask Congress to provide by joint resolution for the acceptance of his proposed endowment and for the establishment of a plan of organization for the Carnegie Institution which would be similar to the plan of organization of the Smithsonian Institution. President Roosevelt telegraphed me to come to the White House, and on arrival laid the plan before me and said that he highly approved it. He added: "You know a great deal more about this matter than I do, so sit down and write a message to Congress, making the proper recommendations, that I can sign and send tomorrow." I objected strongly and said to the President that Mr. Carnegie's idea was unsound, that any attempt to act upon it would have most unfortunate results for the President, for Mr. Carnegie himself and for his undertaking. I pointed out that the demagogs, both in the press and in the two houses of Congress, would at once attack Mr. Carnegie and parade once more all the stories, *ex parte,* about the Homestead strike and the money wrung from the sweat of the toilers and so on, without end. The President replied that he had thought of that and he did not believe it amounted to anything. We carried on the discussion for perhaps an hour and finally the President said: "My mind is made up; please write me that message." So I sat down at the writing desk in the old Cabinet Room and wrote a message to Congress presenting the President's views as I understood them. He, meanwhile, took a book and read. When the message was finished, I handed it to him and he read it very carefully two or three times. He then said: "That is all right. I shall not change a word of it. I shall sign it and send it to Congress in the morning."

At this point I became really alarmed as I saw an important political and educational mistake was about to be made, and I begged the President at least to postpone sending in the message. He, however, insisted upon his own view and his own plan. Finally, in despair, I said to him: "Please get hold of Root and find out what he thinks about this." The President replied: "Root knows nothing about it." I answered: "That may be, but you ought to have his judgment on the matter of policy involved." Finally the President yielded and sent word to Root to come at once to the White House. Root, who had been

peaceably reading in his library at home on a cold winter
night, arrived at the White House about ten o'clock, just
a bit cross at being disturbed at that hour. In a few short
sentences the President stated the matter to Root and
outlined our difference of opinion, but did not tell him
which of us supported the plan. He then handed to Root
the proposed message. "There is the message that I am
going to send to Congress in the morning." Root took the
paper, put on his glasses, and read the message slowly
through. Then, assuming that the plan was mine and
looking at me with great severity, he said to the President:
"Where did this damn fool idea come from?" And then,
in about five minutes of vigorous talk, he demolished the
whole project. Root took my point of view entirely, but
went farther than I did and expressed himself in pretty
vigorous fashion. He handed me back the proposed message, which I folded up and put in my pocket, and the
matter was ended. Some time later, in the spring of 1904,
the Carnegie Institution was incorporated by an act of
Congress as a public but non-governmental undertaking,
which was, of course, the only wise plan to adopt.

JOHN HAY

In calling on John Hay at his house after church one
Sunday, I found Theodore Roosevelt already there and
much interesting discussion followed, particularly as to
the probable results of the war between Japan and Russia.
Mr. Hay said that his personal sympathies were strongly
with Japan, and he evidently had a very low opinion of
Russian public and private morality and of the value of
Russia as a civilizing agent. He was somewhat surprised
to hear that traces of England's influence in Persia had
almost disappeared—as Professor A. V. W. Jackson had
observed on his visit a year earlier—but prophesied that

England would take advantage of the present embarrassment of Russia to reassert itself in Persia and along the Indian frontier generally during the present summer.

It was only a day or two earlier that Hay had remarked, speaking of the letter which General Miles wrote to the Prohibition Committee which had solicited his aid and advice as to their plan of campaign, that Miles should have completed the sentence of his letter which read: "The country is now confronted by a situation," by adding the words: "and I am confronted by the lack of one."

It was not so very long before, that Hay referred to the United States Senate as his "tribal enemy," and when asked which senator he liked least, quickly responded, "The one I saw last." Lodge of Massachusetts had just left his house.

One of the best anecdotes of John Hay is the one concerning his letter to the President enclosing an editorial from the *New York Evening Post* in praise of Tom Johnson. He referred to this editorial as an illustration of the admiration of a mugwump for a good-for-nothing, and added a striking simile.

ATTORNEY-GENERAL KNOX AND THE ISTHMUS OF PANAMA MATTER

This anecdote, highly amusing in itself, and wholly characteristic of both Theodore Roosevelt and Philander C. Knox, is recalled on reading Pringle's *Life of Roosevelt* which goes fully into the whole history of the Panama matter.

At a Cabinet meeting where this question was being discussed and President Roosevelt was showing more than usual sensitiveness to the public criticisms that were being made of him and his action in respect to the revolution at Panama, the President turned to the Attorney-General and said:

"I think, Mr. Attorney-General, that it will be just as well for you to give us a formal legal opinion sustaining my action in this whole matter."

The Attorney-General looked quizzically at the President and said, with a smile:

"No, Mr. President, if I were you I would not have any taint of legality about it."

Knox himself is my authority for the story.

T. R.'S DEFINITION OF A CONSTITUTIONAL KING

Another characteristic anecdote of Theodore Roosevelt has come back to my recollection after many years. During one of my many visits at the White House, President Roosevelt was receiving a foreigner of some consequence, whose name I do not now recall. The visitor was expressing to the President in rather stilted language his conception of the Presidential office and he ended his discourse by saying: "In my judgment, Mr. President, you have more power than any constitutional king."

An odd smile came over Roosevelt's face and he quickly replied with all his emphasis and gesture: "A constitutional king! Why, a constitutional king is nothing but a combination of the Vice-President and the leader of the Four Hundred."

PREPARING FOR THE 1904 CONVENTION

During a visit with Joseph B. Bishop to the White House, President Roosevelt took up the practical political questions relating to the organization and work of the National Republican Convention, to be held at Chicago in June, at which time he was to be nominated for the Presidency. Various plans were discussed and it was finally decided that it would be best to ask Elihu Root to become temporary chairman of the convention, in order to make a speech that would produce a profound public impression. It was felt that the best person to be permanent chairman of the convention was Speaker Cannon, partly because of his strong personality and the affection in which he was held by the masses of the party, partly because of his influence where the situation was somewhat troubled, and partly because he would supplement Root's speech with an almost equally striking one from another point of view.

The question arose as to whether or not ex-Governor Black of New York should be asked to present Roosevelt's name to the convention. It was agreed that Black would do it very well and that his relations to the party organization in New York State were such as to make his choice a politic one. On the other hand, it was recognized that he was not a cordial friend of the President, and that in his law practice he had associated himself with some men who were, to say the least, political nuisances. The matter was not settled, but the President evidently had a strong leaning toward the selection of Black.

A long time was spent in discussing the chairmanship of the National Committee. The newspaper stories that various persons had been offered the post and had declined were without foundation. The whole matter was open. The names that were most frequently mentioned were those of Senators Aldrich and Penrose, Cornelius N. Bliss of New York and Governor Murphy of New Jersey.

THEODORE ROOSEVELT'S OPINION OF PRESIDENT MONROE

At one time while he was in the White House, T. R. had upon his desk a volume which gave him no little amusement. It contained the speeches and addresses made by

President James Monroe during a tour through the northern and eastern states in 1817 and 1818. Many of these speeches were vacuous indeed and T. R. used to read passages from them aloud to friends and visitors and then shriek with laughter. On one occasion when he had a few of his intimate friends about him, he seized this volume and shouted, "Listen to this!" He then read a few hundred words from one of Monroe's addresses, putting into the reading all the sarcasm and cynicism of which he was capable. He then slammed the book on the table and shouted, "Did you ever hear such stuff? Think of a man who could write that sort of thing not only being President of the United States, but having a Doctrine named after him!"

THEODORE ROOSEVELT AND THE ROMANES LECTURE AT OXFORD

In June, 1910, the ship by which I journeyed to Europe passed somewhere in mid-ocean the ship that was bringing Theodore Roosevelt home from his African and European trip. A few of us conceived the notion of sending him a wireless dispatch made up of quotations from the Bible. We achieved this, and sent it off signed by myself, Ogden Mills, Paul Morton, and one or two more of T. R.'s friends, but no reply was received.

When I reached Oxford a few days later, I found that academic capital echoing with various amusing anecdotes and impressions of Roosevelt's visit. One of the best of them was this:

Roosevelt delivered his Romanes lecture in the Sheldonian Theatre and, at the suggestion of Henry Fairfield Osborn, took as his topic "Some Biological Analogies in History," which he discussed at inordinate length. It was a very journalistic and superficial piece of work, but Oxford received it politely and with deferential attention. As the Vice Chancellor, President Warren of Magdalen College, left the Sheldonian after the lecture, he was joined by the University orator and well-known academic wit, Mr. A. D. Godley. "What did you think of the lecture?" asked the Vice Chancellor of Mr. Godley. "Well," replied the latter, "it would appear that the biological analogies in history are three: Longitude, Latitude, Platitude!"

SENATOR ALBERT J. BEVERIDGE

The personality of Albert J. Beveridge, formerly senator from Indiana, was such that he has become the subject of a number of capital anecdotes.

The first relates to Senator Beveridge's ambition to be temporary chairman of the National Republican Convention of 1904. Some weeks before that convention was to meet I happened in upon President Roosevelt in his office at the White House, and found him in a gale of laughter. He said:

"Sit down and hear the funniest thing that ever happened. I have just had a marvellous interview with Beveridge."

The President then went on to tell the following story:

Senator Beveridge had appeared by appointment, and drawing up his chair close to the President said:

"Mr. President, I have come for your final answer. Am I, or am I not, to be temporary chairman of the Chicago convention?"

The President could not escape a direct reply but fenced a little for time, and said something about the importance of the post, the necessity of striking a key-note that would resound throughout the country and so on. Finally the President said:

"Senator, you know we all have the highest admiration

for you, but after considering this question from every point of view and talking it over with my friends we have come to the conclusion that the best man to be temporary chairman of the convention is Root."

Beveridge stiffened, turned a little pale, and then with great dignity said:

"Whom did you say, Mr. President? Root? Elihu Root! What can he say that the country will listen to? Very well, Mr. President, so be it. I am once more alone." Then rising and striking an attitude in imitation of Senator Beveridge, the President said that this interesting interview ended with this peroration:

"So be it, always alone. Alone on the farm, alone at school, alone at the Bar, alone in the Senate, alone in the party! Good morning, Mr. President." It is no wonder that President Roosevelt was in a gale of laughter.

The second incident occurred on the evening before the marriage of Alice Roosevelt and Nicholas Longworth, which took place at the White House on February 17, 1906. On the evening preceding, John Kean, then Senator from New Jersey, gave a large dinner at his house, followed by a reception, to which pretty much all the wedding guests from New York were invited. Senator Beveridge was there. Shortly before midnight he came to me with very solemn mien and said: "Where are you stopping?"

I replied: "At the Shoreham Hotel." He said: "Please walk home with me, I wish your advice." There was something almost portentous in his manner, but as I was accustomed to this it did not surprise me. We walked away from Senator Kean's house, and it was soon obvious that conversation was very difficult because Beveridge had something very much on his mind. We strolled along in the moonlight almost in silence until we reached the apartment house in which he was then living on Vermont Avenue. We entered in silence and ascended to his apartment. He threw open the door, turned on the lights and waving me to a seat disappeared through some curtains into a room beyond. In a moment or two he returned clad in smoking jacket and slippers, still entirely silent, and strode over to the fire, which he freshened up a bit. Then standing with his back to the fire, and swinging slightly backward and forward on his toes, he gazed at me for some seconds. Then came this remarkable question:

"Butler, shall I take the nomination in 1908 or shall I wait?"

Nobody but Beveridge would have thought of asking that question. Of course, I told him to wait.

Beveridge was an earnest and able public servant. That he did not live to complete his *Life of Lincoln* was a tragic loss both to American history and American letters.

WILLIAM JENNINGS BRYAN

The death of William Jennings Bryan in 1925 brought to mind a few stories of him that are of general interest.

A few months after President Harding took office, I was stopping at the White House for a short visit. On returning to the offices just before luncheon, the President asked me whether it might not be well for him to invite Mr. Bryan to lunch, since he was waiting in the anteroom for an opportunity to pay his respects. My answer was that it would be good fun to have Mr. Bryan at the luncheon table. The President therefore took him to the White House and at the table there were only the President and Mrs. Harding, Mr. Bryan, Doctor Sawyer and myself. The President remarked that Mr. Bryan was looking exceedingly well and must have enjoyed a good summer holiday.

"No holiday at all," responded Mr. Bryan cheerily. "I have been speaking on the Chautauqua Circuit and have addressed probably no fewer than 600,000 of our fellow citizens. And, by the way, Mr. President, I have a new opening for my Chautauqua speeches which always makes a hit. I say, 'Ladies and gentlemen, before he entered the White House, President Harding frequently spoke on the Chautauqua Circuit to great audiences. After he left the White House, President Taft addressed Chautauqua audiences in several states. Now, ladies and gentlemen, if one can go from Chautauqua to the White House, and from the White House to Chautauqua, will you not listen with patience to one who has meandered between the two for twenty-five years!' "

This was the first time that I had ever heard Bryan tell a story on himself, and it seemed to me to indicate that he was growing much more mellow than of yore.

Bryan went on to tell a second story on himself which was equally amusing. He said that he had it from the chairman of the Republican State Committee of Massachusetts in the campaign of 1896. It seems that a Republican county chairman who wished a supply of McKinley buttons for his constituency sent a representative to Boston to procure them at a cost of $10. When inquiry was made of the man who sold the buttons, he replied that there was such a demand for McKinley buttons that the price had gone up to $15, but that he could supply Bryan buttons for $10. The inquirer hesitated a moment and then said thoughtfully: "Well, I have only got $10, so you better give me Bryan buttons. I don't suppose the boys will mind so long as they are buttons!"

The last time I ever saw Bryan was when we met on Pennsylvania Avenue in Washington about six months before his death. Bryan was quite a picturesque figure, since he wore a broad-brimmed hat and a long cape with a metal clasp at his throat. As we approached, he waved his hand and hailed me by name. We stopped for a chat almost in front of the New Willard Hotel. Shaking his finger at me, Bryan said: "Butler, do you know what is the matter with you?"

I answered: "My dear Bryan, there are so many things the matter with me that one or two more will not count. Let me know the worst."

"The matter with you is," he answered, "that you will not take me seriously."

"On that point, my dear Bryan," I replied, "it is impossible for us to get up an argument!"

Still another good Bryan story is this: After Mr. Taft had been nominated for the Presidency in 1908 at Chicago, Mr. Bryan received his third nomination at Denver. The following morning Mr. Taft received a telegram from an ecstatic admirer which read substantially as follows: "Hearty congratulations on your certain election in November. Bryan was nominated for the first time at Chicago, for the second time at Kansas City, and for the third time at Denver. He will be nominated for the fourth time at Salt Lake, for the fifth time at San Francisco, for the sixth time at Honolulu and for the seventh time at Manila, thus getting steadily farther and farther away from the White House."

I always got on very well with Bryan despite our differences on almost every conceivable public question. I first met him during the Presidential campaign of 1888,

when he and I were both on the program to address the
gathering at a county fair in mid-Nebraska. At that time
I was much struck with his method of appealing to a
mixed crowd and by the rather exceptional success with
which he met. We were in violent opposition on monetary
questions and on prohibition, but I never doubted the
man's sincerity.

BOIES PENROSE

Senator Boies Penrose was an exceptionally interesting
person, and a most amusing one as well. Graduated from
Harvard College, *magnâ cum laude* and with honorable
mention in political science, he entered the bar in his
home town of Philadelphia and immediately took a keen
interest in politics. As a student of municipal administration, he was most helpful in securing the reform charter
of the city of Philadelphia, adopted about 1886. It was his
work upon this and allied topics which attracted the attention of President Gilman of Johns Hopkins University,
who invited Penrose to become Lecturer on Municipal
Administration at that institution.

The career which was apparently cut out for him was,
however, rudely changed by the influence of Senator
Quay of Pennsylvania, who seized upon Penrose and
quickly led him into the field of earnestly practical politics. There he flourished for the rest of his life. He was
always a figure of great importance at a state or national
convention of the Republican Party, and he had very
great influence in the Senate of the United States where
he sat from 1897 until his death in 1921.

Shortly after the census of 1910 had been completed, a
bill was introduced into the Senate to effect a reapportion-
ment of members of the House of Representatives as contemplated by the Federal Constitution. This bill went to a

committee of which Penrose was an influential member and there it slept. One day Elihu Root, then a senator from New York, who was much interested in this bill, asked me to use my influence with Penrose—which he believed to be considerable—to have the bill reported and passed. So I went to Washington and talked the matter over with Penrose in his committee room at the Capitol. He listened to what I had to say with amused indifference, and then wound up our discussion with these words: "No, Butler, I won't do it. That bill cuts down the number of Representatives in Congress, which would be a very bad thing, for the more there are of 'em, the easier they are to manage." The bill continued to sleep peacefully.

Penrose, like myself, had been a vigorous opponent of the principles incorporated in the Seventeenth Amendment to the Federal Constitution, which was ratified in 1913 and by the terms of which senators were thereafter to be elected by the people instead of by the state legislatures. I had opposed this amendment for the same reason that I opposed the direct primary, and the results of both have fully justified my opposition.

The term of Penrose expired in 1914 and for the first time his re-election to the Senate depended upon the voters of the State of Pennsylvania as a whole. A few months afterwards I met Penrose in Washington and he said, "Butler, give up fighting the direct primary and the direct election of senators. I thought they were going to be bad, but they are wonderful! In Pennsylvania a grateful people has just sent me back to the Senate by a majority of 250,000 at a time when no Republican legislature would have dared to re-elect me." Nothing could more fully record Penrose's scathing cynicism in all that had to do with politics.

TAXATION WITHOUT REPRESENTATION

Following a reception to James Bryce at the Century Club in New York on the evening of February 14, 1913, there was a very interesting conversation among a group of men on various matters of public interest. The group included Thomas F. Clarke, one of the leading men in the administration of the Western Union Telegraph Company, John G. Milburn of the New York bar and two or three more. Mr. Clarke told us this story.

He said he had recently been to Albany to see the Chairman or President of the New York State Tax Commission in reference to a very large increase in the franchise tax assessment of the Western Union Telegraph Company. He added that the franchise tax assessment of the American Telephone and Telegraph Company had been raised from fifty millions to two hundred and fifty millions. Mr. Clarke asked the President of the State Tax Commission what was the ground for the increase. The answer was: "You fellows don't come across to the organization. I've got no orders." Mr. Clarke's next inquiry was, "Well, how did you raise the assessment so much?" The answer came back quickly, "Young man, I raised it by main force."

WOODROW WILSON AS A CANDIDATE FOR PRESIDENT

Aside from the well-known forecasts made by Colonel George Harvey and others on various occasions in New York and at Washington, probably the first serious discussion of Woodrow Wilson as a candidate for the Democratic Presidential nomination in 1912 began as a result of the following editorial written by St. Clair McKelway for the Brooklyn *Eagle,* of which he was editor, and printed in the issue of November 22, 1908:

HE SHOULD BE FORCED OUT, IF HE WON'T GET OUT!

Mr. Bryan announces that he will lead the Democratic party once again if the party really insists. The party should do nothing of the sort. For the first time since Mr. Bryan cast his blight upon it there is material from which its rehabilitation may be secured. There are Democratic governors-elect in Ohio and Indiana, and John A. Johnson has repeated his performance of 1904, carrying Minnesota as the Democratic nominee for the Governorship, while the Republican Presidential candidate swept the state. The Democracy has had enough of Bryan. It should turn elsewhere.

A few days after this editorial was printed, McKelway received a very cordial letter from Wilson, who had seen the editorial, expressing his high approval of it. In reply to Wilson, McKelway expressed the opinion that Wilson himself was one of those who should be most seriously considered in connection with the Democrat Presidential nomination in 1912. Wilson replied, thanking McKelway very warmly for this suggestion but adding that it was much too early to bring forward the name of any possible candidate for 1912 and that he hoped the matter would be dropped for the present. This was told me by Mc-Kelway himself.

The incidents of which McKelway told me followed obviously those recorded in Wilson's life and letters.[1]

The next step was when, on a cold, wet afternoon early in January, 1910, Wilson went from Princeton to Newark, N. J., and called at the office of former United States Senator James Smith, Jr., who was the most powerful man in the Democrat state organization. He had served one term in the United States Senate and was most desirous to be returned to that body. Wilson, greatly to Smith's

[1] Ray Stannard Baker, *Woodrow Wilson: Life and Letters.* New York: Doubleday, Doran & Co., 1931, Vol. III, pp. 11 ff.

surprise, proceeded to ask that he be supported for the Democrat Presidential nomination in 1912 by the state party organization and gave reasons which seemed to him convincing, based upon his obvious personal fitness for the office and the political conditions which the country was then beginning to face. Smith, who knew Wilson only by name, was not quite sure that his visitor was in his right mind and carried on his part of the conversation very cautiously. When Wilson returned to Princeton after spending an hour with Smith, the latter's reflection was that the visitor was a person suffering from megalomania and not to be taken seriously. Somewhat later James R. Nugent, the leader in the Democrat party organization of Essex County, in which Newark is situated, came in and was given the story of Wilson's visit. Nugent immediately said, "I do not see why that is so bad. That man is very able. Who else is there that is as good as he is? Think what it would mean to our organization and to us if we could nominate and elect a President from the State of New Jersey! I certainly think it ought to be carefully considered." Senator Smith was so much impressed by Nugent's judgment that in a few weeks he sent for Wilson and had another long talk with him during which he sounded out Wilson's political mind, so to speak, and tried to get a closer and more intimate understanding of his personality.

The result was that in April of that year Smith invited seven Democrat national committeemen and other party leaders from mid-western states to meet him in confidential conference at Chicago. When this group assembled, Smith presented the name of Woodrow Wilson as a possible Presidential candidate in 1912 and told his associates what he had learned of Wilson's personality and power. Without exception these men all replied that they knew nothing about Wilson and that the country, outside of college and university circles, knew nothing about him. The party leader in Illinois, Roger Sullivan, added that if Smith really wanted to bring Wilson forward as a candidate, the thing to do was to get him to run for Governor of New Jersey that autumn when, if elected, he would become a figure well known to the nation. Smith went back to New Jersey and proposed this course of action to Wilson, who demurred, saying that the governorship was beneath his dignity as President of Princeton and that he did not wish the office. Nevertheless, Smith, whose interest in this whole undertaking had grown greatly, kept up his pressure. One day in the early summer he had Wilson meet himself, Nugent, Colonel George Harvey and two or three of Wilson's personal friends at Seabright, N. J., and pressed the gubernatorial nomination upon him. Wilson finally agreed to accept the nomination but said frankly that, if elected, they must not be surprised if he at once became an active candidate for the Presidential election two years later. All this was told me by Senator Smith himself and confirmed by Roger Sullivan when he and I had a long talk on the whole subject in California two or three years later.

When chosen Governor of New Jersey, Wilson proceeded to carry out his intention of at once becoming a candidate for the Presidency. This caused him to be absent from the State on a good many occasions and for several days at a time. The result of this was a very amusing episode. The Constitution of the State of New Jersey makes no provision for an Acting Governor but explicitly provides that "in case of the death, resignation or removal from office of the Governor, the powers, duties and emoluments of the office shall devolve upon the President of the Senate." It further provides that "in case of the Gov-

ernor's absence from the State or inability to discharge
the duties of his office, the powers, duties and emoluments
of the office shall devolve upon the President of the Senate." The President of the Senate at that time was John
Dyneley Prince, Professor of East European Languages in
Columbia University, and actively engaged in the politics
of Passaic County, which was his home. The State Comptroller happened to be a very legalistically minded person.
Therefore, each time that Wilson was absent from the
state, the Comptroller took note of that fact and at the
end of the month sent a check for his salary as Governor
to Professor Prince covering the days of Wilson's absence
and deducted a like amount from the check sent to
Wilson. The Democrats insisted that the President of the
Senate was only an Acting Governor, but the Republicans,
supported by the Attorney General, held, on the contrary,
that the President of the Senate was, under these circumstances, to act as Governor and therefore was entitled to
the salary of the office during such time as Governor
Wilson might be absent from the state. One day Professor
Prince came into my office at Columbia University, laughing cheerfully, and handed me the Comptroller's check
drawn to him as John D. Prince, Acting Governor, for an
amount which was the Governor's salary for the number of
days which Wilson had been absent from the state during
that month. Prince asked me what I thought he should do
with the check. I told him it gave him opportunity to be a
great public benefactor. All that was necessary was that
he should endorse the check: "Pay to the order of Woodrow Wilson, John Dyneley Prince, Acting Governor,"
and send it to Wilson with a personal note. This Prince
did about a dozen times during the next few months and
each time he received a most cordial and appreciative
note from Wilson. So the constitutional provision in regard

to a Governor and his possible absence from the state did
no financial harm to Wilson.

There is another incident concerning Woodrow Wilson
which is anything but creditable to his reputation for good
manners. On Saturday, May 11, 1912, John Grier Hibben
was to be inaugurated President of Princeton University
in succession to Wilson, who had resigned the Presidency
when he was elected Governor. It was announced that the
President and the Chief Justice of the United States were
coming to Princeton for this distinguished occasion. The
authorities at Trenton were very anxious to know whether
Governor Wilson would be present in person to meet them
on arrival and to show them the hospitality which was
obviously becoming. Moreover, they wished the Governor's military aides to be at the Princeton station when
the distinguished guests arrived. They were unable, after
making many attempts, to get any information from
Wilson as to whether he proposed to be in Princeton for
this occasion or not. This seemed most extraordinary, for
not only was Wilson the former President of the University
and Hibben his long-time colleague, but as Governor of
New Jersey he was ex-officio Chairman of the Trustees of
Princeton University. In this situation the authorities at
Trenton once more turned to Professor Prince as President of the Senate and he came to ask my advice as to
what, if anything, he could do. My reply was that he
should find out from Wilson what his plans were; that
since Wilson would not answer the officials in Trenton,
the only thing to do was for Prince to call him up by
telephone at the moment, because Wilson certainly could
not fail to respond to the President of the Senate. Prince
did this at once, speaking from my office in Columbia
University to Wilson at his house in Princeton. Wilson's

answer was that he would not be out of the state during the ceremony and, therefore, that Prince would have no authority to take any action whatever in the matter. As a matter of fact, Wilson did go out of the state on Friday evening quite secretly for the reasons which he himself has recorded.[1] All through this splendid ceremony and in spite of the most distinguished visitors who came from Washington, Wilson left the company to suppose that he was sitting all day in his house only a few hundred yards from the scene of the great inaugural festivities.

Of all the instances of bad manners on the part of a public man of which I have knowledge, this action of Wilson's was outstanding. The presumption of every one was that Wilson was unwilling to greet President Taft, who would probably be the Republican nominee for the Presidency in the autumn. Doubtless also, he still harbored the bitter feelings caused by his differences and disputes with other important members of Princeton University during the preceding decade.

WILSON LOSES HIS SECRETARY OF STATE

Bryan as Secretary of State was undisguisedly critical of some of Wilson's acts and words after the Great War of 1914–18 had broken out in Europe. After the sinking of the *Lusitania* on May 7, 1915, Wilson addressed a sharp note to the German Government asking for reparation for this act, so far as reparation might be possible. In reply, the German Government refused to accept responsibility for the act and entered upon a typical legalistic argument which could lead nowhere. Public opinion was very much aroused and when the President came to draft his second note on this subject to the German Gov-

[1]Ray Stannard Baker, *Woodrow Wilson: Life and Letters,* Vol. III, p. 313.

ernment, he made it much stronger than the first, so much so that Bryan thought it might lead to involving us in the war. Therefore, when the second note reached the State Department, Bryan sent it back to the President with a statement that he could not sign it or approve it unless certain changes which he indicated were made. The President declined to accept Bryan's suggestions, whereupon Bryan tendered his resignation from the Cabinet. On the following morning, when the Cabinet assembled at eleven o'clock, the chair of the Secretary of State on the President's right hand was vacant. Wilson followed his usual practice at Cabinet meetings which was not to consult his Cabinet but to tell them what he had been doing and to ask if they themselves had any problems to submit. He stated that he had sent a second *Lusitania* note to the German Government and read it to the Cabinet. He added that the reason why the chair of the Secretary of State was vacant was that Bryan had tendered his resignation. In view of Bryan's faithful service to the government, the President suggested that it would be pleasant to send for him to come over from the State Department and allow the Cabinet members to say good-by to their colleague in person. This course was followed and Bryan presently arrived and heard a very agreeable greeting from the President with words of praise for his public service.

When the group dissolved, the Secretary of War, Lindley M. Garrison, left the executive offices in company with Bryan and they walked together up the street toward Lafayette Square. Garrison asked Bryan why he had resigned and Bryan explained to him the differences between Wilson and himself in respect to the note which had just been sent to the German Government. When Bryan and Garrison reached Lafayette Square, newsboys were crying out an extra edition of the evening newspapers containing the second *Lusitania* note. Bryan and Garrison bought copies of these newspapers and together read the note. Bryan drily remarked to Garrison: "This is very odd! The note as the President has finally drafted it omits or changes the statements to which I most strongly objected." Nevertheless, Bryan was out.

This story was told me by Lindley M. Garrison himself with the condition that I should not make it public during his lifetime. The occasion was when we sat side by side at the dinner tendered to Alfred E. Smith following his first election to the Governorship of New York in 1918. The dinner was held in the Ritz-Carlton Hotel during the month of November of that year.

This is a very different story from that told with much detail elsewhere.[1] Nevertheless, I record it precisely as Garrison told it to me. It does not differ much, however, from Bryan's own story of the incident[2] or from that recorded by Wilson himself.[3]

WILSON DURING THE GREAT WAR

At a dinner in New York during the winter of 1925–26, the talk turned largely on matters suggested by *The Intimate Papers of Colonel House,* recently published, and two very striking anecdotes were told.

The first related to a conversation which President Wilson had had early in 1917 when the submarine warfare was under vigorous discussion between the Government of the United States and the Imperial German

[1] J. C. Long, *Bryan: The Great Commoner.* New York: D. Appleton & Company, 1928, pp. 337–342.

[2] *Memoirs of William Jennings Bryan by Himself and His Wife.* Chicago: the United Publishers of America, 1925, pp. 406–414.

[3] Ray Stannard Baker, *Woodrow Wilson: Life and Letters.* New York: Doubleday, Doran & Company, 1935, Vol. V, pp. 357 ff.

Government. During the course of this conversation President Wilson plainly showed that he had developed a new and very bitter antagonism to the German Government because of the fact that in debate in the Reichstag he had been ridiculed and made fun of on account of some of his spoken and written words. It was, we were told, perfectly characteristic of Wilson's vanity that these occurrences in the Reichstag should stir him much more deeply than had those happenings on sea and land that had made so great an impression upon the American people generally. It was suggested that there could be no doubt that Wilson was finally brought to the point of dismissing Bernstorff and looking forward to participation in the war because of his resentment at the facts just stated.

The second anecdote was even more striking. This was that in the month of May, 1917, when the English and French envoys reached the United States and the exact situation as to the military conflict and resources of the combatants was disclosed, Wilson became so much alarmed at what he considered the relative impotence of the Allies and the relative power of Germany that he deliberated as to how the United States could withdraw from farther participation in the war despite the declaration of April 6, 1917. Of course he could not withdraw, but it seemed a most astounding fact that he should even have contemplated such a course.

At the Lotos Club dinner in his honor on Thursday, November 1, 1923, Mr. Lloyd George told me two amusing anecdotes of Woodrow Wilson. I inquired whether he had seen Wilson while in Washington and how he had found him. He said that he had spent an hour or more with him and that his physical condition was very bad indeed. He described Wilson as slipping down in his chair toward the left side through sheer helplessness and only righting himself from time to time with some difficulty. Lloyd George added that Wilson's mind, while doubtless not capable of any sustained effort, was in fine working order for ordinary conversation and repartee. He gave these two illustrations:

The name of Poincaré was mentioned and Wilson promptly said: "When we were in Paris I found that Poincaré was a liar and a sneak and I observe that he has not changed a particle."

Lloyd George asked Wilson his opinion of President Coolidge, and Wilson said that he would reply by citing an anecdote of Oscar Wilde, who, when approached by some one for whom he did not care, adjusted his monocle and staring blandly at the visitor asked: "Are you any one in particular?"

WILSON AND THE SUPREME COURT

When, on January 28, 1916, President Wilson nominated Louis D. Brandeis of Boston to be an Associate Justice of the Supreme Court of the United States, there was furious criticism and opposition to the confirmation of this appointment from many members of the bench and bar.

All this recalled an experience which I had early in life with Woodrow Wilson which, though it did not seem very important then, has grown in significance as the years passed. In 1887 President Cleveland nominated L. Q. C. Lamar of Mississippi, at that time Secretary of the Interior, to be an Associate Justice of the Supreme Court to fill an existing vacancy. Mr. Lamar's personality and character were held in high esteem everywhere, but his nomination to be a member of the Supreme Court was severely criticized on the ground that he had never had previous judicial experience and for more than thirty years had been engaged in active political life and therefore away even from practice at the bar. Shortly after this nomination was made, Woodrow Wilson and I, who were delivering some lectures at Johns Hopkins University and were living together at the University Club, were guests for dinner at the house of President Gilman. The dinner was in honor of Andrew D. White, Mr. Gilman's classmate at Yale, who had just returned from one of his periods of diplomatic service in Europe. After dinner the conversation turned on Mr. Lamar's appointment, and, among others, Andrew D. White expressed grave doubt as to the wisdom of appointing to the Supreme Court a man who, however talented or high-minded, was without judicial experience, and who had been long removed from active practice at the bar. Among those present there was general agreement with this judgment until finally Wilson spoke and expressed with emphasis and precision of language a directly contrary view. He said that men like Mr. Lamar were just what the Supreme Court most needed; that it was high time to appoint to that Court men who had had no judicial experience and who were out of touch with the active practice of the bar; and that he hoped the time would come when some President would be willing to appoint to the Court a man who was not even a lawyer, but who had a large and comprehensive grasp of American political and social principles and problems.

In the light of some of Wilson's words and acts later in life, this extraordinary expression of opinion made thirty years earlier takes on exceptional interest.

WILSON AND THE PANAMA CANAL

Another incident is this: The Round Table Dining Club of New York, of which club Mr. Wilson was a member, asked him to make a special effort to attend one of

the monthly dinners given between the date of his election
to the Presidency in November, 1912, and that of his
inauguration on March 4 following. Mr. Wilson chose
either the January or February dinner and on that evening the members of the Round Table assembled almost in
their full strength to greet their fellow member who had
been chosen President of the United States. After dinner
the conversation naturally turned on politics, and Elihu
Root and Joseph H. Choate seized the opportunity to
discuss with Mr. Wilson the whole question of the Panama
Canal tolls and the impolicy of excepting from payment
of tolls American coastwise shipping. Mr. Wilson listened
attentively, and I remember his saying when the Hay-
Pauncefote Treaty was mentioned that he had never read
it. Mr. Root and Mr. Choate were unusually earnest and
cogent, and at the end of the conversation Mr. Wilson
said, "I think now that I understand the matter and you
can depend upon me to do the right thing when the
time comes." I am confident that it was at this dinner
and through the influence of Mr. Root and Mr. Choate
that Mr. Wilson was given his first understanding of the
meaning of the Panama Canal tolls controversy, and that
his correct and successful attitude in the matter found
its origin in that particular discussion.

CHIEF JUSTICE WHITE AND WILSON

Here is a very amusing and illuminating anecdote of
Chief Justice White.

About the middle of the month of April, 1913, I was in
Washington for the annual meeting of the Trustees of
the Carnegie Endowment for International Peace. As was
my habit in those days, I stopped in the morning at the
office of Mr. Charles G. Glover, President of the Riggs

National Bank, for a chat with him and whoever might happen to be with him at the time. On this particular occasion Chief Justice White was in Mr. Glover's office and we all talked together for a few moments. Suddenly the Chief Justice turned to me and said, "Where are you going from here?"

I replied: "I am going to number 2 Jackson Place for our Carnegie Endowment meeting which is scheduled for half-past ten."

The Chief Justice replied, "Let me walk around the Square with you, as I have plenty of time this morning."

Thereupon we strolled together around Jackson Square, during which time this conversation took place:

Pointing with his thumb to the White House, the Chief Justice said, "How well do you know that man over there?" meaning, of course, President Wilson.

Laughingly I answered, "That is a strange question for a great Democrat to ask of a mere Republican."

The Chief Justice said, "I want to know, because I had an experience with him the other day which is unlike anything that has ever happened to me before."

"What was it?" I asked.

The Chief Justice then told the following story:

A few days after the inauguration of President Wilson, as the Chief Justice was leaving the Capitol after the adjournment of the Court's session for the day he met one of his former constituents from Louisiana who with his wife and daughter had been in attendance upon the inauguration functions. They all greeted the Chief Justice who asked what he could do to make their stay in Washington pleasant. The man and his wife immediately stated that everything was going nicely and that they did not want to trouble the Chief Justice in the least. The Chief Justice observed, however, that the little girl, aged twelve or thirteen perhaps, was tugging at her mother's skirts and trying to attract her attention, so the Chief Justice bent over to her and said, "What is it, little girl? You want something. What can I do for you?"

The child whispered to her mother who tried to persuade her to desist and refrain from asking any favor of the Chief Justice. The latter persisted, however, and finally the little girl confessed that her great ambition was to shake hands with the President of the United States. Her father and mother immediately said that no such thing was possible and must not be attempted, but the Chief Justice broke in with "Come here tomorrow at half-past four and I shall arrange to take you to the White House and present you all to the President who will, I am sure, shake hands with this little girl."

So on the following day they waited for the Chief Justice as he was ready to leave the Capitol, and he took them all to the White House where he had made an appointment for them with the President's secretary. The party was ushered into the President's room and Mr. Wilson rose from his desk and bowed gravely, but in silence. The Chief Justice, with the natural exuberance of his nature, told of the visit of his constituents and of the ambition of this little girl to shake hands with the President of the United States. Again the President smiled and bowed gravely, with his hands behind his back, and said not a word. In one form or another this was repeated for a very few minutes, when the Chief Justice was obliged to retreat with his constituents and without the little girl having had the ambition of a lifetime fulfilled.

So the Chief Justice said with some insistence, "What kind of a man is he anyhow? How well do you know him?"

JOHN SHARP WILLIAMS AND DAVID JAYNE HILL

A most amusing incident took place at the annual meeting of the Trustees of the Carnegie Endowment, held at Washington in April of 1921.

David Jayne Hill was making some remarks about the general international situation and while urging strongly policies that would make for international peace, he vigorously criticized the existing League of Nations and, in particular, insisted that the Government of the United States should have nothing whatever to do with the League. John Sharp Williams, who was then Senator from Mississippi, sat listening to Doctor Hill, his hand at his right ear and a most innocent and childlike look upon his face. When Doctor Hill had finished, Senator Williams got up and in his own peculiar manner, with his inimitable drawl, said substantially this:

"I have listened with great interest to Doctor Hill's speech in favor of peace and against the League of Nations. What he has said reminds me of a story told of General Jubal Early at the second battle of Bull Run. As the battle was about to begin and General Early was riding up toward the lines, he passed a chaplain making for the rear as rapidly as possible. General Early stopped and said to the chaplain: 'Where are you going?'

"The chaplain replied, 'I am going back where it is safer.'

" 'Turn around and go back to the front,' said General Early. 'Aren't you ashamed of yourself? For years you have been praying for a chance to see Almighty God face to face and here at the first chance you really get, I find you running away.' "

Senator Williams sat down and the trustees roared with laughter.

COLONEL HOUSE'S ATTEMPT AT PEACE MAKING, 1916

During the months of March and April, 1916, Colonel House, having returned from Europe, entered upon a series of confidential negotiations with leaders of public opinion in the United States in the hope that he might secure agreement upon a policy which he had already presented to the English and French and German governments that would bring the Great War to an end. This policy was based upon an International Conference of the warring powers to be called by the President of the United States and presided over by him.

One morning I received a very mysterious and confidential message from Colonel House asking me to come to his apartment in East Fifty-third Street for luncheon at one o'clock, but to say nothing about this invitation and to let no one know or see that I was going to his apartment. I therefore made the trip downtown on a Fifth Avenue omnibus, alighting at the Cathedral at the corner of Fifth Avenue and Fiftieth Street. I then walked nonchalantly and apparently uninterested in anything that was going on about me to the house in which was Colonel House's apartment. As I passed eastward on East Fifty-third Street, I noticed, to my great surprise, Elihu Root coming west on the same street. He evidently was as anxious to avoid observation as was I. Therefore, I merely pointed with my finger to the entrance of the building in which Colonel House lived, and Root nodded. We then joined each other and without exchanging a word went into the elevator and said to the operator "Colonel House." We were greeted by the Colonel with great cordiality and taken to luncheon with him alone. When the luncheon was over, the Colonel dismissed his servant, rose from the table and locked the door of the dining room and then, drawing very close to Root and myself, proceeded to out-line his plan for bringing the war to a quick end. He told us what measure of progress he had made with leading Democrats and that it was his hope that Root and I would be willing to present the matter confidentially to those in positions of importance in the Republican party or-ganization so that, if possible, whatever proposal should be made would have the unanimous support of both parties and therefore presumably of the American people.

The plan seemed to us quite chimerical but we listened very respectfully, asked one or two questions and at the end of an hour withdrew together, saying that we would think the matter over.

When Root and I reached the sidewalk, we started to walk westward and neither of us said a word for some time. We crossed Park Avenue and we crossed Madison Avenue and had nearly reached Fifth Avenue, where we were to separate, when Root stopped and said, with fire in his eye, "What a damn fool that man is!" There the matter ended.

ELIHU ROOT AND THE REPUBLICAN NATIONAL CONVENTION OF 1916

The following letter is self-explanatory, dealing, as it does, with some important and hitherto unrecorded in-cidents of the Republican National Convention of 1916. The occasion for the letter was the fact that because of a necessary and immediate operation upon my right eye, I was compelled to withdraw the invitations that had been issued for a dinner at my house in honor of Elihu Root's eightieth birthday. It was written to George Wick-ersham on February 13, 1925.

None of you can imagine my disappointment and sorrow at not being able to assemble, at my own table, in honor of Elihu Root's eightieth anniversary, the surviving members of the group that was gathered five years ago together with that company of friends now added to them. Of those who were with us at the seventy-fifth birthday dinner, Charles R. Miller of the *Times* and Charles Dyer Norton have closed the door behind them for the last time, Pritchett is in distant Santa Barbara, Jim Sheffield is representing the government in Mexico, and Dwight Morrow is recuperating from an illness at Nassau. Every one else is present or accounted for including my unhappy self. The operation on my right eye has been brilliantly successful, but it required four or five days of subsequent darkness in order that the good effects may be permanent.

It rejoices me greatly that the Round Table has been graciously moved to see to it that this anniversary gathering should not fail, and I thank them warmly for this thoughtful act. Elihu Root has many striking capabilities, but not even he can celebrate his eightieth birthday twice. He and I have made a compact that these gatherings are to go on every five years hereafter so long as we are both going under our own steam.

Had I been able to be with you I should have taken this opportunity to tell you all, in confidence, some unwritten history regarding the Republican National Convention of 1916. I was never given a prouder or more grateful task than that of presenting to that convention the name of Elihu Root to be its nominee for the Presidency of the United States. Had there been at that time no division of sentiment in the New York delegation, the whole history of the United States and of the world for the past nine years might have been wholly different.

Barnes and Hilles worked like Trojans, and all through that long night of Friday, following adjournment after two ballots had been taken, I, together with others, labored unceasingly to build up a block of votes sufficient to nominate Root on Saturday morning. Murray Crane was entirely willing to come to the support of Root provided that Theodore Roosevelt would agree not to oppose him. Charlie Warren, however, who is now having difficulty getting himself confirmed to be Attorney General, was obdurate, and so was Reed Smoot, who ought to have known better. About 4:30 on Saturday morning I had my last conference with Boies Penrose and pled with him to release thirty of the thirty-seven delegates from Pennsylvania that he controlled, which would have been sufficient for our purpose. He would not yield an inch but clung to the foolish notion that he could nominate Jim Watson. Shortly before five o'clock on that morning, at the instigation of George Perkins, I talked for thirty minutes with Theodore Roosevelt at Oyster Bay, over a private wire installed in a closet in the room occupied by Perkins in the Blackstone Hotel.

Roosevelt, whose ambition led him to cling to the hope that he might yet be nominated, began by asking me how many votes there were in the convention that could possibly be had for himself. He expressed surprise and disappointment when I told him that the maximum number was between seventy-five and eighty-five, and that if he did get enough to be nominated he would be overwhelmingly defeated by Wilson. He then suggested all sorts of grotesque alternatives, each one more ridiculous than the other, finally settling on Lodge. He would not, however, under any circumstances accept Root, and the jig was up. When I recalled an excited conference at Oyster Bay in September, 1898, attended by Roosevelt, Root, Frederick William Holls, Albert Shaw and myself, at which time Roosevelt's eligibility to run for Governor of New York was only saved by Root's legal acumen, my blood certainly boiled.

I knew perfectly well that the ticket about to be nominated could not possibly be elected, because it could not carry Ohio, and Hiram Johnson and Borah would see to it that it carried neither California nor Idaho. Root would have carried all the states that the Republican ticket carried in that year, and probably six others as well. He would have conducted an entirely different kind of campaign and one on a far higher plane. He would have roused the moral sense of the American people to a full appreciation of the stupendous issues involved in the War and would have allowed the so-called German vote to do whatever it pleased. In such a campaign the German vote would have been a handicap and not an advantage to whosoever made successful appeal to it.

If the Republican Party had had, at that time, enough politicians in places of prominence who knew anything that was real about politics, Wilson would not have been re-elected, our relation to the War would have been entirely different, the form and results of the peace would have been wholly altered, and long before this we should have had both a well-established International

Court with full American support, together with agreed policies for economic, social and political reconstruction following the War, that would have commanded the substantially unanimous assent of the American people. The election of 1920 indicates with emphatic clearness, only in lesser degree, the sort of thing that might have happened in 1916, had full advantage been taken of the opportunity which the personality and policies of Wilson presented.

I have no apologies to make for my part in that struggle, and I have no intention of glossing over what I know personally to have been the facts.

I should like to have said this, with my own lips, in Root's presence to a group of Root's personal friends, as my contribution to the *intimité* of a gathering which, I well know, will never be forgotten by any one of those so fortunate as to be present in person. I can only attend in spirit.

Please give Root my affectionate regards, and to every member of the assembled company my warmest personal greetings.

INDIANA IN THE NATIONAL ELECTION OF 1916

The work of the Republican National Convention of 1916 left me distinctly discouraged. Nevertheless—and probably foolishly—I spent the weeks from early July until early September in campaigning for the Republican ticket in the states of Colorado, Wyoming, Utah, Idaho, Nevada, California, Oregon, Washington, Montana, North Dakota and Minnesota. Early in September I was summoned to a conference in Chicago with the Chairman of the Republican National Committee and a group of his associates and advisers. They asked for an expression of my opinion as to the results at the coming election in the states which I had visited. I told them that to the best of my knowledge and belief the Democrats would carry every state west of the Missouri River with the possible exception of Oregon. I reported that my audiences had been large, attentive and respectful, but that in my judgment they were not in any wise convinced by my arguments. The Chairman and his advisers expressed the opinion that I was a person of very poor judgment and that I did not know what I was talking about. Perhaps after Election Day they may have changed their opinion, for the returns from the states west of the Missouri River were precisely those which I had predicted in September with the exception of South Dakota.

There was present at this conference Will H. Hays, then Chairman of the Republican State Committee in Indiana. He took me aside and asked whether I would not give one more week to the campaign and spend it in the State of Indiana. I demurred for two reasons: first, because I had been away more than two months and there was much work waiting for me at home; and, second, because I was strongly opposed to the Adamson Law which had just been passed by the Congress and was already a matter of excited debate throughout the country. Hays replied that he had supposed that that would be my feeling about the Adamson Law and added that he had thought the matter all over and not only would be quite willing to have me attack it in Indiana, but would arrange for noonday meetings at various railway towns so that I could do so before audiences of railway workers at the noon hour. "Go at it as hard as you like," he added.

The Adamson Law was Chapter 436 of the laws passed by the Sixty-fourth Congress and was approved September 5, 1916. Its title was "An Act to establish an eight-hour day for employees of carriers engaged in interstate and foreign commerce, *and for other purposes.*" It was my intention to emphasize the words "and for other purposes" and to insist that those purposes were purely partisan and political. I objected both on principle and in the public interest to any such hard and fast control, nation-wide in character, of any part of our industrial system. My itinerary for the following week included Lafayette, Crawfordsville, Terre Haute, Columbus and Valparaiso, as well as the crossing of Brown County which proudly boasted that, having not a mile of railway within its borders, it had no interest in this discussion! At each of these towns several hundred railway workers listened to my argument and, while doubtless their reactions were varied, nevertheless they were quiet and attentive. My evening speeches in those same towns before general audiences dealt with the various outstanding issues of the campaign.

The significant thing about this experience is that when the election returns from the State of Indiana were received in November, it was found that that state had cast its electoral vote for the Republican candidate for President and had elected a Republican governor, two Republican United States senators and that out of thirteen representatives in Congress nine of those chosen were Republicans. In Ohio, separated from Indiana only by an imaginary line, where the party organization and the candidates had either supported the Adamson Law or had passed it over in silence, the Democrats gained the electoral vote and also chose the governor, a United States senator and a large majority of the congressmen. Had Ohio voted as did Indiana, the result of that national election would have been wholly different. Woodrow Wilson would have been defeated for re-election.

Perhaps the Adamson Law had something to do with it.

HARDING AND HIS NEWSPAPER

During a conversation a few years ago about our political reminiscences, William Allen White told me this very interesting story of President Harding. After Harding had been nearly two years in the White House, he invited White to call and see him. White naturally expected a conversation on current political questions, perhaps one of exceptional interest and importance. To his great surprise, Harding never mentioned politics at all throughout the conversation, which lasted nearly an hour. Instead, he plunged into a discussion of newspaper costs and problems. He asked White what price he paid for printing paper in Kansas and then compared the sum stated with what he had to pay at Marion, Ohio. Other questions were as to wages paid to various employees on White's newspaper. He passed on to a discussion of matters relating to advertising and circulation, but never a word about politics. Finally, he ended the conversation by saying, "You see, White, that what really interests me is my newspaper. There is nothing in this job here. As a matter of fact, I go to press at the White House every afternoon at three o'clock."

HOW AN AMBASSADOR MAY BE APPOINTED

Following the election of McKinley in 1896, Frederick W. Holls, Theodore Roosevelt, Albert Shaw and I were very keen to have Andrew D. White appointed first Ambassador to Berlin. His knowledge of the German people and his powerful personality had made a great impression in that country when he had served as Minister to Berlin twenty-five years earlier. It was decided that I should make the trip to Canton and present this matter to the President-elect. After a very agreeable luncheon with McKinley, we sat down in his library to discuss both policies and possible appointments. At an appropriate time I presented the urgent request of our group for the appointment of Andrew D. White as Ambassador to Berlin and dwelt with emphasis and at some length upon his outstanding qualifications. McKinley listened most attentively and then said, "I agree entirely with all that you say about Doctor White. He is a very able man and would be an excellent appointment. Unfortunately, however, I have promised that embassy to Boies Penrose, who has just been elected as Senator from Pennsylvania, for some friend of his. I do not now recall the man's name." At this I protested with some vigor and begged McKinley not to make an unsuitable appointment simply because Penrose wanted it. Of course, at the moment, neither McKinley nor I knew who it was that Penrose had in mind. Finally, McKinley said, "You know Penrose very well; why don't you go to him and see if you can't make an arrangement that his man will take some other diplomatic post, in which case I shall be glad to send Doctor White to Berlin."

Greatly encouraged by this, I went off to Philadelphia and presented the matter to Penrose. I began by extolling Doctor White, but Penrose cut me short with, "Oh, I know all about him, but I have a first-rate man and McKinley has promised to appoint him. He is a friend of mine and raised $50,000 for my campaign fund. He wants this place and he has got to have it." Considerable discussion followed in the course of which I ventured to bring forward McKinley's own suggestion that in order to make way for the appointment of Doctor White to Berlin, Penrose's man should take another diplomatic post. At first Penrose was opposed to making any such concession but after a long talk he said that he thought perhaps his man would be glad to go as Minister to Austria. Within thirty minutes I had wired this statement to McKinley, and in due time Doctor White was sent to Berlin as Ambassador and Penrose's friend, who was Charlemagne Tower, went as Minister to Austria. As fortune would have it, his service in that post was followed by appointment as Ambassador to Russia and later as Ambassador to Berlin, so that ultimately he arrived at the destination which Penrose had selected for him originally. Tower did extraordinarily well in all three of these posts and in Berlin was on particularly cordial terms with the Kaiser.

HOW A UNITED STATES JUDGE MAY BE APPOINTED

About a year after Harding assumed the Presidency in March, 1921, there was a vacancy in the United States District Court for the district in which the State of Georgia was included. The Republican organization in that state brought forward two or three names for appointment to the vacant judgeship and urged prompt action on the part of the President. When I reached Augusta on my usual winter holiday in the month of March, 1922, a number of the leading lawyers and other citizens of that city came to me to protest most vigorously against the appointment of any of those persons whom the Republican state organization was pressing upon the President. They gave at some length their reasons for taking this attitude and strongly urged that the place be given to William H. Barrett, a leading member of the Georgia bar and member of a well-known Georgia family, whose character and ability were most excellent.

The situation, as it later developed, seemed sufficiently critical to make a special trip to Washington advisable in order to take up the matter in person with Harding. He, as one of our group of "Little Mothers," was perfectly familiar with Augusta and with Mr. Barrett. So, when I presented the case in some detail, he was already more than usually well informed regarding the man's qualifications. He listened very patiently to what I had to say and then remarked: "Yes, I know Mr. Barrett.

He is an excellent man. Telegraph him your congratulations on his appointment." That was all there was of that.

Judge Barrett has made a most admirable judicial officer and is still fortunately in the public service.

HOW A JUSTICE OF THE SUPREME COURT MAY BE NOT APPOINTED

At about the same time that the appointment of a United States District Judge for Georgia was under consideration, Harding was confronted with the necessity of choosing a new justice of the United States Supreme Court. The person most actively urged upon the President was then a member of the United States Circuit Court for the Second Judicial District. Among his supporters were a number of very influential political leaders as well as prominent Catholics who thought it becoming that since there was no Catholic upon the United States Supreme Court, their candidate, himself a Catholic, should now be advanced to that distinguished post of service. The pressure upon the President was very great and it was more or less assumed that the appointment would shortly be made.

While this was going on I was asked by Elihu Root, John G. Milburn and George W. Wickersham, all intimate friends of mine, to have luncheon with them at the Downtown Club of New York. In no restrained language they gave me their opinion of the proposed appointment and said that no stone must be left unturned to prevent it. The matter was one of which I myself had no personal knowledge whatsoever, but concerning it the opinion of Root, Milburn and Wickersham would be all-controlling with me. They asked me, since I was on intimate terms with the President, to go to him in person and protest against the appointment. This I did at once. Harding was about ready to make the appointment, having been greatly impressed by the candidate's vigorous and influential support. He laid stress upon the importance of not offending or disappointing the Catholics, many of whom were taking active part in the campaign for this candidate. I pressed upon Harding the opinions which Root, Milburn and Wickersham had given and quoted much of their language to him. In fact, I said that in view of what these three men felt, the proposed appointment simply could not be made. He returned to the question of the candidate's religious faith. My answer was that that matter could easily be dealt with by seeking an outstanding member of the bar or judge who was a Catholic from some other part of the country. This Harding did, and Pierce Butler of Minnesota, whose name was suggested by Chief Justice Taft, was his choice for the vacancy on the United States Supreme Court.

The name of the other judge was Manton.

MRS. HARDING AND "THOSE COOLIDGES"

During one of the many visits which my wife and I made to the White House, we were talking one evening after dinner with Mrs. Harding, the President having been called to a conference in another room. We both remarked upon what we thought the admirable and generous proposal of Mrs. John B. Henderson, widow of the former United States Senator from Missouri—the change of whose vote from Nay to Aye would have resulted in the impeachment of Andrew Johnson in 1868—to present her fine house and grounds on Sixteenth Street to the Government as an official residence for the Vice-President of the United States. We gave it as our opinion that this would offer a most satisfactory solution of what had long been a difficult question and that the Vice-President in such a stately residence could relieve the President of very many of his social and public obligations and receptions. A bill had been introduced into the Congress to accept this gift and to make an appropriation for the upkeep of the house and grounds which the Government was to receive. Both my wife and I expressed high approval of all this and our hope that the bill would quickly become a law. Mrs. Harding, who had been growing obviously impatient while we were discussing the matter, burst into flame and almost shouted, "Not a bit of it, not a bit of it. I am going to have that bill defeated. Do you think I am going to have those Coolidges living in a house like that? An hotel apartment is plenty good enough for them."

The bill was defeated and in one year "those Coolidges" were living in the White House itself.

CALVIN COOLIDGE

Late in the spring of 1924, after almost all the delegates had been elected to the National Convention soon to meet at Cleveland, Ohio, I was stopping at the White House for a visit of several days. One evening after dinner, sitting in the library with President Coolidge, Mrs. Coolidge, William M. Butler of Massachusetts, who was shortly to become Chairman of the Republican National Committee, and Coolidge's friends, Mr. and Mrs. Stearns of Boston, during a lull in the conversation I casually remarked that I had taken a great interest in the controversy which had been raging for some months in the public press between the Fundamentalists and the Modernists. "Have you," said Coolidge with his peculiar accent, "how is that?" "Well," I said, "Mr. President, I began as a Modernist, but something that has happened has converted me to Fundamentalism and now I am as strong as a rock for that doctrine." "Why?" said Coolidge curiously. "Because, Mr. President," I replied, "only an all-wise and all-powerful God could have reached out and got Gifford Pinchot, Medill McCormick and Hiram Johnson at one fell swoop!" The rest of the company laughed loudly, but the President's face never changed. When the mirth subsided the President said drily, "Seems to me this is a partiz-an gathering!"

In 1924 or 1925 when there was a vacancy in the United States Supreme Court, Coolidge asked me whether I had any one in mind to suggest for the vacancy. My answer was that I thought it desirable that the appointment should be made from New York. That state, I pointed out, because of its size, its enormous contribution to the support of the Government through taxation and its very distinguished bench and bar, seemed entitled to consideration. This was particularly the case as there had been no justice appointed from New York since Peckham died a quarter of a century earlier other than Justice Hughes, who resigned to accept the Presidential nomination in 1916. We talked over this matter in many of its phases and finally, when the President returned to his request for specific suggestions, I told him that it seemed to me that there were three men specially worthy of consideration. One was William D. Guthrie, who had had a long and distinguished career at the bar and who was very ambitious for high judicial office. The objections in his case would seem to be, first, his age which was getting on toward seventy, and, second, his ultra-legalistic mind which made him approach new and strange problems with stiff inflexibility. Another was Benjamin Nathan Cardozo, by far the ablest legal mind of which I had any knowledge and an absolutely ideal judge. The third was his own college classmate and then his attorney general,

Harlan F. Stone, whom he knew all about. Coolidge reflected a minute or two and said he thought that Guthrie was too old, and that he could not appoint Cardozo despite his merits because there was already one Jew upon the Court and the appointment of another would excite criticism. The matter was dropped without further comment on the President's part. Shortly afterward he appointed Stone to the Court.

There are two other stories of Coolidge which show his lighter side.

In one of our many evening conversations at the White House when serious matters were put aside for a time, the President, looking at the group with a smile, said: "Mr. President of Columbia University, how many of the hundreds of professors in your University do you know personally or could you recognize?" "A great many more, Mr. President of the United States," I replied, "than you know or can recognize of the generals and admirals of the Army and Navy of which you are Commander-in-Chief." All of us, including Coolidge, had a good laugh.

As his term of office was approaching its end, President Coolidge did what was very unusual for him and made an appointment for ten o'clock Sunday morning to see a very important visitor from New York who was pressing for an audience. This man went down to Washington by the midnight train, taking only a handbag and just what was necessary for the journey and for one night in Washington. He appeared at the White House promptly at ten o'clock and his conversation with the President extended over half an hour. The President then looked at his watch and said, in his own inimitable manner, "I am going to church. I shall be glad to have you come with me." The visitor, quite overcome by this very personal invitation, said, "But, Mr. President, I am so sorry—I should have loved to accept this very distinguished invitation and accompany you to church, but I just came down for the night and did not even bring a black coat with me." "In my church," responded the President gravely, "we do not draw any color line."

RELIGIOUS BIGOTRY IN POLITICS

After dinner at my house on the evening of November 11, 1929, Claude G. Bowers, afterwards Ambassador to Spain, told an amusing anecdote of the Presidential campaign of 1928, which illustrated admirably the condition of mind at that time of no small part of the American people.

As the Presidential campaign progressed the religious issue was forced, particularly in the South and Southwest, with something approaching ferocity. In Oklahoma conditions were particularly serious for the Democrat Party and the Democrat candidate by reason of this issue. The authority of the Ku Klux Klan in that section was very great, and it was vigorously exerted to light and to keep burning the fires of religious discord and hate.

The Democrat managers determined to try to meet the situation by sending into that state a woman speaker, whose name was well-known and who, it was thought, would have influence among those women, naturally Democrats, who were being turned against their party's candidate by reason of the religious feeling that had been aroused. For this difficult and perhaps embarrassing task, the Democrat National Committee selected an able and thoroughly competent woman. It was arranged that she should visit Oklahoma and address a mass meeting. The town named was one of which she had never heard and was apparently very small. She concluded, however, that it was a center of a considerable farming population and that a meeting of reasonable size might be anticipated.

On the evening of the day fixed for the meeting her train arrived at the station of this little town shortly after dark. When she alighted on the platform no human being was in sight. The conductor urged her to return to the train and go on to the next station, where a reasonably comfortable hotel would be found. She declined, however, saying that this was the station fixed for her meeting, and that she was to be met there by a committee.

The visitor then entered the station which was deserted, and sat for a time in the dark waiting-room. After some minutes an old man appeared bearing a searchlight lamp, which he thrust into her face. "I am the woman who is to speak here tonight," she replied, "and I have come here for a political meeting. I am waiting for a committee to meet me." "There ain't goin' to be no meetin'," said the man brusquely, "and ain't no committee comin'. I am goin' to lock up here now and you better come and spend the night with me and the old woman because there ain't no hotel round about here." Not a little dazed by the situation, the visitor went with the old man because there was nothing else to do. When they arrived at his house the old woman, as the man called his wife, had gone to bed. The visitor was shown to her room and she passed a perplexed and not very comfortable night. In the morning on coming down to breakfast the old woman was already at table. Looking sharply at the visitor, she said: "So you be the woman speaker, be you?" The visitor replied politely that she was, "and you're for Smith, are you?" "Yes," was the answer. "Well, I ain't," snapped the old woman. "Perhaps if you would let me talk to you," said the visitor, "I might change your mind." "No, you couldn't," snapped the old woman. "Smith's one of them Catholics and they brought in sprinklin'."

Plainly the old woman was an ardent Baptist, and would have nothing to do with any one who was identified with "sprinklin'."

It would be hard to surpass this anecdote in its evidence of a state of mind which in the United States of the twentieth century is amazingly common.

No better political story has come to my attention in recent years than one which my good friend Al Smith himself told a group of friends shortly after the Presidential election of 1928.

After that election was over the Governor spent some time in Florida on a holiday trip. On his way north he stopped at Savannah, where the Mayor tendered him every courtesy and hospitality, including the pleasure of meeting a distinguished company at dinner. On the Governor's right sat one of the grand dames of Georgia, who made no attempt to conceal her admiration for the Governor and for his political course of action. She showered him with compliments and said that of course she had voted for him in November. "But," she added, looking across the table a bit mischievously, "that lady opposite did not vote for you." "Indeed," said the Governor, raising his eyebrows, "I hope that I did not do anything to displease her." "O! I think not," said the other, "but she can tell you about it herself after dinner."

After the company had left the table the lady who had sat at the Governor's right introduced to him the lady who had sat opposite, adding, with a twinkle in her eye, "this is the one who did not vote for you." "That, of course, was your right," said the Governor, bowing politely to the second lady, "but I am sorry that I did or said anything which you did not like." "O! no, Governor," was the response, "it was nothing like that. I admire you more than any man in public life, and I approve entirely of all your policies, but I could not vote for you." "Would you mind telling me why not?" asked the Governor curiously. "Well, you see," was the response, "you are a Catholic, and my husband told me that in this country we must never have Catholics in office." "But," replied the Governor with a twinkle in his eye, "surely you voted for our host, the Mayor of Savannah, and he is a Catholic." "O! yes," responded the woman eagerly, "I voted for him, but he is an Irish Catholic while you are a Roman Catholic."

Perhaps, after all, democracy is not so simple as it sometimes seems.

XII
ON KEEPING OUT OF PUBLIC OFFICE

FROM earliest youth my interest in politics has been very great and my participation in the practical work of politics constant and absorbing. I grew up in a markedly political atmosphere following the Civil War when party feeling and party antagonism were very intense, and when participation in political activity was more general and more widespread than it appears to be now. By inheritance, by association and by training I became a convinced Republican, and when at college I found a philosophical basis for my Republicanism in the political doctrines of Alexander Hamilton and in the teachings of Professor Burgess.

Paterson was an industrial city which felt itself to be founded upon and dependent on the protective tariff policy of the Republican Party. The cotton, steel, locomotive-building, paper-making and silk industries all believed that without the protective tariff they must be forced to the wall by the competition of foreign countries where cheaper labor and a lower standard of living prevailed. Moreover, the Civil War was only some ten or fifteen years away and the Democrat Party was paying the penalty of its opposition to Lincoln and of what had then become the unpopularity of its general attitude during the quarter century preceding. My father was not only a strong Republican but one very active in party work and in party management. He was at various times at the head of the party organization in the City of Paterson and in Passaic County as well as one of the controlling group of leaders in the State of New Jersey. He was invariably a delegate to conventions, city, county and state, and in 1880 was chosen one of the two delegates from the old Fifth Congressional District of New Jersey comprising the counties of Bergen, Morris and Passaic, to the Republican National Convention at Chicago where, after a terrific struggle between the forces of Grant and those of Blaine, General Garfield was nominated on the thirty-sixth ballot.[1]

In those days the conduct of elections was very different from that which now prevails. There were no official ballots, but each party printed its own ballots and pressed them upon the attention of registered voters. Often these ballots were amusingly designed with a view to protecting them against imitation by the enemy. Some years ago I gave to the Department of Politics at Columbia University a scrapbook containing a considerable collection of these old-time ballots, such as were used in my boyhood and youth at the polling place of the Second District, afterwards the Third, of the Third Ward of the City of Paterson, which was in the fire-engine house at the corner of Auburn and Godwin Streets immediately at the rear of the property on which my father's house stood.

On Election Day we boys used to attend the polls from their opening at an early morning hour until their close at seven o'clock in the evening, armed with a supply of

[1]See Chapter X, *Fourteen Republican National Conventions.*

party ballots which we did our best to have taken and used by the arriving voters. These experiences were of themselves a real education in the practical work of politics and in the workings of public opinion. Although I had marched in political parades much earlier and remember distinctly anxiously waiting for news of the decisions of the Electoral Commission in February, 1877, the first election in which I recall taking an active part was that of April, 1879, for Mayor and other city officials of Paterson. The contest was earnestly, even bitterly fought, since the chief issue had to do with compelling the saloons to obey the law as to Sunday and midnight closing, and to break the power of the local brewers in the politics of the city and county. My father was chosen to be the Republican candidate for Mayor and he pressed these issues as vigorously as possible. I participated in a half-dozen ward meetings and gave every hour that I could spare from my college studies to canvass the voters. The Democrat candidate was a popular brewer, and he was elected by a majority of several hundred.

This was the beginning of my practically lifelong fight against the power of the liquor traffic in politics. Great progress was made through regulatory legislation which was entirely practicable and could be made to work, including high license fees and quick punishment for any violation of administrative rules. When the unfortunate —and indeed disastrous—movement for nationwide prohibition began, I opposed it with the utmost vigor, since I knew full well that its only effect could be to undermine obedience to law as well as the moral habits of the American people. It proposed a purely theoretical and wholly impractical way of dealing with the evils of the liquor traffic. Unfortunately, the American people had to be taught these lessons by bitter experience, since the Eighteenth Amendment to the Federal Constitution was in force for some twelve years. During this time the liquor traffic flourished as never before and both public and private morals fell to a grievously low plane. Fortunately, the repeal of the Eighteenth Amendment in 1933 put our nation back on the path of progress.[1]

The average American seems to take it for granted that any one who is keenly interested in politics and who is associated with active political work is of necessity ambitious to hold public office. In my own case this assumption has dogged my entire life and has brought me much amusement and sometimes great annoyance. It has been repeated a thousand times in the press and has been shared even by some personal friends who ought to have known better. There are two reasons why I have never been willing to accept public office either elective or appointive, no matter how honorable or how distinguished. The first reason is that having deliberately chosen a life-career in the establishment of education as a subject of study and intellectual discipline and in the building of a true university, worthy of a modern democratic society, upon the foundation provided by Columbia College, I did not propose to be diverted from it by any temptation, whether financial or political, or for any cause whatsoever. The second reason is that having learned from Professor Burgess the profoundly important distinction between the sphere of government and the sphere of liberty, I proposed to render such public service as I could in the sphere of liberty, carefully avoiding that of government. The more I have observed those who have chosen to render public service in the sphere of government, the more certain I have become of the correctness of my choice. Those who work in the sphere of government do so under limitations

[1]See Vol. II, *Repeal of the Eighteenth Amendment.*

legal, formal, bureaucratic, conventional and other which I could not and would not put up with. The public servant in the sphere of liberty retains his self-control and is not constantly called upon to sacrifice his self-respect. It has been my fortune to know thirteen Presidents of the United States, seven of them very intimately. Of these Theodore Roosevelt was the only one who really enjoyed the work and the responsibilities of that great office. His temperament and his abounding vitality made it possible for him to get contentment and even amusement out of what others found grievous and harassing vexations.

The pressure upon me to accept public office began early and has been unremitting all these years. Only two years after my graduation from college, Garret A. Hobart, afterwards Vice-President of the United States, who was then, together with General William J. Sewell of Camden, the controlling force in the Republican party organization in New Jersey and who was an intimate friend of our family, invited me to stand for election as Member of Assembly from the Second District of Passaic County. He promised me nomination and election without any effort on my part or without any expense, and was kind enough to paint in glowing terms the possible public career of a young man who could command such support as the party organization was willing to give me. My answer, of course, was one of high appreciation of the compliment which the invitation conveyed, but I pointed out that as I was just planning to leave for Europe to continue my studies in Germany and France, it was beyond my power to accept his kind proposal. Both he and my father were greatly disappointed in this attitude on my part but there was no help for it.

Shortly after my return from my first visit to Europe, Mr. Hobart renewed the attack. In 1886 and again in

1888 he proposed to me nomination and election as Representative in Congress, with full organization support, from the Fifth New Jersey District which was then made up of Bergen, Morris and Passaic Counties. There was no doubt that the suggestion was very tempting, not alone for what it meant of itself, but for that to which I was told it might readily lead. Nevertheless, I could not accept the proposal. My work at Columbia was at its very beginning and full of promise. I was just organizing and bringing into existence what is now Teachers College and several literary projects were stirring in my mind. So the door to an official career, then most invitingly held wide open, was closed again. I do not consider my service on the State Board of Education of New Jersey or on the Board of Education of the City of Paterson as public office-holding in the ordinary sense of that term.

Then came the removal of my residence to the City of New York and it was not long before pressure to take public office began again. I have elsewhere mentioned[1] the invitation of President Harrison to become the United States Commissioner of Education in 1889 and that of President Cleveland to succeed Theodore Roosevelt as Chairman of the United States Civil Service Commission in 1895. This latter invitation, I feel quite sure, was made at the suggestion of Mr. Francis Lynde Stetson, a kind friend of mine, who was an intimate friend and personal adviser of President Cleveland. Upon the creation of the Greater New York there ensued a desperate struggle for the mayoralty which was to be a powerful office commanding a great amount of political patronage. Before the difficulties arose which led to the deplorable break in the Republican party ranks at that time, I was approached by leading representatives of both factions with offers of

[1]See Chapter IX, *Some Fortunate Memories.*

their support if I would permit my name to be brought forward as candidate for Mayor. They pointed out that unless I would do this a party breach seemed almost certain since no other name had been suggested upon which both factions could or would agree.

My mind had not been changed in the least, however, regarding public office; in fact it had in the interval become clearer and firmer than ever. It seems incredible that no other name than mine could have been hit upon to avert the split which followed, with the effect of turning over the entire administration of the newly created municipality during the first four years of its existence to Tammany Hall represented by the ease-loving and pliant Mayor Van Wyck. Once more in the early spring of 1901, the Republican party leaders and those who were most influential in the independent or reform movement of that day came to me on the same subject, but once more I declined. That year the outcome was much more fortunate, for Seth Low was agreed upon, nominated and by a narrow majority elected. He gave the city a most excellent administration but unfortunately was defeated for re-election to his own grievous disappointment.

It was a little earlier than this, in 1899, when Governor Theodore Roosevelt asked me to take the chairmanship of the commission which was to be created to revise the charter of the greater city with a view to planning a really modern and scientific form of municipal administration. That was precisely the sort of work which I liked and which I could undertake without any sensible interference with my personal and professional duties. I told the Governor that I would accept this invitation with great pleasure, but upon one condition, namely, that I should be supported in drafting a genuine charter. I had no possible interest in merely re-codifying the great mass of laws affecting the municipality, which was all that the politicians and most of the lawyers concerned had in mind to do.

I explained to the Governor that by a genuine charter I meant a document of not to exceed some twenty-five or thirty pages which would be in effect a constitution with a grant of power to the municipality and the creation of a thoroughly modern and businesslike administrative system, leaving to the municipality its complete home rule under the limitations and forms of what would be in effect a municipal constitution. It was, and is, in my view preposterous that every minute detail of New York City's municipal business should be controlled by the State Legislature and that the salaries paid by New York City taxpayers to school teachers, street cleaners, policemen, firemen and others should be fixed at Albany. The Governor said that he agreed with me entirely but did not know how others might feel. He suggested that I consult leading Democrats and leading Republicans and ascertain whether they would support me in carrying out the program of charter revision which I had outlined. Very brief inquiries convinced me that few if any besides myself desired a real charter or were willing to work for one. On ascertaining that fact, I went back to the Governor and told him that there was no use in my accepting the honor and compliment which he had proposed since I should not be able to accomplish anything that seemed to me worth while. Thereupon, at my suggestion he invited George L. Rives to be chairman of the commission. Mr. Rives accepted and worked with that devotion, ability and unselfishness which were characteristic of him. Professor Frank J. Goodnow of Columbia also rendered important service as a member of the commission.

The most difficult and far-reaching decision was yet to

come. This was in connection with the almost irresistible demand from President Theodore Roosevelt, Governor Odell and the active leaders of the Republican party organization in the State of New York that I accept the nomination for Governor in 1904 with the bluntly expressed purpose, if all went well, of nominating me for President to succeed Roosevelt in 1908. The complete story of this incident will doubtless have interest for others besides myself.

The first hint that I had of the use of my name in connection with the Republican gubernatorial nomination for 1904 was from ex-Judge William N. Cohen of New York, who said to me in the Chicago Club toward the close of the Republican National Convention in June, 1904, that he thought Governor Odell and his friends were planning to nominate me for Governor. I dismissed the matter with a laugh, thinking it an entirely absurd suggestion.[1]

Toward the close of July, I called on Governor Odell at Republican State Headquarters in the Fifth Avenue Hotel, New York, to discuss some aspects of the campaign, and he asked me who was my choice for Governor. I spoke of Root, whose name was then being eagerly discusssed in the press, and mentioned Higgins and Stranahan, in case Root positively declined to permit the use of his name. Governor Odell then said, "Well, you know there is a strong boom for you." I expressed my complete surprise, and he added, "Yes, and it may become serious. The last man who has been talking with me in favor of it is George Aldridge" of Rochester.

I gave no further thought to the matter, and heard no more about it until toward the close of August, when I received the following letter from William L. Ward, Re-

[1]See Chapter X, *Fourteen Republican National Conventions.*

publican National Committeeman for New York, dated
August 22, 1904:

I am in receipt of your favor of the 15th and in reply would
say, that we are getting out an edition of about 500,000 of the
Hay-Root pamphlet, which we will send to our first voters.

I have undertaken the first voter problem for the Eastern States
and do not propose at the present time to send the first voters anything except the above mentioned literature.

I want to congratulate you on the very effective work that you
have already done in sending out your pamphlet. I have practical evidence from a number of people in Westchester County
who were in a doubtful frame of mind, who have been settled
in their ideas to vote for Roosevelt by reason of the Hay-Root
pamphlet, and I know it has made many votes for us in Westchester County.

I was very sorry not to have seen you before you went away
and I trust the first time you are in New York City and are calling at the headquarters you will drop in at my office and see me.

You are doubtless aware that your name is being considered
seriously by the Republican leaders in the State of New York for
the Governorship. This is not a new proposition. This matter was
pretty thoroughly discussed amongst us at Chicago and I feel
very strongly there is no one in the State of New York who, at
this particular time, can get as many votes as you can. You will
attract the Independent vote and satisfy every requirement. The
charges that would be made against Mr. Root, were he the candidate, could not be made against you. We could not be charged
with nominating you for monetary considerations and in the
part of the State where you are not as well known a vigorous
speaking campaign will fully acquaint the people with your kind
and character and you will make friends wherever you appear.

I feel confident that this matter should receive your serious
consideration.

I replied promptly on August 24 as follows:

Your very kind letter of the 22nd has just been received. I am
sure that the Hay-Root pamphlet is as effective a campaign docu-

ment as we could have. Why would it not be well to reprint the *Tribune* editorial of Monday on "The Constitution Club of 1864" and send it to lawyers in New York and elsewhere? It draws a strong parallel between the attacks on Lincoln and those on Roosevelt.

I am very much surprised at what you say about the serious consideration of my name in connection with the nomination for Governor. I knew nothing whatever about the matter, and the only mention of it was made in a joking way by Governor Odell some weeks ago.

If, however, there is on anyone's part a disposition to urge seriously my nomination, will you not kindly say that my position and work at Columbia University make it imperatively necessary that I should not be a candidate for public office or take too active a part in political work. I am always glad to do my part in the ranks as a private, but to do more than that would impair my usefulness here and do harm to the University.

My interest in politics and my participation go back to boyhood. Nearly twenty years ago Mr. Hobart, afterwards Vice-President, offered me a political career in New Jersey. I then chose to stick to my profession, and while my interest and my desire to help the party to victory are even greater than ever, I must, as I have said, do my work in a quiet way and not become a candidate for public office.

Be assured that I highly appreciate the compliment of being thought available for so distinguished an office and that I am grateful for your own kind words.

Mr. Ward wrote me again this letter of August 27:

I am in receipt of your favor of August 24th and I note what you say, sympathize with your feelings, but assure you that your friends in the Organization, including myself, will utilize every argument at hand to change your decision relative to the nomination.

I consider it a critical time for the Republican Party in the State of New York. We must broaden out and take up timber from a new field in order to secure the support of the independent vote and retain the respect of the better class in our Organization. You, to the minds of many of us, fill the bill exactly.

I am in receipt this morning of a very strong letter from Governor Black urging me to do everything I possibly can to secure your nomination. When will you be in New York?

Kindly let me hear from you.

My reply dated two days later was the following:

Accept my thanks for your letter of yesterday—the 27th—but I beg that you will believe me when I say that it is absolutely impossible for me to think of accepting the nomination for Governor. If it were only my own personal wish that was involved, I should certainly surrender it at the request of party leaders like yourself if it was felt that I could serve the party by so doing. But that is not the case. Columbia University is involved, and I must not do anything to injure it. I may say to you in confidence that the Trustees and alumni generally feel that the University suffered because of Mr. Low's candidacy for Mayor in 1897, and for me to become a candidate for Governor now would exasperate them greatly. It would also impair the usefulness of the President of the University if the idea gained ground that he looked forward to political office.

I have thought over the matter long and deeply and am sure that I am right. You will do me a personal favor if you say to your fellow-leaders that my nomination is absolutely out of the question.

Have you thought of Ambassador Choate? He was president of the Constitutional Convention of 1894, is about to withdraw from his embassy, and is a fine figure upon the stump. Large numbers of independents would vote for him and I know of no reason why he would not poll the regular party vote.

I had expected to go to New York tonight to vote at the primaries tomorrow, but family complications here render it impossible. My present plan is to reach New York on September 12, and to leave for St. Louis on the 16th.

Meanwhile the matter had been taken up with the

President by Cortelyou and Root, and the President wrote
me under date of August 25:

WHITE HOUSE,
  WASHINGTON

Oyster Bay, N. Y.

Personal

Dear Murray:
  Cortelyou and Root have been out here. They are red hot to
have you run for Governor. Now, I do not know anything about
it, but, for Heaven's sake! don't commit yourself definitely against
it without ample thought.   Ever yours,
                                    Theodore Roosevelt

Dr. Nicholas Murray Butler,
  Rye Beach, New Hampshire

to which I replied on August 28 as follows:

Dear Mr. President:
  I was just sitting down to answer your letter of the 22nd when
that of the 25th came in. So the latter will come first.
  I am simply amazed at this talk of me for Governor. When
Odell spoke to me of it in July I took it for granted that he was
joking. Except for an occasional meaningless newspaper paragraph, I heard no more of the matter and never gave it a thought
until a letter came from Ward, our National Committeeman,
last Wednesday. He told me that he was in favor of my nomination and asked me to take the matter into "serious consideration."
Now comes your letter saying that both Cortelyou and Root also
want me to run.
  But it is absolutely impossible. As I wrote to Ward, while I
am highly appreciative of the very distinguished honor, I am not
ambitious to hold political office; and, indeed, could not now become a candidate for elective office without serious harm to the
other public interests committed to my care. Nothing injures a
University so much as to give the University itself and the public
reason to believe that the President looks upon his position as
a stepping-stone to political office. The feeling against Mr. Low
on that account was very strong and for me to follow in his
footsteps after only three years of service would injure Colum-

bia University. It is quite out of the question, and I have asked Ward to put a stop to the farther use of my name.

Hobart offered me a political career in New Jersey twenty years ago. He urged me to go to Congress from a safe Republican district, and then to follow a political career. After careful thought, I said "No," and have stuck to my profession ever since. Wall Street tried me with an offer of the presidency of a trust company at a salary nearly as large as yours, but I chose my career with my eyes open and hope to make it a useful one before I get through.

A great University in a democracy is one of the most powerful engines of modern times. My ambition is to make a great University, to have it preserve and inculcate the highest ideals and also to keep it in touch with sound public opinion. That, if accomplished, is a public service that goes way ahead of being Governor of half a dozen States. Selah!

Just a word about your letter of August 22: If you will pardon my bluntness, the tariff part of your letter falls way below the rest of it in execution. It reads as if written by some one else. It struck me as both prolix and jejune—which sounds as if it had a couple of contagious diseases. I am a Protectionist from principle, but I was behind the scenes when the McKinley bill and the Dingley bill were made, and I know personally of the wicked things that were stuck into those bills in order to get them through the impeccable Senate.

It was McKinley's idea, and also Dingley's, that the excesses would be shaved off by reciprocal trade bargains. The Kasson treaties were negotiated in that spirit and for that purpose, and it was a party scandal and a public outrage when they were killed in the Senate. If you will examine the trade statistics under the Blaine reciprocity treaties—which the Democrats terminated by the way—you will see at a glance how both foreign and domestic trade were prospering under them. If the Democrats had sense enough to pitch into specific iniquities of the existing tariff, they could soon put us on the defensive; but when they say that "Protection is robbery," they are simply silly and we can afford to laugh.

Unless we enter on a policy of removing the most serious abuses of the Dingley tariff—and the easiest way to do it is by reciprocal trade agreements—you will have a Democrat House

on your hands after March 4, 1907, and your successor will be a Democrat—which your new-found friend, the *Sun,* thinks identical with Hun. An organized movement is quietly spreading over the country among the business men, that will shortly open some persons' eyes on these matters, particularly perhaps those of the estimable Secretary of the Treasury. What is going on quietly in New England itself, you may see from the enclosed clipping.

Please remember that what I am writing is only intended to have influence upon your general intellectual attitude on the tariff, and not to urge you to say or do any particular thing now. But you ought never to retreat from the position you took on the tariff in your Minneapolis speech, delivered early in September, 1901.

Now that Parker's mushiness is becoming clear, and since the *Post* and *Times* have fallen foul of him and Bailey and the good Shepard because of their weakness on tariff-smashing, and the *Times* and *Eagle* are openly flouting their candidate for joining the Anti-imperialists, the bottom must soon drop out of the Parker canvass. The most cheering news comes from Bar Habor. My sister writes me that the "swells" there are almost solid for Parker. This is truly good news. Their appetite for folly knows no bounds.

As ever yours,
Nicholas Murray Butler

The President,
Oyster Bay, N. Y.

He wrote again under date of August 27, urging my acceptance of the nomination:

Personal

WHITE HOUSE
WASHINGTON

Oyster Bay, N. Y.

Dear Murray:
Last night Littauer came out and told me that Odell was tending more and more to believe that your nomination was by all

odds the strongest nomination that could be made—Root being out of the way. Of course, he could not speak to me authoritatively, and he was most careful to explain that he thought it would cause a little trouble if people got the impression that you were *my* candidate; so I need hardly say, don't allude in any way to my having written you. Odell evidently believes that not only would your nomination be a good thing for the party, but that it would reflect credit upon him, and that while, of course, you would be Governor in all that the name implies, yet that being an individual of both common sense and patriotism, you would try to work with the organization just as I tried to work with it while I was Governor. I think that one reason why Odell wants you to take it is that with Root out of the way, Tim Woodruff is springing to the front, being backed by Platt; and Woodruff certainly is not a man who would add force and dignity to the ticket, or would strengthen it where it is weak, though I dare say he is popular enough in some circles.

If the Republican leaders do ask you to be the nominee for Governor, I most earnestly hope you will accept. The Governorship is a great and dignified office, and though it would at the moment interrupt your career as an educator, it would enable you at the close of your term of service, if you so desired, to go back to that career with immensely added weight. I have always, as you know, felt that the part you had taken in politics—your being delegate to national conventions, etc.—had greatly strengthened your power for good in your educational work, and I think this would strengthen it still more. Moreover, if you are asked, it will be because there is a genuine need of you and I hope you can make up your mind to meet this need. It is not often that we get such a conjunction as a man ideally fit for the office whom the power in control desire to nominate for the office; and I hate to see a failure to take advantage of it.

If you do accept there will, of course, be an effort to show that you are my special ally; and so I should not deem it wise even for you to come down here and see me.

Always yours,
Theodore Roosevelt

Dr. Nicholas Murray Butler,
    Rye Beach, New Hampshire.

But on August 29 he received my reply to his earlier letter, and wrote this letter of that date:

Personal

WHITE HOUSE
WASHINGTON

Oyster Bay, N. Y.

Dear Murray:

In the first place, about you and the governorship I am personally sorry but I am bound to say that I think you are right. I wrote you as I did because I thought I ought to put the case strongly before you for the sake of the party, but down in the bottom of my heart I all along felt just exactly as you express yourself in your letter. By this I do not mean that I was insincere in what I wrote you, for if you were willing to take the position, then I think there was some justification for it; but I entirely sympathize with your unwillingness.

Now, again a word about the tariff. You are quite right in saying that it is the least original part of my speech. Much of it I got from statistics prepared by North, of the Census Bureau. At the same time, as I think I wrote you, most of those who have seen the letter think it one of the very strongest portions of it. Joe Cannon thinks so; Hemenway thinks so; Root thinks so; and Cortelyou thinks so. I do not know what that clipping you sent me was from, but the statement itself was based on a lie. The whole point of the editorial is that Lodge and I favor only reciprocity that does not in any way injure "any" protective interest. Now, as you know, this is Dalzell's position, and at my request Lodge headed the very doubtful but finally victorious fight to strike out the word "any" in this connection from our platform.

I know (though perhaps not as clearly as you do) some of the iniquities perpetrated in both the McKinley and Dingley, as well as the Wilson, tariffs. Do you for a moment imagine that there would not be as many iniquities perpetrated in any new tariff put through either by us or the Democrats? So strongly do I feel this that if we could have the present tariff kept unchanged for a dozen years and no agitation about it, I am confident it would be the best possible thing for this country; but I am perfectly aware that this may be impossible, and that we must do the best we can.

As for the movement in New England for Canadian reciprocity, it is as wholly irrational as anything I know. The New Englanders apparently think we can get a reciprocity with Canada regardless of Canada's consent, or the country's interests outside of New England. They would be violently against a reciprocity treaty which let in Canadian manufactures to the United States and American raw material into Canada—which is the kind of treaty that Canada would be inclined to like, and which Iowa, for instance, would support. The New Englanders think they can take the tariff off hides and keep it on shoes. They may at some time be able to accomplish this feat, but it cannot be done as a regular thing and the principle cannot obtain in any tariff law. The reciprocity agitation in New England is a factor to be reckoned with, just like the free silver agitation in the West. It is not, from a national standpoint, immoral like the free silver movement, but in its present aspect it is just as foolish. I hope we can get reciprocity with Canada. I am doubtful about it, and the reason I am doubtful about it is that the same New Englanders who are howling for it would violently object to having it if we put in the things that Canada will want. However, we may be able to get it.

Always yours,

Theodore Roosevelt

Dr. Nicholas Murray Butler,
    Rye Beach, New Hampshire

Finally, at ten o'clock on the morning of August 29 I received the following letter from Governor Odell written from Long Branch on the previous day, inviting me to dine with him in New York at the Metropolitan Club on the evening of August 30:

You and I should have a little visit this week. Can you run down to New York and take dinner with me at the Metropolitan Club? Please wire me giving date at the 5th Ave. Hotel. It is best to be blind even in telegrams and if you can come I would suggest that you use the name of Jas. Jones which I will understand. You have a good name, but when even our telegraph offices are watched by Dem detectives one has to be very wary.

My reply by telegram was as follows:

James Jones will dine with you at Metropolitan Club tomorrow, Tuesday, August thirtieth at seven thirty.
(unsigned)

I went to New York, voted at the Primaries, and then dined with Governor Odell. He opened up the matter at once very frankly, and stated why he thought Root, despite all his great abilities, would be a weak candidate because of his corporation relations. He added that I had been agreed upon by the leaders to run, and that in all probability my nomination would come by acclamation. If, however, Timothy L. Woodruff decided to make a fight and had the support of Senator Platt, there might be a roll call, but in any event, not fewer than 720 delegates out of the 900 odd would be for me. He added that he wanted me personally to take the nomination, and assured me that I would carry the State by a heavy majority. He asked no pledges whatever, and expressly disclaimed the desire to have any, either open or implied. He talked extremely well and was personally very complimentary.

After Govenor Odell had finished, I thanked him for the great honor, and then told him just why it was that I could not, either now or hereafter, be a candidate for political office. I repeated what I had already written to Mr. Ward, that I had made the choice nearly twenty years ago in New Jersey, and that it was then made once for all. I pointed out the injury that would come to the University if it were felt that its presidency were a stepping-stone to political office. Governor Odell tried for some time to shake my determination, and pointed to the great political possibilities that were open to a successful Governor of New York, while admitting all that I said about the University. Finally, however, he accepted my attitude as final and irrevocable, and after having spent three hours in intimate political conversation, passing finally to the national campaign and its conduct, we walked down Fifth Avenue together as far as the corner of Thirty-ninth Street, where he left me to go to the Union League Club, while I returned to the Hotel Manhattan.

There had been some slight discussion of my name in the newspapers, principally in the *Sun,* but there was also an editorial in the *Evening Journal* of August 23, written by Mr. Arthur Brisbane with Mr. Hearst's consent, to which the following letter from Mr. Brisbane under date of January 20, 1905, refers:

New York Evening Journal
Editorial Rooms
New York

My dear Mr. Butler:

I enclose an editorial which, with Mr. Hearst's consent, I published in our paper sometime ago.

I was interested to hear from Governor Odell that he had actually offered you the nomination for the Governorship, and that you had declined it. He told me that in confidence, of course. I am very sorry that you did not take the nomination. You would have been elected by an overwhelming majority, and it seems to me that you could have done extraordinarily good work. I do not see how the Republican machine dared to offer you the nomination, however, as they must have a good many interests that need "protecting," and that you would not protect.

I wonder—that is why I am writing you—if you could hand the enclosed clipping to one of your secretaries and get him to have its original identified. My impression is that Goethe said it, and of course any one of your wise men would know. I should not bother you with the quotation, except that I think it might possibly interest you in case you have not looked at it. I quote it from memory entirely—I have not seen it for a good many years.

Yours very sincerely,
A. Brisbane

When I did go down to Oyster Bay a day or two later I passed, on the road between the station and the President's house, Mr. Riggs, the political correspondent of the *Sun,* returning from the President's. On reaching the house I said to the President that Riggs had seen me and that undoubtedly there would be something about me and the Governorship in the *Sun* the next day. The President said no, that there would not be anything, because Riggs had asked him flatly whether I was going to run, and he had told Riggs that I had been offered the nomination but had absolutely declined. Next morning the *Sun* stated simply that I would not permit my name to be considered for the nomination.

There the matter was dropped and nothing further was said or done about it. Shortly afterward State Senator Frank W. Higgins of Cattaraugus County was nominated by the Republicans and elected Governor in November.

There was one curious side to this whole incident which seemed to me then and still seems to me ludicrous. Theodore Roosevelt in 1904 had much the same notion that Lincoln had in 1864 that he was unpopular and could not be re-elected. One of his reasons for urging upon me the nomination for Governor was that what he called my personal and political strength would assure our carrying New York State in November which otherwise he felt he might lose. I roared with laughter at this absurd suggestion and reminded him of Lincoln's anxiety forty years earlier. I believed that he would sweep New York by a very large majority in November and that any good Republican could be elected Governor. The event proved that my judgment was correct.

Some wise man has said that the shadow of the Presidency never falls across a man's life but once, and undoubtedly in my case it did so fall in the month of August,

1904. The decision then taken, which made my powerful political friends think I must be insane or feeble-minded, has never been regretted by me. When we were preparing for the calamitous Convention of 1912 and a group of us were in conference at the National Republican Club in New York, one man said to me rather bitterly, "If you had had more sense and had not been such a fool in 1904, the party would now be engaged in re-electing you to the Presidency and all this horrible mess would have been avoided." Congressman Lucius Littauer of Gloversville, who had known all about the happenings of 1904, interjected with: "Let that go—that water has gone over the dam."

There was still another movement to secure for me the Presidental nomination, of which I knew nothing whatever at the time or for some years afterwards. The facts were recorded by Senator Joseph B. Foraker of Ohio in his volume of recollections.[1] The statement which Senator Foraker there makes is this:

I received a large number of other letters of a congratulatory character, among them the following from Nicholas Murray Butler, now President of Columbia University. Mr. Butler doesn't know, and probably never will know until these notes are published, that it seemed to me in 1912 that he would be a good man, the best I could think of, for the Republicans to unite upon as a compromise candidate for the Presidency. I ventured to make the suggestion where I thought it might do some good, but found the lines so tightly drawn between Taft and Roosevelt that it went unheeded. A race for the White House between the Presidents of Columbia and Princeton would have been enough to arouse lively interest in the campaign, among college men at least, and, with the Republicans united, Columbia would have won easily. How the situation may develop for 1916 is not now clearly foreseen,

[1]Joseph Benson Foraker, *Notes of a Busy Life*. Cincinnati: Stewart & Kidd Company, 1916. Vol. II, pp. 69–70.

but it may be safely assumed that, unless something shall occur in connection with the European War, or on some other now unforeseen account, to increase greatly the popularity of the President, he can be easily defeated by Butler or any other equally able and equally sound representative of real Republicanism.

His letter was as follows:

New York, April 4, 1900.

Hon. J. B. Foraker,
United States Senate
Washington, D. C.

My dear Senator Foraker:

Accept my cordial congratulations upon your brilliant and effective leadership in the struggle which ended yesterday, for the passage of a bill for the civil government of Puerto Rico. I have been reading its provisions with care, and it seems to me to offer the ideal solution of the problems presented by our outlying possessions.

You have contributed in a most important way, in this measure, to the development of our national history, and to the expansion of our institutions, without exposing them to the danger of disintegration through the operation of strange and alien forces.
I am,
                    Cordially yours,
                         Nicholas Murray Butler

During his seven and one half years of service in the Presidency Theodore Roosevelt made three separate and very urgent appeals to me to accept high public office both at home and in the diplomatic service. He argued that I need not allow acceptance of his proposals to interfere with my chosen career since he was certain that I could, at his request, arrange for a leave of absence from the Presidency of Columbia for two years or even more, and he thought this very desirable on personal, as well as on public grounds. He was very kind about the matter, but our minds never met. He never really accepted my point of view although he professed to understand it, but thought me very queer and very stubborn.

President Taft, who had learned of my unwillingness to interrupt my academic service by accepting public office, nevertheless suggested to me that perhaps I would accept appointment as Ambasador to Berlin. The President based this suggestion on my long familiarity with the German people and their political and intellectual leaders.

When 1912 came around and the rift in the Republican Party had made itself manifest, I was again urged to run for Governor of New York. My nomination would not have averted the naming of a third candidate by the newly organized Progressive Party, but the organization leaders believed that even under such circumstances and because of what they said was my strong personal following among the Democrats, I could be elected. Nevertheless, I declined to allow my name to be used and urged the nomination of either James W. Wadsworth, Jr., or Job E. Hedges. The convention at Saratoga in the following September put both men upon the State ticket, naming Hedges for Governor and Wadsworth for Lieutenant Governor. A heated campaign followed and Job E. Hedges, who would have made an excellent Governor, was badly defeated because of the strength of the Progressive movement in the State which was behind the candidacy of our good friend, Oscar S. Straus. Hedges used to tell in his own inimitable way a most amusing story of that campaign. As Election Day drew near, he found himself scheduled to speak one evening at a small town in the western part of the State. He arrived on a gloomy October afternoon, with rain pouring in torrents, and burdened with the feeling that he was engaged in a hopeless contest. On reaching his hotel he was waited upon by a committee of local Republicans who, after greeting him, said that be-cause of the fact that Hedges' own father had been a sol-dier in the Civil War and had lost his life, the few sur-viving Civil War veterans in that town were to be guests of honor at the evening meeting and would occupy seats upon the platform. One of these men, they said, was sub-ject to epileptic fits and usually had one attack each day. So far as they knew he had not then had his daily con-vulsion, and they begged Hedges not to be disturbed or upset if the man should be stricken while speaking was in progress. On reaching the hall, Hedges found a half dozen veterans seated on the stage and greeted them cordially. He then plunged into his speech, in the course of which he sarcastically described a speech reported to have been made a night or two earlier in Sullivan County by Mr. Straus. The latter, so the newspaper reports said, had promised that if elected Governor he would, among other things, labor so to improve the health of the people of the State that the chief diseases which ravaged the population, including tuberculosis, would disappear. Hedges was greatly amused by the fact that this particular promise was made to the voters of Sullivan County, no small part of the prosperity of which was due to the at-traction which its climate and elevation had for tubercu-losis patients. Hedges rang the changes on this topic for a moment or two and then shouted to his audience, "I shall make no promises that I cannot keep. If elected Governor I shall do the best I can to improve the health conditions of our people, but I cannot undertake to banish tubercu-losis or any other disease from among us, because that is absolutely impossible."

At that very moment the aged veteran had his daily at-tack and fell to the floor with a cry. Hedges, in telling the story, went on to say that his army veteran admirer, on hearing his chosen candidate say that he could not abolish disease, thought there was no use in refraining from having his usual attack, so went ahead and had it.

Job Hedges, by the way, was not only a most attractive personality but a man of much larger political importance than the general public appreciated. He had a delightful gift of humor and that led him to be known and classed as a wit, which is apparently a fatal disqualification in the American mind for the holding of high public office. While every one liked Hedges and appreciated him, they rarely thought of him, as he was entitled to be thought of, as a serious and excellent candidate for such an office as Governor or United States Senator.

After all that took place at the Republican National Convention of 1912, it rather amused me to find myself, a few months later, receiving the Republican electoral vote for Vice-President. This fact quickly led to the statement in the press and in various books of reference that I was the Republican candidate for the Vice-Presidency in that year. Of course nothing of the kind happened.

Vice-President Sherman was renominated with President Taft but unfortunately died a very few days before the election in November. Some little time later, when the Electoral College was about to meet, Senator Reed Smoot of Utah called me by telephone from Washington and asked whether I had any objection to the eight Republican electoral votes, four from Utah and four from Vermont, being cast for me for Vice-President. I told Smoot I had no possible objection to this being done, provided there was no chance of electing a Republican Vice-President. I said if there was such a chance he would have to get some other candidate. We chaffed each other over the telephone for a few minutes and that ended the matter. The eight Republican electoral votes had to be cast for somebody, and under the circumstances it was a matter of complete indifference whether they were cast for me or not.

My next encounter with opportunity for public office came in the late spring of 1914. William Barnes and James W. Wadsworth, Jr., asked me to meet them at the Union League Club in New York and said that in their judgment I could and should be elected United States Senator. They offered me their support for the nomination and urged my acceptance. Such an offer coming from them was almost equivalent to receiving the nomination itself. It took but a few moments for me to dispose of this matter and to say to them both that in my judgment Wadsworth himself was the best fitted Republican in the State for the Senatorship. Barnes, on learning that I would not permit my name to be used, agreed with this and went at once to work to bring about the nomination and election of Wadsworth, who made a most excellent Senator for two terms. He has both principles and courage to stand for them.

Still the spectre of public office would not down and numerous individuals throughout the country who were influential in party management as well as many Republican and independent journals began in a scattering sort of way to bring my name forward as a candidate for the Republican Presidential nomination in 1920. So far as I have been able to ascertain, this movement first took something like form in the States of Washington, California, Colorado, Minnesota, Iowa and Illinois. I paid no attention to the matter and merely made polite and formal responses to the numerous letters that began to reach me. To begin with, I did not desire the nomination and, moreover, did not believe that if I did so desire it, it could be brought about. For this there were two chief reasons. President Wilson was at the very height of his unpopularity and, despite the fact that he had been admitted to the bar and was trained as a lawyer, he figured in the public mind only as that nebulous sort of person known as "a college president." It cannot be doubted that he had made that particular calling unpopular, for the moment at any rate, and my political sense told me that this fact would operate to influence the minds of many delegates to the coming convention. In the second place, my views as to international policy, international association and international peace, which had been frequently and freely expressed, while in line with the best traditions of the nation and particularly those of the Republican party since McKinley's time, were not at all acceptable to the small but well-organized and ruling group of reactionary Senators at Washington who were seeking to make political capital out of President Wilson's failings of temperament and mistakes of policy by leading or forcing the Republican Party to support a policy of impossible and grotesque international isolation. Despite these views, party leaders of undoubted authority in different parts of the country, including men like former Governor Franklin Murphy of New Jersey and Charles D. Hilles of New York, kept writing me that my name was much talked of and that something might readily happen in the near future. As the likelihood of this increased, I became subject to the usual solicitations, flatteries and expressions of devotion and advice from the typical hangers-on and political parasites. Long years of experience had taught me to treat all these approaches with polite and discreet indifference. The mistake which I made at that time was in not putting a stop to what followed before it had gone far enough to make such a step embarrassing. A group of high-minded and earnest personal friends organized, without my knowledge, a committee to push my candidacy and before I knew anything about it had collected some funds and had opened modest headquarters at the Hotel Commodore in New York. Municipal Court Judge John R. Davies, a political neighbor and friend and a most earnest party worker, was at the head of this group. What I should have done was to put a stop to the matter at once, but not having done this then did not see just how to do it later on. This committee procured a stupendous amount of indorsement and support, most of which is recorded in the printed records and documents of that undertaking. The press in all parts of the country was surprisingly friendly and commendatory, although here and there there were signs of the two objections which I myself understood and foresaw. An interesting and, indeed, very flattering incident in connection with all this is that three of the men whose names were presented to the convention assured me personally that they looked upon me as the man who should be nominated for the Presidency. These men were Harding, Lowden and Governor Sproul of Pennsylvania. My own choice for the nomination was former Governor Frank O. Lowden of Illinois, but because they knew that they could not control him, the Senatorial clique would not permit his nomination.

As matters progressed, however, it was impossible for my supporters to secure the unanimous vote of the New York delegation because of the insistent demands of those who were urging the name of General Leonard Wood. This of itself was an almost fatal weakness, but in addition the promised Western support, which was always said to be forthcoming, for one reason or another never came. I was not in the least disappointed or surprised at the result.

After his election Harding summoned me to Marion for a conference and Saturday, December 18, was selected as the date. Accompanied by Judge John R. Davies, I made the trip from New York to Marion and immediately on my return dictated the following memorandum of what took place:

In one of his letters written to me during the campaign, Senator Harding said that after election he wished to have a long conference on matters of public policy. A few days after the elction I received a letter from Senator Harding, written from Point Isabel, Texas, asking me to come to Marion, and to designate a date between December 10 and December 20 that would be convenient. I suggested Saturday, December 18, and as that proved agreeable to Senator Harding, the date was fixed upon.

Leaving New York, with Judge John R. Davies as companion, I reached Marion a few minutes behind schedule time, about eight o'clock on Saturday morning, December 18. Mr. Christian, Senator Harding's secretary, was waiting at the station with Senator Harding's automobile, and I was taken to Senator Harding's house, where breakfast was waiting. Senator and Mrs. Harding had as house guests over night Harry M. Daugherty of Columbus, Senator Harding's campaign manager and intimate friend, and Senator James A. Reed of Missouri, a so-called Senate "irreconcilable," with whom Senator Harding had been discussing his proposed international policy. Mr. Daugherty said that he had waited overnight particularly, to see me, because he wished to discuss some political matters. These matters, which related in part to appointments and in part to political procedure, were briefly discussed before Mr. Daugherty left.

So soon as breakfast was finished, Senator Harding took me to the adjoining house, which he had used as headquarters during the campaign, and where his secretaries and stenographers were installed. For three and one-half

hours he and I were in unbroken and most intimate conference on questions of persons and policy.

In opening our conference, Senator Harding touched,
first, on his plans for international relations. He said that
as a result of his experiences in the Senate, his independent study of the questions, his experiences during the
campaign and his interpretation of the results of the
election, he had arrived at the conviction that there were
three fundamental principles which the American people
wish to have made the basis of any dealing with the
Peace Treaty problem:

1. They did not want to join the League of Nations as urged
by President Wilson and as now organized;

2. They did want to take part in some Association of Nations
that would furnish an effective method of establishing world
peace and of making possible reduction of armaments;

3. They did not want a separate peace with Germany, as contemplated by the so-called Knox Resolution.

Senator Harding stated that he found among his advisers pretty general assent to the first two of these principles, but that agreement on the third was more difficult.
He felt, however, that this third principle was important,
and he hoped in time to have it prevail.

I replied by strongly urging support of all three of
these principles, pointing out particularly how unfortunate it would be to make a separate peace with Germany,
and so divorce ourselves from the Allies at the very moment when we were to ask them to accept very drastic
proposals of ours for the reconstruction of the existing
form of international association. I understood that Senator Harding assented to this proposition.

I then addressed myself to the question of the method
of making effective the first and second of the funda-

mental principles named by Senator Harding. Anticipating that the discussion would take this form, I had prepared a careful Memorandum, a copy of which is printed elsewhere.[1] I laid stress upon the fact that there would be grave difficulties and embarrassments, amounting perhaps to impossibilities, in the way of wholly neglecting the present League of Nations and endeavoring to form a new association entirely outside of it. I called attention to the fact that the Assembly in its meeting at Geneva had received suggestions of amendment from the Scandinavian countries and from Argentina, and that all these suggestions had been referred to a Committee on Amendment for consideration and report at a later meeting of the Assembly. This action opened the way, in my judgment, to have the results of any negotiations that might be carried on by the United States immediately upon Senator Harding's inauguration, considered and acted upon by this Committee on Amendment and reported to the Assembly of the League of Nations in due time for adoption. This method of procedure seemed to me to be the simplest and the least likely to create friction.

I strongly urged that if the methods suggested by Senator Harding were not followed, some other method be devised that would remodel and reconstitute the existing League of Nations rather than to start all over again and run the risk of new perils, new friction and new delays. Senator Harding was very much interested in this Memorandum, and asked a good many questions about it. He took a copy of it to put with his own papers, and said that he would reserve judgment as to all methods of procedure until he had procured substantial agreement on his three fundamental principles. He expressed himself as believing that the plan suggested by me was highly

[1]See Volume II, *The Treaty of Versailles at Washington.*

practical and might be found, on fuller consideration, to be the best way to deal with these matters.

Then followed some more general discussion regarding the interdependence of the economic and the political situations, both national and international, this being the point chiefly emphasized in the press, following my visit to Marion. I laid stress upon the fact that emergency tariff legislation and forced action by the Federal Reserve Board in aid of farmers and cotton planters would probably do more harm than good, since relief could only be had by increasing trade and commerce and not by throwing new obstacles in its way, or by holding products out of the market to await higher prices. Perhaps an hour and a half were spent in the fullest possible discussion of these problems. I went over with Senator Harding, and then left with him, copies of a letter from Lord Weardale, of an article signed "Mesmes," which appeared in the French weekly journal *L'Opinion* for November 13, 1920, and a very striking article entitled "America, Ourselves and the League," which appeared in the London *Spectator* for December 4, 1920. Senator Harding read this last article carefully, and then took for later study a pamphlet copy of my speech delivered during the campaign at New London, Conn., on October 16, 1920, on which the *Spectator* editorial was based.

From this our conversation drifted to general questions relating to organization of the Administration. I stated that I would repeat to Senator Harding what I had said to Theodore Roosevelt when the latter so unexpectedly became President in September, 1901, namely, that there is such a thing as a generation in politics, and that an administration is likely to be more successful if the President chooses his close advisers and fellow-workers from men of about his own age, or from those who are a little

younger. Men of a distinctly older generation are not so
likely to work well with a President who is much their
junior. I illustrated how this had operated in the case of
the Roosevelt administration, and pointed out the changes
in that administration which the application of this principle had brought about. I said that of course there would
occasionally be exceptions based upon the peculiar capacity, experience or public standing of a given individual, but that in the long run the rule would hold good.
Senator Harding agreed absolutely with this thought, and
added: "It is for just that reason that Elihu Root seems
to me quite impossible as Secretary of State." He added:
"No one admires Senator Root more than I do, or has
more esteem for him as a statesman, but the fact must
be recognized that his career lies behind him, and that at
seventy-six years of age he is not the man to be Secretary
of State in my Administration." Senator Harding went
on to say that the appointment of Elihu Root was being
vigorously urged upon him by men for whose judgment
he had the greatest respect and in whom he had every
confidence, but he himself felt that for what might be
called psychological reasons the appointment should not
be made. I differed with Senator Harding, and strongly
urged the appointment of Root to be Secretary of State.
I urged that Root was an exception to the rule of which
we had been speaking and that his fitness was so pre-
eminent, particularly at a critical time in the history of
our international relations like the present, that the country would almost expect his appointment and would
heartily applaud it. Senator Harding said very little in
reply, but was evidently not convinced.

The conversation turned then for a few moments on
the duties of the Secretary of State, on his responsibilities
in connection with the problems of foreign policy that

were immediately pressing and upon the better organization and equipment of the Department of State for its work. Suddenly Senator Harding, swinging around in his chair and looking me straight in the face, said: "Now, Murray Butler, look me straight in the eye and tell me what you would like in my Administration." I answered, looking Senator Harding straight in the eye, "I want nothing whatever. I am not a candidate for any public office, however distinguished, either elective or appointive. My objective is always and everywhere public opinion and not public office. My wish is to help the Administration advance certain policies and to effect certain great benefits for the people of the United States and of the world, but I prefer to be permitted to do that by being in the confidence of the Administration rather than by holding any office whatever under it."

In reply Senator Harding said: "I always think of you first, or among the very first, in connection with the Cabinet, and I have supposed that the only appointment that would tempt you, or that you would be willing to accept, would be that of Secretary of State. For the psychological reasons of which we have been speaking there are difficulties in tendering you that appointment, but it is for you if you will take it. Whether you take it or not I want you to feel on most intimate terms with the Administration, and to know that your judgment and advice are always wanted and will always be sought. Perhaps if the Cabinet post cannot be managed you would be willing to go to England as Ambassador." I replied by expressing my profound appreciation of these marked and most distinguished compliments, but stated that I had no wish or intention of accepting any political office of any kind, and that I was not in financial position to accept the Ambassadorship to Great Britain, even for two or three years. I added that a reasonable term of office as Ambassador to Great Britain would be very agreeable and added that undoubtedly I could obtain leave of absence from my work at Columbia to hold such a post for a short time. On the other hand, I pointed out that knowing as I did what recent Ambassadors had been obliged to spend to maintain their position in London, I, living on an academic salary, could not under any circumstances accept such a burden of responsibility.

Senator Harding then asked whether, if a little later a new commission was appointed to undertake international negotiations with a view to solving the problem of the Peace Treaty, I would be willing to accept service upon it. I replied that I would be willing to render service of that sort, which would be brief and temporary, and in which perhaps I might be of some real use. Senator Harding said: "Well, we shall see about that. In any event, I want to find a way to pay you the most distinguished honor in my power." Then the conversation passed to another topic.

Senator Harding distinctly said that he had not made up his mind finally as to any single member of his Cabinet, and that he had offered no Cabinet appointment to anybody. He added that the nearest he had come to making up his mind was in regard to the Department of Agriculture, for the head of which he thought he knew exactly the right man. He said the difficulty was to find a Secretary of Agriculture who was really a practical farmer and would satisfy the farmers, and was not merely a professor of farming or an editor of a farm paper. He asked whether I knew anything about Professor Bailey, formerly of Cornell University, who was supported by the New York Grange for the post. I told Senator Harding of Professor Bailey's personality, age, publications, experience at Cornell University and general relations to the farm movement, particularly in New York State.

The next question discussed related to the Department of Labor, and Senator Harding outlined with definiteness and clearness the sort of administration he desired for that department. He expressed himself as intending to get rid of the extremely radical element, which had found such large place there during the Wilson Administration. He asked me to make confidential inquiry and to report concerning the qualifications of T. B. O'Connor of Buffalo, a member of the Longshoreman's Union and an Irishman, who, it appears, had made a strong statement in favor of Senator Harding from the labor point of view during the campaign and in antagonism to Samuel Gompers. Senator Harding expressed the opinion that Mr. O'Connor might prove to be the sort of man of which he was in search. I undertook to make these inquiries but said it would take some little time, since I would not dare begin them immediately following my visit to Marion, lest the purpose of the inquiry might be suspected.

The Treasury Department was then touched upon, and Senator Harding said excellent men were being suggested from different parts of the country, but that he had about decided that it would be best for the Administration to find its Secretary of the Treasury in the Middle West rather than in New York or in New England. No names were mentioned for this post, but Senator Harding was quite clear that the appointment of any New Yorker to the Treasury, no matter how fit or how free of Wall Street influence he might be, would be attacked by the radical press as indicating the control of the Administration by big business. Senator Harding thought that this was one of those psychological situations which it was the part of wisdom to avoid.

Following the discussion of some other matters, partly of persons and partly of policies, the conversation ranged over the whole field of domestic administration, including the best time to call the new Congress in special session, the best program for the new Congress to follow and the steps to be taken to put the administrative departments at Washington upon a more efficient and business-like basis.

Senator Harding then returned to my Memorandum in regard to the international situation, which he held in his hand, and asked me what my suggestion would be if an alternative to that plan were necessary. I replied that I earnestly hoped that the separate treaty of peace with Germany might be avoided, and that, serious as were many of the errors in the Versailles Treaty, a way might be found, and ought to be found, to make a settlement of the war issues in common with our late Allies, since public opinion in Great Britain, in France and in Italy, to say nothing of public opinion in Germany, would be certain to misinterpret any separate treaty between the United States and Germany, and to regard it as a more or less complete abandonment of the Allies in their attempt to hold Germany to its obligations as a chief author of the war. I said that if it became impossible to secure the ratification of the Versailles Treaty with adequate reservations, then it would be incumbent upon the United States, in good faith toward its own ideals, its own traditional policies and its late Allies, to propose some alternative plan to the League of Nations by which the causes of war might be reduced to a minimum, an international judicial tribunal with adequate jurisdiction and authority established and an immediate limitation of armaments made possible. I proceeded to outline a project which I had had in mind for some weeks for meeting the situation if worst should come to worst and if the United

States would not accept the Versailles Treaty, no matter with what reservations. I proposed to Senator Harding that in that case he, as President, should call a conference at Washington, to be attended by representatives of the principal Allied Powers, with a view to approaching the problems left by the war and raised by reconstruction, from their economic side. I pointed out that if such a conference were called primarily for the purpose of stopping the stupendous expenditure on military, and particularly on naval, armaments, it would be certain to have the support of public opinion, not only in the United States but throughout the world, and that, once called, such a conference could not avoid facing the underlying questions both in Europe and in the Orient which had led and were leading to the building up of armaments. I suggested that if such a conference got under way, it might readily enlarge the scope of its discussions, and, by adjourning from time to time, bring into existence that very association of nations which Senator Harding himself had emphasized in his campaign speeches. Senator Harding asked me what I thought the effect of such an act would be on the existing League of Nations. I replied that, in my judgment the League of Nations could not fail to applaud such an act, because its purposes were in line with its own. I added that if such a conference were successful, the existing League of Nations might readily become a very useful and influential institution for the European nations alone.

At about half-past twelve Senator Harding said that he wanted me to go with Senator New, who had just arrived from Washington, to the Marion Club, in order to meet and shake hands with the members of that body, who had been very helpful to the Senator during the summer in receiving the various delegations and visitors that had come to Marion. Before ending the conversation he repeated, in the most earnest way, his statement that he wanted me to feel that I was really a member of the Administration, wholly in its confidence and free to bring counsel and advice on any subject at any time, as well as to answer when called upon.

On leaving the building, Senator Harding and I were photographed several times and then I joined Senator New and Doctor Sawyer, Senator Harding's physician, and was driven to the Marion Club. There the various members were introduced and greeted and the Guest Book was signed.

I returned to Senator Harding's house for luncheon, to which Judge Davies had also been invited. The luncheon party consisted of Senator and Mrs. Harding, Senator and Mrs. New, Doctor Sawyer, Judge Davies and myself. The conversation was of the most intimate personal and political character. After luncheon Judson Welliver, who was in charge of the publicity work, came in and told me that the newspaper men were waiting for me in their little building adjoining. I then went with Mr. Welliver and discussed the political situation with some fifteen or twenty newspaper men for half an hour, and handed them the statement which I had written.

After this I continued in conference with the Senator until the latter said it was time to start upon the automobile trip to Galion, Ohio, where I was to catch the fast New York Central train to New York. During this conversation Senator Harding took me into an adjoining room and said: "If you really cannot accept the State Department, the best man that I see for that place is Senator Fall." I made no attempt to conceal my amazement, and remonstrated bluntly, saying, "Why, Senator, that man's reputation in Pueblo before he ever left Colorado for New Mexico was such that you must not think of him for Cabinet office." Harding replied, "You are entirely mistaken. You have listened to rumors circulated by jealous enemies of his. Fall is a very able man. I sat with him on the Committee on Foreign Relations and he is the best-posted man of the whole lot, particularly as to all Latin American matters." With this the matter dropped and Senator Harding and I returned to the room where Mrs. Harding was and said good-by.

It is significant that at no time in this conversation was the name of Charles Evans Hughes mentioned, or that of David Jayne Hill. Mr. Hughes was ultimately appointed Secretary of State, but before that appointment was settled upon Doctor Hill was seriously considered, with the urgent and organized support of an influential group of Senators.

Senator Harding escorted me and Judge Davies to the motor and saw us safely off for Galion, twenty-six miles distant.

The visit was notable in every way and highly gratifying. Senator Harding was frankness and cordiality personified, and his good judgment and sound common sense were apparent in everything he said and did. While cherishing no animosities, he showed perfect familiarity with the various troublesome elements in his political party, and a good understanding of the value, or valuelessness, of different individuals in counsel or co-operation. In conversation some months later Harding told me that he had appointed Taft to be Chief Justice of the United States and Hughes to be Secretary of State because he felt that they, having been nominated by Republican National Conventions as candidates for the Presidency, had a particularly strong claim upon a Republican President.

Immediately upon his inauguration Harding summoned

me to the White House and asked me to make it my stopping place whenever I came to Washington. This I was very glad to do.

Three months later Harding returned to the attack and we had this correspondence:

THE WHITE HOUSE
WASHINGTON
(CONFIDENTIAL)

June 7, 1921

My dear Dr. Butler:

It is exceedingly important to make a very early nomination for our Ambassador to Japan. You know something of the efforts made to secure the services of Dr. David Jayne Hill. You have already told me that you do not think it agreeable to your plans to take up a period of diplomatic service, but I have thought that perhaps the very great importance of this post, during the next year or two, would make an appeal to you that might persuade you to enter the service for a time. I cannot let the occasion pass without making you a tender of this nomination. It is a very fine opportunity for a really great and helpful service. I am frank to say that I would not want you to accept it at too great a sacrifice. If you could work your plans in such a way that you might serve without undue sacrifice I should be delighted to send your nomination to the Senate. Please let me have an early expression of your judgment concerning the matter.

Very truly yours,
Warren G. Harding

(CONFIDENTIAL)

June 8, 1921

To the President
White House
Washington, D. C.

My dear Mr. President:

I am profoundly touched and highly honored by the proposal contained in your letter of the 7th. Your feeling as to the importance of the post at Tokio, particularly during the next year or two, is one which I fully share. It certainly offers a most inviting opportunity for large public service.

To my great regret, however, I find it out of the question to act upon the suggestion which you have so generously made. This is due in part to personal reasons, of which I have spoken in our confidential talks on matters of public policy, and in part to my present obligations here at Columbia University. We are entering upon several large and important projects for which I am personally more or less responsible, and while I might readily arrange to be absent for a few weeks, or even for a few months if necessary, I could not at present, in justice to myself or to my life work, remain out of the country for a longer period.

I value more than I can say this new mark of your confidence, and assure you that I most sincerely wish that conditions were such as to permit me to accept this post and to serve your Administration and our country to the full extent of my power.

With warmest regard, my dear Mr. President, and grateful appreciation of the honor which you have done me,

I am,

Always faithfully yours

Nicholas Murray Butler

(CONFIDENTIAL)

June 9, 1921

To the President
 White House
  Washington, D. C.

My dear Mr. President:

May I offer a suggestion that has occurred to me in reference to your forthcoming appointment of an Ambassador to Japan?

Knowing the Pacific Coast as I do, I feel it would be a master stroke—politically, psychologically and strategically—to select the new Ambassador from one of the Pacific Coast States. There are in those States men of the highest type of Americanism who, while fully understanding and appreciating the local feeling there regarding the Japanese, could adequately represent our entire country. A man of this type having the confidence of his own neighbors, would at once disarm the possible criticism that the prejudices and susceptibilities of the Pacific Coast were not considered in our negotiations with Japan.

It is perhaps of little value to make a general suggestion of this sort without accompanying it with some specific illustrations

of what I have in mind to ask you to consider. There are at least
four men, all strong Republicans, all great admirers of yours and
supporters of your Administration, living on the Pacific Coast
any one of whom would I think make a most acceptable Ambassador, particularly under present conditions.

Beginning at the North, I would name, first, Henry Suzzallo,
President of the State University of Washington, at Seattle. Suzzallo was born in California, was educated at Stanford University, and is now approaching fifty years of age. He is a strong
executive, a fine speaker and a man of sterling commonsense,
political and other. I should call him easily the first citizen of the
State of Washington, in view of the universal regard and esteem
in which he is held. Had he so wished, I think he might have
gone to the Senate last year, and I know that he has refused a
strong invitation to stand for Governor. He is very diplomatic
in his manner and in his methods, and while pretty well known
all over the country, is intimately known on the Coast from
Vancouver to San Diego.

Coming South, the second name that I would propose for consideration is that of Edgar D. Piper, Editor of the *Oregonian,*
Portland, Oregon. Mr. Piper is probably known to you personally; I can testify to the regard in which he is held in Oregon, to
the influence of his paper, and to his firm grasp on public affairs.
He has a most attractive personality. Inasmuch as I saw Mr.
Piper in Washington a few weeks ago he probably called upon
you at the White House.

The third name, and from some points of view the most de-
serving of consideration, is that of Alfred Holman, Editor of
the *Argonaut,* San Francisco, California. We have, I think, no
American journalist who writes more powerful editorials than Mr.
Holman, and he knows Pacific Coast sentiment and public men
through and through. He was himself born in Oregon a little
more than sixty years ago, and had important relations with
the *Portland Oregonian* and with the *Seattle Post Intelligencer*
before making his home in California, which he did some twenty
years ago.

The fourth name is that of Mr. John Percival Jefferson, of
Santa Barbara, California. Mr. Jefferson, who is perhaps sixty-
five years of age, was born in Delaware and educated at West
Point. He left the army to engage in engineering and commer-

cial pursuits, and having acquired a competence moved to California, where he made his home in Santa Barbara some years ago. Mr. Jefferson has travelled extensively in the Orient. He knows Japan and the Japanese, China and the Chinese, and also the Pacific Islands as intimately as any one whom I know. He is a man of marked ability, delightful manner and large personal influence in his community.

No one of these men has, so far as I recall, said or written anything which could possibly give offence either in Japan or in China. On the other hand, all of them know intimately and fully appreciate the Oriental problem as the Pacific Coast sees it. I am glad, therefore, to make these suggestions, in the hope that you may find them useful in considering this very grave and important problem.

With Mrs. Butler and my daughter I am sailing on Tuesday next, to spend some weeks in Europe. On my return I shall hope for an opportunity to come to Washington, and after a game of golf tell you something of my latest impressions and information.

With warmest regards and every good wish, I am,

Faithfully yours,

Nicholas Murray Butler

THE WHITE HOUSE
WASHINGTON

(CONFIDENTIAL)

June 13, 1921

My dear Dr. Butler:

When you called on Saturday I had not seen the very interesting letter you addressed to me under date of June 9. If I had had the information it contains I would have been glad to have discussed with you some of the suggestions contained therein. I think exceedingly well of Mr. Piper. My own estimate of Mr. Holman is very high, but I do not think him available because of political conditions which would be encountered immediately in his own state. I have already told you that I have suggested the name of Mr. Cravath and there is inquiry about his availability for service. I am so anxious to have an outstanding representative there. I cannot cease wishing that you might have found it possible to go.

I hope you have a most delightful trip abroad. I should like to repeat the request expressed personally the other night, that you take a few moments off to write me in confidence if you learn anything that you think I ought to know.

Please convey a message of bon voyage to Mrs. Butler and your daughter and be assured that we wish you a most delightful vacation.

Very truly yours,
Warren G. Harding

(CONFIDENTIAL)

June 14, 1921

To the President
   White House
      Washington, D. C.

My dear Mr. President:

I thank you cordially for your gracious note of the 13th, which reaches me just as I am going on board the *Aquitania*.

Since seeing you on Saturday last, I have received confidential information that the British Government also feels keenly the importance of the Tokio appointment, since they believe that one of the most outstanding problems before us all today is the establishment of a plan of mutual understanding and cooperation between the Powers having large interests on the Pacific Ocean. It may be that you will shortly receive, if you have not already received, a suggestion that within the next year a conference of the Pacific Coast Powers be arranged, in order that representatives of the United States, Great Britain, Japan, China, Australia, New Zealand, Canada, and possibly Peru and Chile, should endeavor to map out policies and plans of action that would protect the rights and interests of all while avoiding the necessity for huge armaments on the part of any. In case such a conference should be suggested, would it not be advisable to propose that it be held at San Francisco? That would appeal to the pride of our California friends and it would reduce to a minimum any possible criticism from that quarter of the results of such a conference.

On thinking over farther the name that you now have in mind, I am disposed to think the gentleman exceptionally well equipped for this particular task. I had myself not thought of him before in that connection.

Today there has come to me a confidential invitation to meet privately, shortly after reaching London, the group of members of the House of Commons who call themselves the Committee on Foreign Relations. The House of Commons has, as you know, no such standing committee in our sense, but this group of prominent members of the House meets regularly to consider and discuss questions of foreign policy, with a view to influencing the action of the Government and public opinion. I am advised that they wish to talk with me informally and with the utmost frankness. This they can do with a private and unofficial person, while they might find it difficult or embarrassing in the case of a formally accredited representative.

If it will not tax your patience too much, I shall certainly write you as fully as circumstances permit regarding my various conferences on public matters in England, France and Belgium.

It was a great pleasure to see both you and Mrs. Harding looking and seeming so well on Saturday. I only hope that the summer will bring you increased satisfaction, and that the Congress will not delay too long in giving us that revision of the tax laws for which the world of commerce and industry is waiting. My wife and daughter join me in cordial regards to Mrs. Harding and yourself. I count upon coming down to see you as soon as practicable after my return in September. I am adding my summer address, in case for any reason you should wish to have any communication sent to me.

I am, my dear Mr. President
Always faithfully yours,
Nicholas Murray Butler

Mail address from June 14 to Sept. 5, 1921:

C-o Brown, Shipley & Co.
123 Pall Mall
London, S. W.

Cable address from June 14 to Sept. 12, 1921:

Murray Butler
C-o Shiprah
London

The matter ended in the appointment on June 29, 1921, of Charles Beecher Warren as Ambassador to Japan.

Harding was one of the kindest men who ever lived, but he was without any serious qualifications for the Presidency. He had a good mind, but made little use of it. He had no wide or accurate knowledge of public questions or of the foundations in history, economics and public law on which those questions rest. He was good-natured, lazy and weak when pressure was put on him by a stronger will than his own, which happened to be that of a friend. He would not have consciously done a wrong act in his great office but he had neither the intellect nor the character to prevent himself from being made use of for unworthy purposes by unworthy men who loudly professed their personal and political friendship. On one occasion I remember coming into the White House offices about six o'clock in the evening and being urged by Mr. Christian, the President's secretary, to persuade the President to go to the White House and rest before dinner. Christian added that the President was very tired and was at that moment sitting before a huge pile of letters in his private office. I went in and found him precisely as his secretary described, but with a look of extreme dejection on his face. In reply to my urging that he come over to the White House and lie down before dinner, he said with a weary groan that he must go through this pile of letters which he had not as yet found time to examine. Having known the way in which McKinley and Theodore Roosevelt did business in that office I said to Harding, "Do you mind my looking at some of them?" He replied, "No, look at any of them you please." Taking the first two or three letters off the top of the pile which must have contained not fewer than one hundred, I glanced at them hastily and said, "Oh, come on, Mr. President, this is ridiculous. Even in my office they do not burden me with reading or answering letters like these." I shall never forget Harding's answer, for while it was very pathetic, it did him great credit. These were his words: "I suppose so, but I am not fit for this office and should never have been here." Other Presidents might truthfully have said the same thing, but it may be doubted whether any of them has been or will be frank enough to make the confession which broke from poor Harding's lips that evening.

On Friday, May 4, 1923, President Harding called me by telephone and asked me to come to Washington at once as there was something very important of which he wished to speak. I replied that of course his invitation was a command, but that it put me in very great difficulties. I had some important engagements for Saturday and Sunday and was to sail on the following Saturday for England to deliver a series of lectures on the Watson Foundation at various British universities. I asked whether we could not discuss the matter by telephone. The President hesitated a moment and said, "No, that would be impossible, but since you cannot do any work on Sunday, please arrange to come down by the night train on Saturday, spend Sunday and return again by the night train that evening." I did this and had a most extraordinary experience at the White House. The President came into my sitting room before I had finished breakfast and from that time on, until I left at half-past eleven to return to the railway station, he hardly ever let me out of his sight for a moment. Evidently, there was something very much on his mind and he was trying to bring himself to tell me what it was. Several times during the morning, afternoon and evening he seemed to be on the point of unbosoming himself, but he never did so. He came down to the porch of the White House to say farewell, as I took the automobile back to the station, and even then seemed to be trying to tell me something which troubled him. I have never been able to guess what that something was. The record shows, however, that almost immediately after my visit he drew his will and sold the *Marion Star*. It was not long before he started on the journey to Alaska and the Pacific Coast from which he was never to return.

It has always been my opinion that Harding had some sort of premonition that he would not live out his term and that things would not go well during his administration. The basis for this opinion was all sorts and kinds of little things which were observable in the day-by-day life of the White House and which it would not be easy to describe or define. Harding was happiest when playing cards or when playing golf. Not being myself a card player I knew nothing of the details of that game, but we had many games of golf together, on the golf courses at Washington, at Augusta, Ga., when he came there, and for one season at St. Augustine, Fla., where we passed some two weeks together in 1922 at the Ponce de Leon Hotel. When the news of his tragically sudden death reached me I was in London and, not knowing what might happen politically, returned home by the first ship. President Coolidge telegraphed me to come to the White House for a consultation and I did so at the earliest opportunity and at that time established the very agreeable personal relations with him which fortunately continued throughout his life. He repeated President Harding's invitation to make the White House my stopping place when in Washington. This I was always very glad to do.

President Coolidge was by training and temperament wide as the poles asunder from Harding. He had all the caution, circumspection and intellectual limitations of the rural New Englander. With those characteristics he combined a firm faith in the fundamental principles of the American political and social order as these have existed and developed for two centuries. He was wholly lacking in imagination and his days were filled with seriousness. The lighter side of life and its amusements meant little to him. He went through this part of his official routine with a sort of patient resignation but the expression of his face was about the same when he opened a baseball game as it was when he sat and listened to his favorite preacher at church on Sunday morning. His own written style as exhibited in his speeches and public papers while still in public office in Massachusetts was simple, direct and clear, and in many respects resembles the best seventeenth-century English. It is a misfortune that as President he had permitted so many of his formal addresses to be written for him by members of his staff. These have made him seem prolix, jejune and ordinary to a degree. Curiously enough, these long addresses have put this so-called silent man in the position of using in his public addresses and papers more words during his five and a half years in the White House than were used by Theodore Roosevelt and Wilson together in their fifteen and a half years of the Presidency. A Washington correspondent with time on his hands made and published this computation, and I have no reason to doubt its correctness. President Coolidge never invited me to accept appointment to office.

Two more urgent invitations to accept candidacy for public office were still to come. Returning from Europe during the midsummer of 1925, I received a wireless message when still a day or two out of New York, telling me of a confidential visit that I should receive when the ship reached Quarantine Station. When the first official boat came alongside at Quarantine, there stepped from it to our ship my old friend, the Chairman of the New York County Republican Committee, Mr. Samuel S. Koenig. After a hurried greeting we withdrew to a quiet corner for the confidential conference which he desired. His wish was, before I had time to be interviewed by newspapermen or to see people generally, to tell me that it was the desire of the Republican organizations of the whole city of New York that I should accept their nomination for mayor. The notion struck me as so preposterous that I had difficulty in adjusting myself to the situation, but Mr. Koenig was very much in earnest and it was always my desire to give him all the help I could in his arduous and little appreciated task of holding together the organization of a minority party in the city of New York. I told him that I did not see how I could possibly consider the matter but that since a final answer was imperative within twenty-four hours I would fairly and honestly consider the proposal and let him have my answer the following morning. As a matter of fact the nomination had already been offered to a half-dozen different men, no one of whom felt able to accept it. The purpose in offering it to me, since success in the election was quite out of the question, was explained to be that it would probably lead to something more important later on. This was, however, an old story and the picture had no attraction. My reply to Mr. Koenig was that I would give him all possible help in his coming municipal campaign, but that I could not accept the nomination that was so kindly offered.

The latest, and doubtless the last, proposal of this nature was more important, more serious and more difficult to deal with. This had to do with the nomination for governor in 1926, with the expressed notion that if I were successful at the polls there would be no difficulty in bringing about my nomination for President in 1928. Rumblings of this began early in the summer but I paid no attention to them. Suddenly about the middle of August I was summoned from Southampton to New York for a conference of several hours' duration at the Hotel Ambassador with Senator Wadsworth and Charles D. Hilles. We went over the situation in all its aspects, and I listened once again to the now familiar arguments which were earnestly and kindly presented by men who were genuine friends. My answer was the usual negative. I went farther and pointed out that no man of the ordinary office-holding or office-seeking type could defeat Governor Smith, who was making a most excellent governor, and that if he was to be defeated we must find a candidate who had a fine character, large intelligence and good administrative experience. My own preference was Mr. Hilles himself. Although my mind was made up, the matter did not end there, and pressure upon me was continued, accompanied by all sorts of promises as to 1928, until twenty-four hours before the State Convention met. The day of its meeting was Monday and I spent Sunday in attendance upon a series of political conferences at the Hotel Ambassador and at the Metropolitan Club. Finally after much searching of hearts and prolonged debate, Congressman Mills was selected for the nomination. Despite his ability, his grievous and outstanding defects of temper and temperament led him to make a most fatuous campaign. Governor Smith defeated him overwhelmingly in November and thereby established himself as the powerful figure in national politics which led to his nomination for the Presidency at Houston in 1928.

There is a certain type of man who can accept official public service and do great good for the country without personal inconvenience or distress. He is, however, of a type which is rather rare and greatly needs encouragement. Men of this sort have made most admirable representatives or senators in Congress and have often spent the best years of an active life in that form of public service, gaining influence and authority as their knowledge and experience grew. Names of several such men come readily to mind. On the other hand there are men of large ability, great competence in public affairs and lofty patriotism who simply cannot accept the limitations which attend upon the exercise of public office in our American democracy. Those limitations upon one's patience and one's desire to achieve are doubtless greater in the case of legislative office than in that of any other, but they always exist. It is the business of constitutions and laws to see that they do exist and the psychology of the crowd does the rest. As I have said, no man in my time has been so happy, and on the whole so successful, in public office as Theodore Roosevelt. Whether President of the United States Civil Service Commission, or Commissioner of Police in the city of New York, or Assistant Secretary of the Navy, or Lieutenant Colonel of the Rough Riders, or Governor of the State of New York or President of the United States, he was always the same eager, vigorous, forward-moving personality. He rode and fished and shot and boxed and took almost every known form of hard physical exercise. He knew how to play, both mentally and physically, and he loved play for its own sake. He was an omnivorous reader with a taste as wide as the capacity of the printing press. He took his official tasks very seriously, but he always took them and made certain that they did not take him. With every other important office-holder of my knowledge the contrary has been the case. He has either lacked the spirit of play entirely or it had been crushed out of him by the burden of his cares and responsibilities. The result is that Theodore Roosevelt stands out in my memory as the only happy President. There may have been others, but I doubt it. Franklin Roosevelt comes nearest to it.

Having many times declined to be an ambassador to one of the chief capitals and having known all the ambassadors for a lifetime, I have acquired some very distinct ideas concerning them, their qualifications and their duties. The day is past when an ambassador is wholly satisfactory if he confines himself to the effective representation of his government in its business with another government. The useful ambassador must now be ambassador to a people as well as to a government. He must and should appear on various occasions, academic, literary, scientific, social and other, and participate by spoken word in dignified and honorable fashion. He must and should meet all sorts and conditions of people in the country where he is at the moment accredited. All this means that the so-called service man who has come up from the ranks in the diplomatic service is usually the poorest possible person to appoint as ambassador to a capital such as London or Paris or Rome or Berlin or Madrid or Tokio. He has been too long out of touch with his own countrymen to render the type of ambassadorial service which is now so important. The most useful type of ambassador at such posts is a man of personal distinction and professional achievement, chosen in later middle life with his reputation thoroughly well-made, who has both the independence and the competence to speak for the people of the United States as well as for the government. It was precisely these qualifications which made James Russell Lowell and Joseph H. Choate the perfect ambassadors to Great Britain, and it is similar qualifications which made it possible for Myron T. Herrick to bind together the people of the United States and those of France as they had never been bound together before. Years ago Andrew D. White did a like service in Berlin and there have been other less conspicuous illustrations of the same fact. Similarly, James Bryce was by far the most effective ambassador that Great Britain has ever sent to Washington.

Unfortunately, the great cost of maintaining a modern embassy and the stubborn niggardliness of the Congress of the United States combine to make it wholly impossible for any number of men of high qualifications, but limited means, to accept these appointments. Every one of our embassies, and our legations as well, should be built, furnished and maintained by the government as is the White House, and a thoroughly satisfactory allowance granted for official entertainment. In other words, the foreign representatives of the United States should be treated in the same way that the President is treated. Their salaries, no matter how much they are likely to be increased hereafter, will always be too small and will be scarcely adequate for their own personal and family expenditures. The whole standard of our diplomatic service would be raised and its effectiveness multiplied many times if these policies were adopted. The cost to the government would be inconsiderable, particularly when put in contrast with the amounts now annually wasted with such jolly nonchalance.

Twice—first in 1894 and again in 1915—I declined election to membership in the New York State Constitutional Convention despite my very great interest in its work. Nevertheless, I found it possible to accomplish much in which I was interested by making several visits to Albany, by appearing before committees of the Constitutional Convention and by correspondence. The Convention of 1915 invited me to address its members in the Assembly Chamber at Albany on June 15 on the occasion of the 700th anniversary of Magna Carta.[1]

In recent years there have been two highly important public commissions upon which I was privileged to serve. Both of these commissions did a thoroughly good job and service upon them gave to each member new and almost unexampled opportunity to gain intimate present-day knowledge of the functions of government. One was the State Reorganization Commission, of which Charles Evans Hughes was chairman, appointed on the joint initiative of the Governor, the President pro tempore of the Senate and the Speaker of the Assembly of the State of New York, for the purpose of "framing suitable legislation to combine the functions and departments of the State" following the adoption by the people of a constitutional amendment which made such readjustment possible. Among the members of this Commission were John W. Davis, former Governors Charles S. Whitman and Nathan L. Miller, John Lord O'Brian, Morgan J. O'Brien, William Church Osborn, Henry L. Stimson and George W. Wickersham.

The work of this Commission is summarized in its report submitted to the Senate and Assembly under date of February 26, 1926. Perhaps no more sweeping rearrangement and simplification of a state government has ever been made. More than one hundred and eighty separate administrative departments, commissions and boards were regrouped under eighteen major departments. These recommendations were promptly enacted into law. The several constitutional amendments recommended by the

[1]Cf. *Is America Worth Saving?* New York: Charles Scribner's Sons, 1920, pp. 253–275.

Commission, some of which were of far-reaching importance, have now all been added to the State Constitution.

The second commission, that known as the City Committee on Plan and Survey, of which Judge Morgan J. O'Brien was chairman, and among whose members were John H. Finley, Frederick H. Ecker, Herbert H. Lehman, Henry H. Curran and Dwight W. Morrow, was appointed by Mayor Walker in 1926. The report of this Committee, of which I was vice-chairman, submitted to the Mayor under date of June 5, 1928, was, and remains, of outstanding importance for the better administration of the business of the city of New York. It dealt with housing and zoning, port and terminal facilities, traffic regulation, sanitation and harbor pollution, highways and bridges, parks and recreational facilities, finance, budget and revenue, and departmental reorganization.

Membership on these two very important bodies, while carrying with it real opportunity for public service, was not in the ordinary sense holding public office.

Three invitations, urgently pressed, which lay quite outside the field of political life, may be mentioned for the sake of the record. One was the very confidential invitation to become President of the Erie Railroad, tendered me by J. Pierpont Morgan in 1901. Another was a similar invitation, also most confidential, to become President of the Union Pacific Railroad system, given me in most complimentary terms by Edward H. Harriman in 1903. In each case the salary and emoluments proposed seemed as fantastic as they were fabulous. Both invitations were declined with appreciative thanks. Mr. Harriman afterwards compromised by handing me his check for $100,000 to establish at Columbia University a fund in memory of his father, the Reverend Orlando Harriman, who was graduated with the Class of 1835. Mr. Morgan also compromised by accepting an invitation to become a Trustee of the University in which post he served from 1903 to 1913. Both Mr. Morgan and Mr. Harriman knew perfectly well that I had no competence to administer a railway system. They told me that that would be taken care of, but that I was wanted to represent the corporation before public opinion, before the Congress and before various state legislatures. No occupation could have appealed to me less than that, no matter what compensation was offered. The third invitation was from Levi P. Morton and Thomas Fortune Ryan to become president of an important trust company in the city of New York at a huge salary, for which post likewise I had no competence and no desire.

A reading of this record will make it plain why I have never had any patience with the doctrine that history is to be interpreted only, or primarily, in terms of economics. History itself contradicts this assumption from the very beginning of Western civilization. The economic motive and economic interest have always been present and always will be present. As men rise in the scale of humanity, however, the purely economic motive is steadily subordinated to the higher and finer appeals made by the intellectual life and the ambition for service to one's fellow men through the upbuilding of human institutions. There is far more happiness and satisfaction to be found in such a career than in one guided and shaped solely by the gain-seeking impulse, no matter how successful such gain-seeking may be.

END OF VOLUME I

INDEX

Abelard, 130
Abelard (Compayré), 204
Académie Française, 129, 171
Academy of Moral and Political Science, 108
Academy of Music, New York City, 87-88
Acta Columbiana, 84
Adams, John Quincy, 10, 219
Adams, John T., Republican National Convention (1916), platform, 255-256
Adamson Law, 349-350
Addington, Doctor, regimen for gout, 25
Agnew, Cornelius R., 80
Agnus, Felix, Republican National Convention (1916), platform, 255-256
Agriculture, Department of, Harding discusses, 398-399
Ainley, Hefford, 102
Ainley, Joseph H., 102
Alabama, Weeks's campaign (1916), 247
Alabama, University of, 70
Alaska, 99
Albany, N. Y., 95; Academy, 197
Albany *Evening Journal*, 257
Alcott, A. Bronson, 93
Alcuin (West), 204
Alderman, Edwin A., 201
Aldrich, George W., delegate (1904), 236-237; dislike of Hughes, 253; favored Butler's nomination, 371
Aldrich, Nelson W., Senator, Rhode Island, 285, 319
Alexander, Archibald, 67-68; lectures on philosophy, 69; counsel on graduate study, 92-93, 104, 126; examination for Ph.D., 100; Butler as graduate student of, 159; illness and absence of, 159; resignation, 160; report on department of philosophy, 160
Alger, Russell A., Republican National Convention (1888), 218
Allies, 337
Allison, Senator, Iowa, Republican National Convention (1888), 218
All Souls College, Oxford, 7
Alumni, Columbia College, 138

Ambassador, appointment, 351-352; United States, to Great Britain, 397-398; qualifications and duties, 417-418; financial burdens, 418
America, public morality, effect of prohibition movement on, 15; example of true meaning of liberty, the ideal of Washington and Jefferson, 292
"America, Ourselves and the League," 395
American Academy of Arts and Letters, 166
American College in Rome, 4
American Geographical Society, 166
American industry, and tariff acts, 290-291
American Journal of Education, 95
American Journal of Philology, 94
Americans, European misconception of, 124; and international relations, 393
American Telephone and Telegraph Company, 328
American University, The (Burgess), 96
Amherst College, 58, 97
Ancestry, reason for pride in, 33
Angell, James B., Committee of Ten, 196
Anglo-Saxon, 65
Anmeldungs-Buch, 113, 121
Ann Arbor, 112
Annin, William E., and J. R. Young, 302-303
Anson, Sir William, 7
Anthon, Charles, chair named for, 171
Apologia, 1-19
Apponyi, Count, 12
Aquitania (ship), 408
Arabian Nights, 57
Argentina, League of Nations, 394
Armaments, limitation, 400-401
Arnold, Matthew, 7; Fitch's interpretation, 204
Arnold, Thomas, Fitch's interpretation, 204
Arnold, Thomas Kerchever, editor, Latin textbook, 57
Arrowsmith, Robert, and *Columbiad* prank, 84-85
Art education, introduction, 189
Arthur, Chester A., Republican National Convention (1880), 209; campaign (1884), 308

Pennsylvania *Magazine of History and Biography*, 29 *n*

Penrose, Boies, 319; Republican National Convention (1912), on the behavior of the delegates, 241-242; political situation in Pennsylvania (1916), 247-249; attitude toward T. Roosevelt, 249; Republican National Convention (1916), 268, 346-347; on Fairbanks, 271; on T. Roosevelt's suggestion of Lodge, 274; opposition to Root, 275, 288; and Harding's nomination, 278; career, 326-327; suggests Tower as ambassador, 352-353

Perkins, George W., and T. R., 249, 347; Progressive party convention (1916), conferee with Republicans, 258-275; silence on Root, 271

Permanent court of international justice, 291

Perry, Edward Delavan, brought to Columbia, 163; limerick on Doumic, 171

Persia, England's influence, 316-317

Perth, Scotland, 103

Peru, conference of Pacific Coast Powers, 408

Peterson, *Familiar Science*, 56-57

Pfleiderer, theologian, 105, 124

Phelps, William Walter, 209

Philadelphia, Pa., 112; home of Colonel Benjamin Loxley, 29; of Morgan J. Rhys, 30; Mt. Moriah Cemetery, 30; Republican National Convention (1900), 224, 227, 228; J. R. Young, congressman, 302; Drexel Institute, 305; Penrose and reform charter, 326

Philadelphia Evening Telegraph, 274

Philadelphia Press, 285

Phillips, J. H., 201

Philolexian Society, 83-84

Philology, 94

Philosophical Society, student, organized by Butler, 159

Philosophie der Griechen (Zeller), 120

Philosophy, German, 93; degree of doctor of, 93, 94, 100; Hegel, 111; Harris, 192; Herbartian, 194-195

Philosophy of Religion (John Caird), 8

Pinchot, Gifford, 357

Pine, John B., 135; statutes of 1890-1892, 158; search for site, 165 ff.; and Industrial Education Association, 181; committee on proposals for Teachers College, 185

Piper, Edgar D., 406-407

Pitt, William, and Gilbert Buchanan, 24

Pius XI, Pope, 13

Platform, Republican, 282-283; drafting, 284-286; pledges broken, 291

Platt, Frank H., 235

Platt, Thomas C., Republican National Convention (1880), 209; (1896), gold plank, 223; and the nomination of T. R. for the vice-presidency, 225-226; organization, 245; support of Woodruff's candidacy, 378, 381

Plumb, Senator, 209

Poincaré, Henri, 108, 130

Poincaré, Raymond, 109; Wilson on, 338

Poland, of the Committee of Fifteen, 194

Political leaders, foreign, 3-8, 12-13; American, 10-12, 209

Political organization, participation in, 9-12

Politics, Behind the Scenes in, 293-362; religious bigotry in, 359-362; and economic interdependence, 395

Portland, Ore., 35

Portland Oregonian, 406

"Post-Positive *Et* in Propertius, The," 94

Potter, Henry C., 156, 306

Potter, Horatio, 42

Potter, William B., considered as Barnard's successor, 156

Powell, Committee of Fifteen, 194

President of the United States, personal acquaintance with, 10-12, 367; correspondence, 10; nominated at National Conventions, 208; child who wished to shake hands, 340-342; administration, advantages of workers of same generation, 395-396

Preston, Miss., 201

Price, Thomas R., 137

Priestley, Joseph, 30

Prime, Samuel Irenæus, *Memoirs of the Rev. Nicholas Murray*, 28 *n.*

Prime Ministers of England, 4-5

Prince, John Dyneley, brought to Columbia, 163; and Wilson, 332, 333-334

Princeton Theological Seminary, 31

Princeton University, 54, 90, 112; undergraduate societies, 84; Osborn, 162; college admissions, 198; inauguration of Hibben, 333-334

Pringle, *Life of Roosevelt*, 317

Pritchett, 346

Progressive party, in 1912, 247, 249, 255, 386; National Convention (1916), 257; discussions with Republican conferees on Roosevelt, 257-275

Prohibition, attitude toward, 15; effect on American public morality, 15, 365-366; Committee, 317